An OPUS book

The Russian Revolution

OPUS General Editors

Keith Thomas
Alan Ryan
Peter Medawar

Sheila Fitzpatrick

The Russian Revolution

Oxford   New York

OXFORD UNIVERSITY PRESS

1982

Oxford University Press, Walton Street, Oxford OX2 6DP

London Glasgow New York Toronto
Delhi Bombay Calcutta Madras Karachi
Kuala Lumpur Singapore Hong Kong Tokyo
Nairobi Dar es Salaam Cape Town
Melbourne Auckland

and associates in
Beirut Berlin Ibadan Mexico City Nicosia

British Library Cataloguing in Publication Data
Fitzpatrick, Sheila
    The Russian Revolution.—(OPUS)
    1. Russia—History—Nicholas II. 1894–1917
    2. Russia—History—1917
    I. Title II. Series
    947.08 DK258
ISBN 0–19–219162–4

Library of Congress Cataloging in Publication Data
Fitzpatrick, Sheila.
    The Russian Revolution. (OPUS)
    Bibliography: p. Includes index.
    1. Soviet Union—History—Revolution, 1917–1921.
    I. Title. II. Series.
DK265.F48 917.084'1 82–3611 AACR2
ISBN 0–19–219162–4

Set by Western Printing Services Ltd, Bristol
Printed in Great Britain by
The Thetford Press Ltd
Thetford, Norfolk

Contents

Acknowledgements

The first draft of this book was written in the summer of 1979, when I was a Visiting Fellow at the Research School of Social Sciences of the Australian National University, Canberra. I would like to express my gratitude to Professor T. H. Rigby, who arranged my invitation to A.N.U. and subsequently made very helpful comments on the manuscript; and to my husband, Jerry Hough, who was a constant source of intellectual stimulus and encouragement; and to the students in my courses at Columbia University and the University of Texas at Austin, who were the first audience for much of this book.

Introduction

Since revolutions are complex social and political upheavals, historians who write about them are bound to differ on the most basic questions – causes, revolutionary aims, social support and impact on the society, political outcome, and even the timespan of the revolution itself. In the case of the Russian Revolution, the last question presents peculiar problems. While the great French Revolution has a clear conventional starting-point (1789) and an end which can be no later than Napoleon's defeat and the Bourbon restoration in 1814–15, the Russian Revolution tends to be given either a very narrow definition (February to October 1917)[1] or an open-ended one. There was no Romanov restoration in Russia. Nor, by any reasonable definition, did the revolutionary upheaval end when the Bolsheviks took power in October 1917, since a civil war remained to be fought. Did the Bolsheviks' Civil War victory in mid-1920 mark the end of the revolution? Should we look further forward, to some later definitive 'betrayal of the revolution' (as Trotsky and others have suggested) or an equally definitive achievement of revolutionary objectives? Or should we perhaps accept the view, sometimes expressed by both Soviet and anti-Soviet commentators, that the revolution continues up to the present day?

In his *Anatomy of Revolution*, Crane Brinton suggested that revolutions have a life-cycle passing through phases of increasing fervour and zeal for radical transformation until they reach a climax of intensity, which is followed by the 'Thermidorian' phase of disillusionment, declining revolutionary energy and gradual moves towards the restoration of order and stability.[2] The Russian Bolsheviks, bearing in mind the same French-Revolution model that lies at the basis of Brinton's analysis, feared a Thermidorian degeneration of their own revolution, and half suspected that one had occurred at the end of the Civil War, when economic collapse forced them into the 'strategic retreat' marked by the introduction of the New Economic Policy (NEP) in 1921.

Yet at the end of the 1920s, Russia plunged into another upheaval – Stalin's 'revolution from above', associated with the industrialization drive of the First Five-Year Plan, the collectivization of agriculture, and a 'proletarian cultural revolution' directed primarily against the old intelligentsia – whose impact on society was greater even than that of the February and October Revolutions of 1917 and the Civil War of 1918–20. It is only after this upheaval ended in the early 1930s that we find increasing signs of a classic Thermidor: the waning of revolutionary fervour and belligerence, new policies aimed at restoring order and stability, revival of traditional values and culture, solidification of a new political and social structure. But perhaps even this Thermidor of the mid 1930s was not the end of the Russian Revolution. In a final internal upheaval, reminiscent of earlier surges of revolutionary terror though not involving basic structural or ideological change, the Great Purge of 1937–8 swept away many of the surviving Old Bolshevik revolutionaries and effected a wholesale turnover of personnel within the regime's newly acknowledged and privileged elite.

In setting a timespan for the Russian Revolution, the first judgement that has to be made concerns the nature of the 'strategic retreat' of NEP in the 1920s. Although the Bolsheviks' avowed intention in 1921 was to use this peaceful interlude to gather strength for a later renewal of the revolutionary assault, there was always the possibility that their intention would change as revolutionary passions subsided and stability returned to the society. Some scholars believe that Lenin, in the last years before his death in 1924, came to feel that Russia's future movement towards socialism could best be achieved by evolutionary rather than revolutionary means. Nevertheless, Russian society remained highly volatile and unstable during the NEP period. The Bolsheviks feared counter-revolution, remained preoccupied with the threat from 'class enemies' at home and the capitalist nations abroad, and constantly expressed dissatisfaction with NEP and unwillingness to accept it as an outcome or permanent settlement of their Revolution. In my judgement, NEP remained a retreat, and the Bolsheviks' mood remained belligerent and revolutionary.

A second judgement has to be made on the nature of Stalin's 'revolution from above' that ended the NEP interlude in the late 1920s. To some historians, Stalin's revolution does not deserve the name, since it was something artificial and imposed by the regime – an assault on the nation by its rulers rather than a true revolutionary upheaval. Others reject the idea that there was any real continuity between Stalin's revolution and Lenin's. I accept the characterization of Stalin's revolution as a 'revolution from above' (that is, an upheaval produced by a ruling party aiming at radical transformation of the society and prepared to fight for it), but see important elements of continuity linking Stalin's revolution with Lenin's. However, the real question is not whether the two episodes were alike, but whether they were part of the same process. Napoleon's revolutionary wars can be included in our general concept of the French Revolution, even if we do not regard them as an embodiment of the spirit of 1789; and a similar approach seems legitimate in the case of the Russian Revolution. In commonsense terms, a revolution is coterminous with the period of upheaval and instability between the fall of an old regime and the firm consolidation of a new one. In the late 1920s, the permanent contours of Russia's new regime had yet to emerge.

This book therefore treats the February and October Revolutions of 1917, the Civil War, the interlude of NEP and Stalin's First Five-Year Plan revolution as successive stages in a single process – the Russian Revolution. That process, I believe, was essentially completed with the end of the First Five-Year Plan in 1932. The regime declared a revolutionary victory and began to emphasize order, stability and normalization. The population relaxed, thankful that the revolutionary struggle was over. To be sure, the relaxation was somewhat premature: the Great Purge was still to come, and the Purge had scarcely ended before the country plunged into the even greater misfortune of the Second World War. But the Purge, as this author sees it, was less an integral part of the Russian Revolution than a monstrous postscript, added under the stress of impending war (see below, pp. 156–9). The institutional and social structure and the cultural norms that were to last throughout the Stalin period had been established before the Great Purge, and did not change as a result of it. By the mid 1930s, Russia's new regime had already settled into its mould.

As the foregoing discussion shows, even establishing the timespan of the Russian Revolution involves some subjective judgement on the historian's part. This is still more true of the interpretation of causes, effects and overall significance of the Revolution. The natural question for the general reader to ask is: What was the revolution all about? Historians, if they are willing to answer the question at all, give a wide range of answers.

The Bolsheviks believed that their revolution was a workers' revolution, leading Russia to socialism by way of a transitional period of proletarian dictatorship under the Bolshevik (Communist)[3] Party. This scheme is reflected in most Soviet scholarly works, which particularly emphasize the links between the working class and the party. Non-Soviet Marxists have usually denied that it was a real workers' revolution, or at least that it continued to be so after the Bolsheviks seized power in October 1917, or after the revolt of the Kronstadt sailors in 1921. Trotsky, one of the leaders of the October Revolution, later defeated by Stalin in the leadership struggles of the 1920s and finally deported from the Soviet Union in 1929, saw the Bolshevik Revolution in retrospect as a workers' revolution that Stalin betrayed. In Trotsky's interpretation, the outcome of the revolution was not socialism but a dictatorship resting on the support of an essentially bourgeois bureaucracy.[4] This interpretation has had great influence on Western Marxists, and also (perhaps surprisingly) on Western Soviet scholarship as a whole.

In Western scholarship, however, the political and ideological aspects of the Revolution have been much more prominent than the social ones. Viewing the Stalinist dictatorship as the most significant outcome of the Revolution, scholars have investigated its possible origins in Lenin's concept of the party and his prerevolutionary writings on party organization, treated the October seizure of power as a Bolshevik coup rather than a popular revolution, and seen the 'dictatorship of the proletariat' established in October 1917 as nothing more than a façade for the dictatorship of the Bolshevik Party. In the decade after the Second World War – the period of rapid development of Soviet studies in the United States – Stalin's dictatorship was described as 'totalitarian', implying a close similarity to Hitler's Nazi regime in Germany, and the Revolution and the early years under Lenin's leadership were seen as part of the progression towards totalitarianism. Recently, a number of scholars have objected to this characterization of Lenin and the Revolution.[5] But it is still generally accepted for the Stalin era, and the resulting discontinuity has yet to be satisfactorily explained.

Political analysis has often come uncomfortably close to political partisanship in Western Sovietology, and this clearly has some connection with the impact of the Cold War on the formative years of American Soviet studies. But it has outlived the Cold War, and in fact was never the exclusive prerogative of any one ideological group. Unlike historians of the French and American Revolutions, or even of the European fascist regimes of the 1930s, historians of the Russian

Revolution remain preoccupied with questions of moral judgement. A strongly negative moral judgement was always implicit in the totalitarian model; and those scholars who now reject it often seem more interested in changing the moral judgement (rescuing Lenin and the Revolution from the condemnation that, they feel, only Stalin deserves) than trying a less judgemental approach. The failure of one eminent British historian, E. H. Carr, to make explicit moral judgements or even agree that this was the historian's proper task was widely criticized,[6] sometimes in terms of outrage and indignation.

One might expect economic interpretations to figure prominently in the historiography of the Russian Revolution, but this is not really the case. Russia's admitted backwardness and the 'premature' nature of the Revolution put Soviet Marxists on the defensive from the beginning, and their analyses have dealt less with inexorable laws of economic development than with the idiosyncrasies of Russia's situation in 1917 that made the laws less inexorable than usual. In the Stalin era, when Russia's prerevolutionary backwardness was much emphasized, the whole issue of economic prerequisites of revolution tended to be ignored: it was the *political* prerequisites that mattered, that is, the organizing role of the Bolshevik Party before October 1917. This approach had little in common with Marxism: in many ways, it was a mirror-image of the contemporary totalitarian-model scholarship in the West.

The one line of interpretation that does stress economic factors (though not causes) is Western, and places the Russian Revolution in a context of modernization. Here the significant outcome of the Revolution is the economic breakthrough at the end of the 1920s and the rapid industrialization of the first Five-Year Plans. Russian Marxism is seen as the modernizing wing of the late nineteenth-century revolutionary movement, the Marxists being distinguished from their Populist opponents by their belief in the inevitability of capitalist industrialization on the Western model and their urban, industrial orientation. In Russia, as later in the Third World, Marxism was both a revolutionary ideology (by virtue of its denunciation of capitalist and colonial exploitation) and an ideology of economic development out of backwardness. As Adam Ulam puts it, Stalin's forced-pace industrialization was carried out through 'terror and totalitarianism', but it was nevertheless 'the logical complement of Marxism, "revolution fulfilled" rather than "revolution betrayed"'.[7]

The themes of <u>dictatorship and modernization</u> – 'terror and progress', in Barrington Moore's phrase[8] – are prominent in my inter-pretation of the Russian Revolution. But a third theme is also promi-nent, that of class struggle and workers' revolution. Finding no way to fit it neatly into either a totalitarian interpretation or a modernization one, Western scholars have often tended to dismiss the class element. But the Bolsheviks came to power in 1917 as a workers' party (albeit with intelligentsia leadership, like the other revolutionary parties), and they could neither have taken power nor held it through the Civil War period without the support of urban workers and the radicalized soldiers and sailors of the old Tsarist Army and Navy. Did they really, as has been suggested, cut all significant ties with the working class as soon as the new regime had firmly established itself in power and consolidated its dictatorship?

Before attempting to answer this question, it must be said that it leads us straight into a minefield of value judgements. Historians who assert that the Bolshevik Party and the Revolution were in some sense working-class are almost invariably implying qualified approval or sympathy with the Revolution. Those who assert the contrary (even non-Marxists, for whom the question might seem neutral) are imply-ing disapproval and condemnation. The terms 'proletarian' and 'working-class' are applied selectively by Western and Soviet historians alike: thus, the people who organize soviets and factory committees, volunteer for the Red Army and attend classes in Marx-ism are 'proletarians', while those who loot, brawl, break machinery, beat up intellectuals and Jews and rape women from the old upper classes are not.

However, the fact is that the Bolsheviks' working-class support in 1917 came both from the first group (the 'conscious proletariat', in Bolshevik terminology) and the second, and both types of attitude and behaviour can legitimately be called working-class. It is possible to judge the Bolsheviks' fidelity to the workers' revolution in terms of their policies on worker self-management, soviet democracy and trade-union representation of labour's economic interests. But class hatred and a willingness to crush the class enemy by violent and coercive means was also a part of the workers' revolution. If the Bolsheviks' dictatorship served that end, it surely was to some degree a product of the revolution and an instrument of the class.

This is borne out if we look further into the proposition, generally accepted by Western scholars as evidence of a severing of the working-class–Bolshevik connection, that the dictatorship of the proletariat was quickly transformed into a dictatorship of the party. In functional political terms, this proposition is obviously true, but its significance depends on whether the party could or could not be described as working-class. In 1917, a majority of party members were urban workers, but their proportional weight declined in the Civil War years, mainly as the result of peasant recruitment via the Red Army. In the 1920s, with the party's hold on power secure and the tasks of economic reconstruction and modernization before it, a quite reasonable strategy for the party leadership would have been to turn away from the working class (which was dispersed and partially disaffected, and had in any case served its revolutionary purpose) and woo the old educated elite, particularly the technical experts and managers, whose services would be most useful in the future. But the leadership did not follow this strategy. Instead, the Bolsheviks became increasingly insistent on the party's proletarian identity, and backed this up in the years 1924–32 by a massive drive to recruit workers into the party and re-establish the old proletarian predominance in total party membership. It was very difficult for 'bourgeois experts' to gain admittance to the party, even though many in this group had come to see the Bolsheviks' modernizing and nation-building objectives as congenial, and were aware of the advantages in terms of personal security and career advancement that were associated with party membership. During the First Five-Year Plan, when the experts' services were particularly needed by the regime, they were astonished to find themselves once again labelled class enemies, subject to public denunciation and police harassment.

It is clear, then, that a real relationship between the Bolshevik Party and the working class existed, and continued into the early 1930s. Yet in the First Five-Year Plan period, when the relationship was most emphasized (and demonstrated in practice by the party's recruitment policies and the regime's ability to rally active working-class support in its confrontation with the peasantry over collectivization), the working class as such was scarcely improving its political, social and economic position. Real wages and living standards fell as a result of the industrialization drive; the trade unions were muzzled when they tried to protest; and the powers of management *vis-à-vis* labour markedly increased.

What were the workers getting out of the special relationship? Or, to reverse the question, what was the regime getting out of it? To find an answer, it is necessary to return once again to the elusive concept of proletarian dictatorship. In strict Marxist terms, this meant that the proletariat would rule *as a class*; and it was probably so understood by many workers and Bolsheviks in 1917. But its operational meaning was different. Having taken power, the Bolsheviks had to find the men to run things. The initial selection was haphazard, but the criteria were clear: party members, workers, and soldiers and sailors who had actively supported the Revolution were the most reliable organizers, and the most likely to understand Bolshevik policies and objectives. Perhaps later, when the Civil War was over, there would be time to consider fundamental organizational reforms, but for the time being it was necessary to get 'our men' into positions of authority, either replacing or sharing command with 'their men' – the officials, officers and professionals inherited from the old regime. As it turned out, this approach worked, more or less, and it lasted. The way in which workers became 'masters' of Russian society after the October Revolution was not by an abolition of the old status hierarchy. It was by moving in very large numbers into the old masters' jobs.

Thus the essence of the special relationship between the party and the working class after 1917 was that the regime got 'cadres' (administrators and managers) from the working class, and workers got responsible, high-status jobs from the regime. The party's policies of worker recruitment were part of this process: in the 1920s, a substantial proportion of workers who joined the party were subsequently 'promoted' into white-collar jobs and left the factory bench forever. This, of course, made it quite difficult for the party to achieve its objective of making factory workers the majority group; and the party's statisticians had to introduce a special category of 'workers by social position' for those who had joined the party as workers but were now in other occupations, primarily administration. Although it took some time for the Bolshevik leaders (being good Marxists) to realize it, the regime's commitment to the working class had much less to do with workers *in situ* than with working-class upward mobility.

Earlier in this introduction, I raised the very broad and ambiguous question: 'What was the revolution about?' My answer could be roughly summarized as 'terror, progress and upward mobility'. But that is what the revolution (in this interpretation) *turned out* to be about. The Bolsheviks had other slogans inscribed on their banners in 1917 – 'soviet democracy', 'power to the working class', even the time-honoured *liberté, égalité, fraternité*. They believed or partly believed these slogans. They were enthusiasts with great expectations. Even for a historian as 'alien, indifferent and polemically-disposed' as Sukhanov, the Menshevik chronicler of 1917,[9] there is pathos in these expectations, and their inevitable disappointment.

The Revolution has achievements to its credit as well as failures. But the cost of the achievements was very high. With revolutions, as with all reckless undertakings, there is always the question whether, had the revolutionaries been able to foresee the future, they would ever have gone out to fight, and the allied question of whether in some cosmic sense it was all worth while. But, as has already been suggested, the second question is dangerous ground for historians. In dealing with historical events, the judgement of worth is very close to a statement of personal preferences; and the historian is not really in the same situation as a citizen casting his vote at the polls. We may dislike dictatorship and approve of upward mobility, or conceivably even reverse these preferences. But history has not consulted us, and we really have to deal with what seems to have happened and how it fits together. The Russian Revolution is now a part of history, not an aspect of contemporary politics. In this book, I have tried to treat it as such.

1 The Setting

At the beginning of the twentieth century, Russia was one of the great powers of Europe. But it was a great power that was universally regarded as backward by comparison with Britain, Germany and France. In economic terms, this meant that it had been late to emerge from feudalism (the peasants were freed from legal bondage to their lords or the state only in the 1860s) and late in industrializing. In political terms, it meant that until 1905 there were no legal political parties and no central elected parliament, and the autocracy survived with undiminished powers. Russia's towns had no tradition of political organization or self-government, and its nobility had similarly failed to develop a corporate sense of identity strong enough to force concessions from the throne. Legally, Russia's citizens still belonged to 'estates' (urban, peasant, clergy and noble), even though the estate system made no provision for new social groups like professionals and urban workers, and only the clergy retained anything like the characteristics of a self-contained caste.

The three decades before the 1917 Revolution saw not impoverishment but an increase in national wealth; and it was in this period that Russia experienced its first spurt of economic growth as a result of the government's industrialization policies, foreign investment, modernization of the banking and credit structure and a modest development of native entrepreneurial activity. The peasantry, which still constituted 80 per cent of Russia's population at the time of the Revolution, had not experienced a marked improvement in its economic position. But, contrary to some contemporary opinions, there had almost certainly not been a steady deterioration in the peasantry's economic situation either.

As Russia's last Tsar, Nicholas II, sadly perceived, the autocracy was fighting a losing battle against insidious liberal influences from the West. The direction of political change – towards something like a Western constitutional monarchy – seemed clear, though many members of the educated classes were impatient at the slowness of change and the stubbornly obstructionist attitude of the autocracy. After the 1905 Revolution, Nicholas gave in and established a national elected parliament, the Duma, at the same time legalizing political parties and trade unions. But the old arbitrary habits of autocratic rule and the continued activity of the secret police undermined these concessions.

After the Bolshevik Revolution of October 1917, many Russian emigrés looked back on the prerevolutionary years as a golden age of progress which had been arbitrarily interrupted (as it seemed) by the First World War, or the unruly mob, or the Bolsheviks. There was progress, but it contributed a great deal to the society's instability and the likelihood of political upheaval: the more rapidly a society changes (whether that change is perceived as progressive or regressive) the less stable it is likely to be. If we think of the great literature of prerevolutionary Russia, the most vivid images are those of displacement, alienation and lack of control over one's destiny. To the nineteenth-century writer Nikolai Gogol, Russia was a troika careering in darkness to an unknown destination. To the Duma politician Aleksandr Guchkov, denouncing Nicholas II and his Ministers in 1916, it was a car steered along the edge of a precipice by a mad driver, whose terrified passengers were debating the risk of seizing the wheel. In 1917 the risk was taken, and Russia's headlong movement forward became a plunge into revolution.

The society

The Russian Empire covered a vast expanse of territory, stretching from Poland in the west to the Pacific Ocean in the east, extending into the Arctic north, and reaching the Black Sea and the borders of Turkey and Afghanistan in the south. The hub of the Empire, European Russia (including some of the area that is now the Ukraine) had a population of 92 million in 1897, with the total population of the Empire recorded by that year's census at 126 million.[1] But even European Russia and the relatively advanced western regions of the Empire remained largely rural and non-urbanized. There were a handful of big urban industrial centres, most of them the product of recent and rapid expansion: St Petersburg, the imperial capital, renamed Petrograd during the First World War and Leningrad in 1924; Moscow, the old and (from 1918) future capital; Kiev, Kharkov and Odessa, together with the new mining and metallurgical centres of the Donbass, in what is now the Ukraine; Warsaw, Lodz and Riga in the west; Rostov and the oil city of Baku in the south. But most Russian provincial towns were still sleepy backwaters at the beginning of the twentieth century – local administrative centres with a small merchant population, a few schools, a peasant market and perhaps a railway station.

In the villages, much of the traditional way of life remained. The peasants still held their land in communal tenure, dividing the village fields into narrow strips which were tilled separately by the various peasant households; and in many villages, the *mir* (village council) would still periodically redistribute the strips so that each household had an equal share. Wooden ploughs were in common use, modern farming techniques were unknown in the villages, and peasant agriculture was not much above subsistence level. The peasants' huts were clustered together along the village street, peasants slept on the stove and kept their animals with them in the house, and the old patriarchal structure of the peasant family survived. The peasants were not much more than a generation away from serfdom: a peasant who was sixty at the turn of the century was already a young adult at the time of the Emancipation of 1861.

Of course the Emancipation had changed peasant life, but it had been framed with great caution so as to minimize the change and spread it over time. Before Emancipation, the peasants worked their strips on the village land, and they also worked the masters' land or paid him the equivalent of their labour in money. After the Emancipation, they continued to work their own land, and sometimes worked for hire on their former masters' land, while making 'redemption' payments to the state to offset the lump sums that had been given the landowners as immediate compensation. The redemption payments were scheduled to last for forty-nine years (although in fact the state cancelled them a few years early), and the village community was collectively responsible for the debts of all members. This meant that individual peasants were still bound to the village, though they were bound by the debt and the *mir*'s collective responsibility instead of by serfdom. The terms of the Emancipation were intended to prevent a mass influx of peasants into the towns and the creation of a landless proletariat which would represent a danger to public order. They also had the effect of reinforcing the *mir* and the old system of communal land tenure, and making it almost impossible for peasants to consolidate their strips, expand or improve their holdings, or make the transition to independent small-farming.

While permanent departure from the villages was difficult in the post-Emancipation decades, it was easy to leave the villages temporarily to work for hire in agriculture, construction, mining or in the towns. In fact such work was a necessity for many peasant families: the money was needed for taxes and redemption payments. The peasants who worked as seasonal labourers (*otkhodniki*) were often away for many months of the year, leaving their families to till their land in the villages. If the journeys were long – as in the case of peasants from central Russian villages who went to work in the Donbass mines – the *otkhodniki* might return only for the harvest and perhaps the spring sowing. The practice of departing for seasonal work was long-established, especially in the less fertile areas of European Russia where the landlords had exacted payment in money rather than labour from their serfs. But it was becoming increasingly common in the late nineteenth and early twentieth century, partly because more work was available in the towns. In the years immediately before the First World War, about nine million peasants took out passports for seasonal work outside their native village each year, and of these almost half were working outside agriculture.[2]

With one in every two peasant households in European Russia including a family member who left the village for work – and a higher proportion in the Petersburg and Central Industrial Regions and the western provinces – the impression that old Russia survived almost unchanged in the villages may well have been deceptive. Many peasants were in fact living with one foot in the traditional village world and the other in the quite different world of the modern industrial town. The degree to which peasants remained within the traditional world varied not only according to geographical location but also according to age and sex. The young were more likely to go away to work, and in addition the young men came in contact with a more modern world when they were called up for army service. Women and the aged were more likely to know only the village and the old peasant way of life. These differences in peasant experience showed up strikingly in the literacy figures of the 1897 census. The young were very much more literate than the old, men were more literate than women, and literacy was higher in the less fertile areas of European Russia – that is, the areas where seasonal migration was most common – than in the fertile Black Earth region.[3]

The urban working class was still very close to the peasantry. The number of permanent industrial workers (somewhat over three million in 1914) was smaller than the number of peasants who left the villages for non-agricultural seasonal work each year, and in fact it was almost impossible to make a hard-and-fast distinction between permanent urban-dwelling workers and peasants who worked most of the year in the towns. Even among the permanent workers, many retained land in the village and had left their wives and children living there; other workers lived in villages themselves (a pattern that was particularly common in the Moscow area) and commuted on a daily or weekly basis to the factory. Only in St Petersburg had a large proportion of the industrial labour force severed all connection with the countryside.

The main reason for the close interconnection between the urban working class and the peasantry was that Russia's rapid industrialization was a very recent phenomenon. It was not until the 1890s – more than half a century after Britain – that Russia experienced large-scale growth of industry and expansion of towns. Even then, the creation of a permanent urban working class was inhibited by the terms of the peasants' Emancipation in the 1860s, which kept them tied to the villages. First-generation workers, predominantly from the peasantry, formed a large part of the Russian working class; and few were more than second-generation workers and urban dwellers. Although Soviet historians claim that more than 50 per cent of industrial workers on the eve of the First World War were at least second-generation, this calculation clearly includes workers and peasant migrant workers (*otkhodniki*) whose fathers had been *otkhodniki*.

Despite these characteristics of underdevelopment, Russian industry was in some respects quite advanced by the time of the First World War. The modern industrial sector was small, but unusually highly concentrated, both geographically (notably in the regions centred on Petersburg and Moscow and the Ukrainian Donbass) and in terms of the size of the industrial plants. As Gerschenkron has pointed out, comparative backwardness had its own advantages: industrializing late, with the aid of large-scale foreign investment and energetic state involvement, Russia was able to skip over some of the early stages, borrow relatively advanced technology and move quickly towards large-scale modern production.[4] Enterprises like the famous Putilov metalworking and machine-building plant in Petersburg and the largely foreign-owned metallurgical plants of the Donbass employed many thousands of workers.

According to Marxist theory, a highly concentrated industrial proletariat in conditions of advanced capitalist production is likely to be revolutionary, whereas a pre-modern working class that retains strong ties to the peasantry is not. Thus the Russian working class had contradictory characteristics for a Marxist diagnosing its revolutionary potential. Yet the empirical evidence of the period from the 1890s to 1914 suggests that in fact Russia's working class, despite its close links with the peasantry, was exceptionally militant and revolutionary. Large-scale strikes were frequent, the workers showed considerable solidarity against management and state authority, and their demands were usually political as well as economic. In the 1905 Revolution, the workers of St Petersburg and Moscow organized their own revolutionary institutions, the soviets, and continued the struggle after the Tsar's constitutional concessions in October and the collapse of the middle-class liberals' drive against the autocracy. In the summer of 1914, the workers' strike movement in Petersburg and elsewhere assumed such threatening dimensions that some observers thought that the government could not take the risk of declaring a general mobilization for war.

The strength of working-class revolutionary sentiment in Russia may be explained in a number of different ways. In the first place, limited economic protest against employers – what Lenin called trade unionism – was very difficult under Russian conditions. The government had a large stake in Russia's native industry and in the protection of foreign investment, and state authorities were quick to provide troops when strikes against private enterprise showed signs of getting out of hand. That meant that even economic strikes (protests over wages and conditions) were likely to turn political; and the widespread resentment of Russian workers against foreign managers and technical personnel had a similar effect. Although it was Lenin, a Russian Marxist, who said that by its own efforts the working class could develop only a 'trade-union consciousness' rather than a revolutionary one, Russia's own experience (in contrast to that of Western Europe) did not bear him out.

In the second place, the peasant component of Russia's working class probably made it more revolutionary rather than less. Russian peasants were not innately conservative small proprietors like, for example, their French counterparts. The Russian peasantry's tradition of violent, anarchic rebellion against landlords and officials, exemplified in the great Pugachev revolt of the 1770s, was manifest once again in the peasant uprisings of 1905 and 1906: the Emancipation of 1861 had not permanently quietened the peasants' spirit of revolt because they did not regard it as a just or adequate emancipation and, increasingly land-hungry, asserted their right to the land that had been withheld. Moreover, the peasants who migrated to towns and became workers were often young, freed from family constraints but still unused to the discipline of the factory, and bearing the resentments and frustrations that go with dislocation and incomplete assimilation to an unfamiliar environment.[5] To some extent, the Russian working class was revolutionary just because it had not had time to acquire the 'trade-union consciousness' of which Lenin wrote – to become a settled industrial proletariat, capable of protecting its interests by non-revolutionary means, and understanding the opportunities for upward mobility that modern urban societies offer those with some education and skills.

However, the 'modern' characteristics of Russian society, even in the urban sector and the upper educated strata, were still very incomplete. It was often said that Russia had no middle class; and indeed its business and commercial class remained comparatively weak, and the professions had only recently acquired the status normal in industrialized societies. Despite increasing professionalization of the state bureaucracy, its upper ranks remained dominated by the nobility, traditionally the state's service class. Service prerogatives were all the more important to the nobility because of its economic decline as a landowning group after the abolition of serfdom: only a minority of noble landowners had successfully made the transition to capitalist, market-oriented agriculture.

The schizoid nature of Russian society in the early twentieth century is well illustrated by the bewildering variety of self-identifications offered by subscribers to the city directories of St Petersburg, the largest and most modern of Russia's cities. Some subscribers kept to the traditional forms and identified themselves by social estate and rank ('hereditary noble', 'merchant of the First Guild', 'honoured citizen', 'State Counsellor'). Others clearly belonged to the new world, and described themselves in terms of profession and type of employment ('stockbroker', 'mechanical engineer', 'company director' or, as representative of Russia's achievements in female emancipation, 'woman doctor'). A third group consisted of persons who were uncertain which world they belonged to, identifying themselves by estate in one year's directory and by profession in the next, or even giving both identifications at once, like the subscriber who listed himself quaintly as 'nobleman, dentist'.

In less formal contexts, educated Russians would often describe themselves as members of the intelligentsia. Sociologically, this was a very slippery concept, but in broad terms the word 'intelligentsia' described a Westernized educated elite, alienated from the rest of Russian society by its education and from Russia's autocratic regime by its radical ideology. However, the Russian intelligentsia did not see itself as an elite, but rather as a classless group united by moral concern for the betterment of society, the capacity for 'critical thought' and, in particular, a critical, semi-oppositionist attitude to the regime. The term came into common use around the middle of the nineteenth century, but the genesis of the concept may be found in the latter part of the eighteenth century, when the nobility was released from the obligation of compulsory service to the state, and some of its members, educated but finding their education under-utilized, developed an alternative ethos of obligation to 'serve the people'.[6] Ideally (though not altogether in practice), intelligentsia membership and bureaucratic service were incompatible. The Russian revolutionary movement of the second half of the nineteenth century, characterized by small-scale conspiratorial organization to fight the autocracy and thus liberate the people, was largely a product of the intelligentsia's radical ideology and political disaffection.

By the end of the century, when the development of high-status professions had provided educated Russians with a broader range of occupational choice than had existed earlier, an individual's self-definition as an *intelligent* often implied relatively passive liberal attitudes rather than active revolutionary commitment to political change. Still, Russia's new professional class inherited enough of the old intelligentsia tradition to feel sympathy and respect for the committed revolutionaries, and lack of sympathy for the regime, even when its officials tried to pursue reforming policies or were assassinated by revolutionary terrorists.

Moreover, some types of professional avocation were peculiarly difficult to combine with total support for the autocracy. The legal profession, for example, blossomed as a result of the reform of the legal system in the 1860s, but the reforms were much less successful in the long term in extending the rule of law in Russian society and administration, particularly in the period of reaction that followed the assassination of Emperor Alexander II by a group of revolutionary terrorists in 1881. Lawyers whose education had led them to believe in the rule of law were likely to disapprove of arbitrary administrative practices, untrammelled police power and governmental attempts to influence the working of the judicial system.[7] A similar inherent adversary relationship to the regime was associated with the zemstvos, elected local-government bodies that were institutionally quite separate from the state bureaucracy and frequently in conflict with it. In the early twentieth century, the zemstvos employed around 70,000 professionals (doctors, teachers, agronomists and so on), whose radical sympathies were notorious.

Engineers and other technical specialists working for the state or in private enterprises had less obvious reason to feel alienated from the regime, especially given the energetic sponsorship of economic modernization and industrialization that came from the Ministry of Finance under Sergei Witte in the 1890s and subsequently from the Ministry of Trade and Industry. Witte, indeed, made every effort to rally support for the autocracy and its modernization drive among Russia's technical specialists and businessmen; but the problem was that Witte's enthusiasm for economic and technological progress was obviously not shared by a large part of Russia's bureaucratic elite, as well as being personally uncongenial to Emperor Nicholas II. Modernization-minded professionals and entrepreneurs might not object in principle to the idea of autocratic government (though in fact many of them did, as a result of their exposure to radical politics as students of the Polytechnical Institutes). But it was very difficult for them to see the *Tsarist* autocracy as an effective agent of modernization: its record was too inconsistent, and its political ideology too clearly reflected nostalgia for the past rather than any coherent vision of the future.

The revolutionary tradition

The task which the Russian intelligentsia had taken on itself was the betterment of Russia – first, drawing up the social and political blueprints for the country's future, and then, if possible, taking action to translate them into reality. The yardstick for Russia's future was Western Europe's present. Russian intellectuals might decide to accept or reject different phenomena that were observed in Europe, but all were on the agenda for Russian discussion and possible inclusion in the plans for Russia's future. In the third quarter of the nineteenth century, one of the central topics of discussion was Western European industrialization and its social and political consequences.

One view was that capitalist industrialization had produced human degradation, impoverishment of the masses and destruction of the social fabric in the west, and therefore ought to be avoided at all costs by Russia. The radical intellectuals who held this view have been retrospectively grouped under the heading of 'Populists', though the label implies a degree of coherent organization which did not in fact exist (it was originally used by the Russian Marxists to differentiate themselves from all the various intelligentsia groups that disagreed with them). Populism was essentially the mainstream of Russian radical thought from the 1860s to the 1880s.

The Russian intelligentsia generally accepted socialism (as understood by Europe's pre-Marxist socialists, especially the French 'utopians') as the most desirable form of social organization, though this was not seen as incompatible with the acceptance of liberalism as an ideology of political change. The intelligentsia also reacted to its social isolation by a fervent desire to bridge the gulf between itself and 'the people' (*narod*). The strain of intelligentsia thought described as Populism combined an objection to capitalist industrialization with an idealization of the Russian peasantry. The Populists saw that capitalism had had a destructive impact on traditional rural communities in Europe, uprooting peasants from the land and forcing them into the cities as a landless and exploited industrial proletariat. They wished to save the Russian peasants' traditional form of village organization, the commune or *mir*, from the ravages of capitalism, because they believed that the *mir* was an egalitarian institution – perhaps a survival of primitive communism – through which Russia might find a separate path to socialism.

In the early 1870s, the intelligentsia's idealization of the peasantry and frustration with its own situation and the prospects for political reform led to the spontaneous mass movement which best exemplifies Populist aspirations – the 'going to the people' of 1873–4. Thousands of students and members of the intelligentsia left the cities to go to the villages, sometimes envisaging themselves as enlighteners of the peasantry, sometimes more humbly seeking to acquire the simple wisdom of the people, and sometimes with the hope of conducting revolutionary organization and propaganda. The movement had no central direction and no clearly defined political intent as far as most of the participants were concerned: its spirit was less that of a political campaign than a religious pilgrimage. But the distinction was hard for either the peasantry or the Tsarist police to grasp. The authorities were greatly alarmed, and made mass arrests. The peasants were suspicious, regarding their uninvited guests as offspring of the nobility and probable class enemies, and often handing them over to the police. This débâcle produced deep disappointment among the Populists. They did not waver in their determination to serve the people, but some concluded that it was their tragic fate to serve them as outcasts, revolutionary desperadoes whose heroic actions would be appreciated only after their deaths. There was an upsurge of revolutionary terrorism in the late 1870s, motivated partly by the Populists' desire to avenge their imprisoned comrades and partly by the rather desperate hope that a well-placed blow might destroy the whole superstructure of autocratic Russia, leaving the Russian people free to find its own destiny. In 1881, the 'People's Will' group of Populist terrorists succeeded in assassinating Emperor Alexander II. The effect was not to destroy the autocracy, but rather to frighten it into more repressive policies, greater arbitrariness and circumvention of law, and the creation of something close to a modern police state.[8] The popular response to the assassination included antisemitic pogroms in the Ukraine, and rumours in Russia's villages that nobles had murdered the Tsar because he had freed the peasants from serfdom.

It was in the 1880s, in the wake of the two Populist disasters, that the Marxists emerged as a distinct group within the Russian intelligentsia, repudiating the utopian idealism, terrorist tactics and peasant orientation that had previously characterized the revolutionary movement. Because of the unfavourable political climate in Russia and their own repudiation of terrorism, the Marxists made their initial impact in intellectual debate rather than by revolutionary action. They argued that capitalist industrialization was inevitable in Russia, and that the peasant *mir* was already in a state of internal disintegration, propped up only by the state and its state-imposed responsibilities for the collection of taxes and redemption payments. They asserted that capitalism constituted the only possible path towards socialism, and that the industrial proletariat produced by capitalist development was the only class capable of bringing about true socialist revolution. These premisses, they claimed, could be scientifically proven by the objective laws of historical development that Marx and Engels had explained in their writings. The Marxists scoffed at those who chose socialism as an ideology because it was ethically superior (it was, of course, but that was beside the point). The point about socialism was that, like capitalism, it was a predictable stage in the development of human society.

To Karl Marx, an old European revolutionary who instinctively

applauded the struggle of 'People's Will' against the Russian autocracy, the early Russian Marxists clustered around Georgii Plekhanov in
emigration seemed too passive and pedantic – revolutionaries who
were content to write articles about the historical inevitability of
revolution while others were fighting and dying for the cause. But the
impact on the Russian intelligentsia was different, because one of the
Marxists' scientific predictions was quickly realized: they said that
Russia *must* industrialize, and in the 1890s, under Witte's energetic
direction, it did. True, the industrialization was as much a product of
state sponsorship and foreign investment as of spontaneous capitalist
development, so that in a sense Russia did take a separate path from
the West.[9] But to contemporaries, Russia's rapid industrialization
seemed dramatic proof that the Marxists' predictions were right, and
that Marxism had at least some of the answers to the Russian intelligentsia's 'great questions'.

Marxism in Russia – as in China, India and other developing countries – had a meaning rather different from that which it had in the
industrialized countries of Western Europe. It was an ideology of
modernization as well as an ideology of revolution. Even Lenin, who
could scarcely be accused of revolutionary passivity, made his name as
a Marxist with a weighty study, *The Development of Capitalism in
Russia*, that was both analysis and advocacy of the process of economic
modernization; and virtually all the other leading Marxists of his
generation in Russia produced similar works. The advocacy, to be
sure, is presented in the Marxist manner ('I told you so' rather than 'I
support . . .'), and it may surprise modern readers who know Lenin
only as an anti-capitalist revolutionary. But capitalism was a 'progressive' phenomenon to Marxists in late nineteenth-century Russia, a
backward society that by Marxist definition was still semi-feudal. In
ideological terms, they were in favour of capitalism because it was a
necessary stage on the way to socialism. But in emotional terms, the
commitment went deeper: the Russian Marxists admired the modern, industrial, urban world, and were offended by the backwardness
of old rural Russia. It has often been pointed out that Lenin – an
activist revolutionary willing to give history a push in the right direction – was an unorthodox Marxist with some of the revolutionary
voluntarism of the old Populist tradition. That is true, but it is relevant
mainly to his behaviour in times of actual revolution, around 1905 and
in 1917. In the 1890s, he chose Marxism rather than Populism because
he was on the side of modernization; and that basic choice explains a

great deal about the course of the Russian revolution after Lenin and his party took power in 1917.

The Marxists made another important choice in the early controversy with the Populists over capitalism: they chose the urban working class as their base of support and Russia's main potential force for revolution. This distinguished them from the old tradition of the Russian revolutionary intelligentsia (upheld by the Populists and later, from its formation in the early 1900s, by the Socialist-Revolutionary (SR) Party), with its one-sided love affair with the peasantry. It distinguished them also from the liberals (some of them former Marxists), whose Liberation movement was to emerge as a political force shortly before 1905, since the liberals hoped for a 'bourgeois' revolution and won support from the new professional class and the liberal zemstvo nobility.

Initially, the Marxists' choice did not look particularly promising: the working class was tiny in comparison with the peasantry, and, in comparison with the urban upper classes, lacked status, education and financial resources. The Marxists' early contacts with the workers were essentially educational, consisting of circles and study groups in which intellectuals offered the workers some general education plus the elements of Marxism. Historians differ in their assessment of the contribution that this made to the development of a revolutionary labour movement.[10] But the Tsarist authorities took the political threat fairly seriously. According to a police report in 1901,[11]

Agitators, seeking to realize their goals, have achieved some success, unfortunately, in organizing the workers to fight against the government. Within the last three or four years, the easygoing Russian young man has been transformed into a special type of semi-literate *intelligent*, who feels obliged to spurn family and religion, to disregard the law, and to deny and scoff at constituted authority. Fortunately such young men are not numerous in the factories, but this negligible handful terrorizes the inert majority of workers into following it.

Clearly Marxists had an advantage over earlier groups of revolutionary intellectuals seeking contact with the masses: they had found a section of the masses willing to listen. Although Russian workers were not far removed from the peasantry, they were a much more literate group, and at least some of them had acquired a modern, urban sense of the possibility of 'bettering themselves'. Education was a means of upward social mobility as well as the path towards revolution envisaged by both revolutionary intellectuals and the police. The Marxist teachers, unlike the earlier Populist missionaries to the peasantry, had something more than the risk of police harassment to offer their students.

From workers' education, the Marxists – illegally organized from 1898 as the Russian Social-Democratic Labour Party – progressed to an involvement in more directly political labour organization, strikes and, in 1905, revolution. The match between party-political organization and actual working-class protest was never an exact one, and in 1905 the socialist parties had great difficulty keeping up with the working-class revolutionary movement. Between 1898 and 1914, nevertheless, the Russian Social-Democratic Labour Party ceased to be a preserve of the intelligentsia and became in the literal sense a workers' movement. Its leaders still came from the intelligentsia, and spent most of their time living outside Russia in European emigration. But in Russia, the majority of members and activists were workers (or, in the case of professional revolutionaries, former workers).[12]

In terms of their theory, the Russian Marxists started off with what seemed to be a major revolutionary disadvantage: they were obliged by their theory to work not for the coming revolution, but for the revolution after next. According to orthodox Marxist prediction, Russia's entry into the capitalist phase (which took place only at the end of the nineteenth century) would inevitably lead to the overthrow of the autocracy by a bourgeois liberal revolution. The proletariat might support this revolution, but it seemed unlikely to have more than a secondary role. Russia would be ripe for proletarian socialist revolution only after capitalism had reached its maturity, and that time might be far in the future.

This problem did not seem very pressing before 1905, since no revolution was in progress and the Marxists were having some success in organizing the working class. However, a small group – the 'legal Marxists', headed by Petr Struve – came to identify itself strongly with the objectives of the first (liberal) revolution on the Marxist agenda, and to lose interest in the ultimate goal of socialist revolution. It was not surprising that modernization-minded opponents of the autocracy like Struve should have joined the Marxists in the 1890s, since there was at that time no liberal movement for them to join; and it was equally natural that around the turn of the century they left the Marxists to participate in the establishment of the liberal Liberation movement. The heresy of legal Marxism was nevertheless roundly denounced by Russian Social-Democratic leaders, especially by Lenin. Lenin's violent hostility to 'bourgeois liberalism' was somewhat illogical in Marxist terms, and caused some perplexity to his colleagues. In revolutionary terms, however, Lenin's attitude was extremely rational.

At around the same time, the Russian Social-Democratic leaders repudiated the heresy of Economism, that is, that the workers' movement should stress economic rather than political goals. There were in fact few articulate Economists in the Russian movement, partly because Russian workers' protests tended to progress very quickly from purely economic issues like wages to political ones. But the emigré leaders, often more sensitive to trends within European Social Democracy than to the situation inside Russia, feared the revisionist and reformist tendencies that had developed in the German movement. In the doctrinal struggles over Economism and legal Marxism, the Russian Marxists were putting clearly on record that they were revolutionaries, not reformists, and that their cause was the socialist workers' revolution and not the revolution of the liberal bourgeoisie.

In 1903, when the Russian Social-Democratic Party held its Second Congress, the leaders fell into dispute over an apparently minor issue – the composition of the editorial board of the party newspaper *Iskra*.[13] No real substantive questions were involved, though to the extent that the dispute revolved around Lenin it might be said that he himself was the underlying issue, and that his colleagues considered that he was too aggressively seeking a position of dominance. Lenin's manner at the congress was overbearing; and he had recently been laying down the law very decisively on various theoretical questions, notably the organization and functions of the party. There was tension between Lenin and Plekhanov, the senior Russian Marxist; and the friendship between Lenin and his contemporary Yulii Martov was on the point of breaking.

The outcome of the Second Congress was a split in the Russian Social-Democratic Labour Party between 'Bolshevik' and 'Menshevik' factions. The Bolsheviks were those who followed Lenin's lead, and the Mensheviks (including Plekhanov, Martov and Trotsky) constituted a larger and more diverse group of party members who thought Lenin had overreached himself. The split made little sense to Marxists inside Russia, and at the time of its occurrence was not regarded as irrevocable even by the emigrés. It proved, nevertheless, to be permanent; and as time passed the two factions acquired more clearly distinct identities than they had had in 1903. In later years, Lenin was sometimes to express pride in being a 'splitter', meaning by this that he considered large, loosely-knit political organizations to be less effective than smaller, disciplined radical groups demanding a high degree of commitment and ideological unity.

In the years after 1903, the Mensheviks emerged as the more orthodox in their Marxism (not counting Trotsky, a Menshevik until mid-1917 but always a maverick), less inclined to force the pace of events towards revolution and less interested in creating a tightly-organized and disciplined revolutionary party. They had more success than the Bolsheviks in attracting support in the non-Russian areas of the Empire, while the Bolsheviks had the edge among Russian workers. (In both parties, however, Jews and other non-Russians were prominent in the intelligentsia-dominated leadership.) In the last prewar years, 1910–14, the Mensheviks lost working-class support to the Bolsheviks as the workers' mood became more militant: they were perceived as a more 'respectable' party with closer links to the bourgeoisie, whereas the Bolsheviks were seen as more working-class as well as more revolutionary.[14]

The Bolsheviks, unlike the Mensheviks, had a single leader, and their identity was in large part defined by Lenin's ideas and personality. Lenin's first distinctive trait as a Marxist theoretician was his emphasis on party organization. He saw the party not only as the vanguard of proletarian revolution but also in a sense as its creator, since he argued that the proletariat alone could achieve only a trade-union consciousness and not a revolutionary one.

Lenin believed that the core of the party's membership should consist of full-time professional revolutionaries, recruited both from the intelligentsia and the working class, but concentrating on the political organization of workers rather than any other social group. In *What Is To Be Done?* (1902), he insisted on the importance of centralization, strict discipline and ideological unity within the party. These, of course, were logical prescriptions for a party operating clandestinely in a police state. Nevertheless, it seemed to many of Lenin's contemporaries (and later to many scholars) that Lenin's dislike of looser mass organizations allowing greater diversity and spontaneity was not purely expedient but reflected a natural authoritarian bent.

Lenin differed from many other Russian Marxists in seeming actively to desire a proletarian revolution rather than simply predicting that one would ultimately occur. This was a character trait that would surely have endeared him to Karl Marx, despite the fact that it required some revision of orthodox Marxism. The idea that the liberal bourgeoisie must be the natural leader of Russia's anti-autocratic revolution was never really acceptable to Lenin; and in *Two Tactics of Social Democracy*, written in the midst of the 1905 Revolution, he insisted that the proletariat – allied with Russia's rebellious peasantry – could and should play a dominant role. Clearly it was necessary for any Russian Marxist with serious revolutionary intentions to find a way round the doctrine of bourgeois revolutionary leadership, and Trotsky was to make a similar and perhaps more successful effort with his theory of 'permanent revolution'. In Lenin's writing from 1905, the words 'dictatorship', 'insurrection' and 'civil war' appeared increasingly frequently. It was in these harsh, violent and realistic terms that he conceived the future revolutionary transfer of power.

The 1905 Revolution and its aftermath; the First World War

Late Tsarist Russia was an expanding imperial power with the largest standing army of any of the great powers of Europe. Its strength *vis-à-vis* the outside world was a source of pride, an achievement that could be set against the country's internal political and social problems. In the words attributed to an early twentieth-century Minister of Interior, 'a small victorious war' was the best remedy for Russia's domestic unrest. Historically, however, this was a rather dubious proposition. Over the past half century, Russia's wars had tended neither to be successful nor to strengthen society's confidence in the government. The military humiliation of the Crimean War had precipitated the radical domestic reforms of the 1860s. The diplomatic defeat that Russia suffered after its military involvement in the Balkans in the late 1870s produced an internal political crisis that ended only with Alexander II's assassination. In the early 1900s, Russian expansion in the Far East was pushing it towards a conflict with another expansionist power in the region, Japan. Though some of Nicholas II's ministers urged caution, the prevailing sentiment in court and high bureaucratic circles was that there were easy pickings to be made in the Far East, and that Japan – an inferior, non-European power, after all – would not be a formidable adversary. Initiated by Japan, but provoked almost equally by Russian policy in the Far East, the Russo-Japanese War broke out in January 1904.

For Russia, the war turned out to be a series of disasters and humiliations on land and at sea. The early patriotic enthusiasm of respectable society quickly soured, and – as had also happened during the 1891 famine – attempts by public organizations like the zemstvos to help the government in an emergency only led to conflicts with the bureaucracy and frustration. This fuelled the liberal movement, since autocracy always seemed least tolerable when it was most clearly perceived as incompetent and inefficient; and the zemstvo nobility and professionals rallied behind the illegal Liberation movement, directed from Europe by Petr Struve and other liberal activists. In the last months of 1904, with the war still in progress, the liberals in Russia organized a banquet campaign (modelled on that used against the French King, Louis Philippe, in 1847), through which the social elite demonstrated support for the idea of constitutional reform. At the same time, the government was under other kinds of pressure, including terrorist attacks on officials, student demonstrations and workers' strikes. In January 1905, Petersburg workers held a peaceful demonstration – organized not by militants and revolutionaries, but by a renegade priest with police connections, Father Gapon – to bring their economic grievances to the attention of the Tsar. On Bloody Sunday (9 January), troops fired on the demonstrators outside the Winter Palace, and the 1905 Revolution had begun.

The spirit of national solidarity against the autocracy was very strong during the first nine months of 1905. The liberals' claim to leadership of the revolutionary movement was not seriously challenged; and their bargaining position with the regime was based not only on support from the zemstvos and the new unions of middle-class professionals but also on the heterogeneous pressures coming from student demonstrations, workers' strikes, peasant disorders, mutinies in the armed forces and unrest in the non-Russian regions of the Empire. The autocracy, for its part, was consistently on the defensive, seized by panic and confusion, and apparently unable to restore order. Its prospects for survival improved markedly when Witte managed to negotiate peace with Japan (the Treaty of Portsmouth) on remarkably advantageous terms in late August 1905. But the regime still had a million of its troops in Manchuria, and they could not be brought home on the Trans-Siberian Railway until the striking railwaymen were brought back under control.

The culmination of the liberal revolution was Nicholas II's October Manifesto (1905), in which he conceded the principle of a constitution and promised to create a national elected parliament, the Duma. The Manifesto divided the liberals: the Octobrists accepted it, while the Constitutional Democrats (Cadets) formally withheld acceptance and hoped for further concessions. In practice, however, the liberals withdrew from revolutionary activity at this time, and concentrated their energies on organizing the new Octobrist and Cadet parties and preparing for the forthcoming Duma elections.

However, the workers remained actively revolutionary until the end of the year, achieving greater visibility than before and becoming increasingly militant. In October, the workers of Petersburg organized a 'soviet' or council of workers' representatives elected in the factories. The practical function of the Petersburg Soviet was to provide the city with a kind of emergency municipal government at a time when other institutions were paralysed and a general strike was in progress. But it also became a political forum for the workers, and to a lesser extent for socialists from the revolutionary parties (Trotsky, then a Menshevik, became one of the Soviet's leaders). For a few months, the Tsarist authorities handled the Soviet in a gingerly manner, but early in December it was dispersed by a successful police operation in other cities; and the news of the attack on the Petersburg Soviet led to an armed uprising by the Moscow Soviet, in which the Bolsheviks had gained considerable influence. This was put down by troops, but the workers fought back and there were many casualties.

The urban revolution of 1905 stimulated the most serious peasant uprisings since the Pugachev revolt in the late eighteenth century. But the urban and rural revolutions were not simultaneous. Peasant rioting – consisting of the sacking and burning of manor houses and attacks on landowners and officials – began in the summer of 1905 and rose to a peak in the late autumn, subsided, and then resumed on a large scale in 1906. But even in late 1905 the regime was strong enough to begin using troops in a campaign of village-by-village pacification. By the middle of 1906, all the troops were back from the Far East, and discipline had been restored in the armed forces. In the winter of 1906–7, much of rural Russia was under martial law, and summary justice (including over a thousand executions) was dispensed by field courts martial.

Russia's landowning nobility learnt a lesson from the events of 1905–6, namely that its interests lay with the autocracy (which could perhaps shield it from a vengeful peasantry) and not with the liberals.[15] But in urban terms, the 1905 Revolution did not produce such clear consciousness of class polarization: even for most socialists, this was not a Russian 1848, revealing the treacherous nature of liberalism and the essential antagonism of bourgeoisie and proletariat. The liberals – representing a professional rather than capitalist middle class – had stood aside in October, but they had not joined the regime in an onslaught on the workers' revolution. Their attitude to the workers' and socialist movements remained much more benign than that of liberals in most European countries. The workers, for their part, seem to have perceived the liberals rather as a timorous ally than a treacherous one.

The political outcome of the 1905 Revolution was ambiguous, and in some ways unsatisfactory to all concerned. In the Fundamental Laws of 1906 – the closest Russia came to a constitution – Nicholas made known his belief that Russia was still an autocracy. True, the autocrat now consulted with an elected parliament, and political parties had been legalized. But the Duma had limited powers; Ministers remained responsible solely to the autocrat; and, after the first two Dumas proved insubordinate and were arbitrarily dissolved, a new electoral system was introduced which virtually disfranchised some social groups and heavily over-represented the landed nobility. The Duma's main importance, perhaps, lay in providing a public forum for political debate and a training-ground for politicians. The political reforms of 1905–7 bred parliamentary politicians just as the legal reforms of the 1860s had bred lawyers; and both groups had an inherent tendency to develop values and aspirations that the autocracy could not abide.

One thing that the 1905 Revolution did *not* change was the police regime that had come to maturity in the 1880s. Due process of law was still suspended (as in the case of the field courts martial dealing with the rebellious peasantry in 1906–7) for much of the population much of the time. Of course there were understandable reasons for this: the fact that in 1908, a comparatively quiet year, 1,800 officials were killed and 2,083 were wounded in politically motivated attacks[16] indicates how tumultuous the society remained, and how much the regime remained on the defensive. But it meant that in many respects the political reforms were only a façade. Trade unions, for example, had been made legal in principle, but individual unions were frequently closed down by the police. Political parties were legal, and even the revolutionary socialist parties could contest the Duma elections and win a few seats – yet the members of revolutionary socialist parties were no less liable to arrest than in the past, and the party leaders (most of whom returned to Russia during the 1905 Revolution) were forced back into emigration to avoid imprisonment and exile.

With hindsight, it might seem that the Marxist revolutionaries, with

1905 under their belts and 1917 already looming on the horizon, should have been congratulating themselves on the workers' spectacular revolutionary début and looking confidently towards the future. But in fact their mood was quite different. Neither Bolsheviks nor Mensheviks had got more than a toehold in the workers' revolution of 1905: the workers had not so much rejected as outpaced them, and this was a very sobering thought, particularly for Lenin. Revolution had come, but the regime had fought back and survived. Within the intelligentsia, there was much talk about abandoning the revolutionary dream and the old illusions of social perfectibility. From the revolutionary standpoint, it was no gain to have a façade of legal political institutions and a new breed of self-important, chattering liberal politicians (to summarize Lenin's view of them, which did not greatly differ from Nicholas II's). It was also deeply, almost unbearably disappointing for the revolutionary leaders to return to the familiar dreariness of emigré life. The emigrés were never more prickly and contentious than in the years between 1905 and 1917; indeed, the Russians' continual petty bickering became one of the scandals of European Social Democracy, and Lenin was one of the very worst offenders.

Among the bad news of the prewar years was that the regime was embarking on a major programme of agrarian reform. The peasant revolts of 1905–7 had persuaded the government to abandon its earlier premiss that the *mir* was the best guarantee of rural stability. Its hopes now lay in the creation of a class of small independent farmers – a wager on 'the sober and the strong', as Nicholas's chief Minister, Petr Stolypin, described it. Peasants were now encouraged to consolidate their holdings and separate from the *mir*, and land commissions were established in the provinces to facilitate the process. The assumption was that the poor would sell up and go to the towns, while the more prosperous would improve and expand their holdings and acquire the conservative petty-bourgeois mentality of, say, the French peasant farmer. By 1914, about 40 per cent of peasant households in European Russia had formally separated from the *mir*, although, given the legal and practical complexity of the process, only a relatively small number had completed the later steps towards establishing themselves as proprietors farming their own consolidated and self-contained blocks of land.[17] The Stolypin reforms were 'progressive' in Marxist terms, since they laid the basis for capitalist development in agriculture. But, in contrast to the development of urban capitalism, their short- and

medium-range implications for Russian revolution were highly de-
pressing. Russia's traditional peasantry was prone to revolt. If the
Stolypin reforms worked (as Lenin, for one, feared that they might),
the Russian proletariat would have lost an important revolutionary
ally.

In 1906, the Russian economy was bolstered by an enormous loan
(two and a quarter billion francs) which Witte negotiated with an
international banking consortium; and both native and foreign-owned
industry expanded rapidly in the prewar years. This meant, of course,
that the industrial working class also expanded. But labour unrest
dropped down sharply for some years after the savage crushing of the
workers' revolutionary movement in the winter of 1905–6, picking up
again only around 1910. Large-scale strikes became increasingly common in the immediate prewar years, culminating in the Petrograd
general strike of the summer of 1914, which was sufficiently serious for
some observers to doubt that Russia could risk mobilizing its army for
war. The workers' demands were political as well as economic; and
their grievances against the regime included its responsibility for
foreign domination of many sectors of Russian industry as well as its
use of coercion against the workers themselves. In Russia, the Mensheviks were conscious of losing support as the workers became more
violent and belligerent, and the Bolsheviks were conscious of gaining
it. But this did not noticeably raise the spirits of the Bolshevik leaders
in emigration: because of poor communications with Russia, they
were probably not fully aware of it, and their own position in the
emigré Russian and socialist community in Europe was increasingly
weak and isolated.[18]

When war broke out in Europe in August 1914, with Russia allied
with France and England against Germany and Austria-Hungary, the
political emigrés became almost completely cut off from Russia, as
well as experiencing the normal problems of alien residents in wartime. In the European socialist movement as a whole, large numbers of
former internationalists became patriots overnight when war was declared. The Russians were less inclined than others to outright patriotism, but most took the 'defensist' position of supporting Russia's war
effort as long as it was in defence of Russian territory. Lenin, however,
belonged to the smaller group of 'defeatists' who repudiated their
country's cause entirely: it was an imperialist war, as far as Lenin was
concerned, and the best prospect was a Russian defeat which might
provoke civil war and revolution. This was a very controversial stand,

even in the socialist movement, and the Bolsheviks found themselves very much cold-shouldered. In Russia, all known Bolsheviks – including Duma deputies – were arrested for the duration of the war.

As in 1904, Russia's declaration of war produced a public surge of patriotic enthusiasm, much jingoistic flag-waving, a temporary moratorium on internal strife and earnest attempts by respectable society and non-governmental organizations to assist the government's war effort. But once again, the mood quickly turned sour. The Russian Army suffered crushing defeats and losses (a total of five million casualties for 1914–17), and the German Army penetrated deep into the western territories of the Empire, causing a chaotic outflow of refugees into central Russia. Defeats bred suspicion of treason in high places, and one of the main targets was Nicholas's wife, Empress Alexandra, who was a German princess by birth. Scandal surrounded Alexandra's relationship with Rasputin, a shady but charismatic character whom she trusted as a true man of God who could control her son's haemophilia. When Nicholas assumed the responsibilities of Commander in Chief of the Russian Army, which took him away from the capital for long periods, Alexandra and Rasputin began to exercise a disastrous influence over ministerial appointments. Relations between the government and the Fourth Duma deteriorated drastically: the mood in the Duma and among the educated public as a whole was captured in the phrase with which the Cadet Pavel Milyukov punctuated a speech on the government's shortcomings – 'Is this stupidity or is it treason?' Late in 1916, Rasputin was murdered by some young nobles close to the court and a right-wing Duma deputy, whose motives were to save the honour of Russia and the autocracy.

The pressures of the First World War – and, no doubt, the personalities of Nicholas and his wife, and the family tragedy of their young son's haemophilia[19] – threw the anachronistic traits of the Russian autocracy into sharp relief, and made Nicholas seem less like an upholder of the autocratic tradition than an unwitting satirist of it. The 'ministerial leapfrog' of incompetent favourites in the Cabinet, the illiterate peasant faith-healer at court, the intrigues of the high nobility leading to Rasputin's murder and even the epic story of Rasputin's stubborn resistance to death by poison, bullets and drowning – all these seemed to belong to an earlier age, to be a bizarre and irrelevant accompaniment to the twentieth-century realities of troop-trains, trench warfare and mass mobilization. Russia not only had an educated public to perceive this, but also possessed institutions like the Duma, the political parties, the zemstvos and the industrialists' War Industries Committee which were potential agents of transition from the old regime to the modern world.

The autocracy's situation was precarious on the eve of the First World War. The society was deeply divided, and the political and bureaucratic structure was fragile and overstrained. The regime was so vulnerable to any kind of jolt or setback that it is hard to imagine that it could have survived long, even without the War, although clearly change might in other circumstances have come less violently and with less radical consequences than was the case in 1917.

The First World War both exposed and increased the vulnerability of Russia's old regime. The public applauded victories, but would not tolerate defeats. When defeats occurred, the society did not rally behind its government (a relatively normal reaction, especially if the enemy becomes an invader of the homeland, and the reaction of Russian society in 1812 and again in 1941–2) – but instead turned sharply against it, denouncing its incompetence and backwardness in tones of contempt and moral superiority. This suggests that the regime's legitimacy had become extremely shaky, and that its survival was very closely related to visible achievements or, failing that, sheer luck. The old regime had been lucky in 1904–6, an earlier occasion when war defeats had plunged it into revolution, because it got out of the war relatively quickly and honourably, and was able to obtain a very large postwar loan from Europe, which was then at peace. It was not so lucky in 1914–17. The war lasted too long, draining not only Russia but the whole of Europe. More than a year before the Armistice in Europe, Russia's old regime was dead.

2 1917: The Revolutions of February and October

In February 1917, the autocracy collapsed in the face of popular demonstrations and the withdrawal of elite support for the regime. In the euphoria of revolution, political solutions seemed easy. Russia's future form of government would, of course, be democratic. The exact meaning of that ambiguous term and the nature of Russia's new constitution would be decided by a Constituent Assembly, to be elected by the Russian people as soon as circumstances permitted. In the meantime, the elite and popular revolutions – liberal politicians, the propertied and professional classes and the officer corps in the first category; socialist politicians, the urban working class and rank-and-file soldiers and sailors in the second – would coexist, as they had done in the glorious days of national revolutionary solidarity in 1905. In institutional terms, the new Provisional Government would represent the elite revolution, while the newly revived Petrograd Soviet would speak for the revolution of the people. Their relationship would be complementary rather than competitive, and 'dual power' (the term applied to the coexistence of the Provisional Government and the Soviet) would be a source of strength, not of weakness. Russian liberals, after all, had traditionally tended to see the socialists as allies, whose special interest in social reform was comparable to and compatible with the liberals' own special interest in political democratization. Most Russian socialists, similarly, were prepared to see the liberals as allies, since they accepted the Marxist view that the bourgeois liberal revolution had first place on the agenda and the socialists were bound to support it in the struggle against autocracy.

Yet within eight months the hopes and expectations of February lay in ruins. 'Dual power' proved an illusion, masking something very like a power vacuum. The popular revolution became progressively more radical, while the elite revolution moved towards an anxious conservative stance in defence of property and law and order. The Provisional Government barely survived General Kornilov's attempted coup from the right before succumbing in October to the Bolsheviks' successful coup from the left, popularly associated with the slogan of 'All power to the soviets'. The long-awaited Constituent Assembly met but accomplished nothing, being unceremoniously dispersed by the Bolsheviks in January 1918. On the peripheries of Russia, officers of the old Tsarist Army were mustering their forces to fight the Bolsheviks, some under the monarchist banner that had seemed banished forever in 1917. The revolution had not brought liberal democracy to Russia. Instead, it had brought anarchy and civil war.

The headlong passage from democratic February to Red October astonished victors and vanquished alike. For Russian liberals, the shock was traumatic. The revolution – *their* revolution by right, as the history of Western Europe demonstrated and even right-thinking Marxists agreed – had finally occurred, only to be snatched from their grasp by sinister and incomprehensible forces. Mensheviks and other non-Bolshevik Marxists were similarly outraged: the time was not yet ripe for proletarian socialist revolution, and it was inexcusable that a Marxist party should break the rules and seize power. The Allies, Russia's partners in the war in Europe, were aghast at the débâcle and refused to recognize the new government, which was preparing to pull Russia out of the war unilaterally. The diplomats barely even knew the names of Russia's new rulers, but suspected the worst and prayed for a speedy resurrection of the democratic hopes they had welcomed in February. Western newspaper readers learned with horror of Russia's descent from civilization into the barbarous depths of atheistic Communism.

The scars left by the October Revolution were deep, and made more painful and visible to the outside world by the emigration of large numbers of educated Russians during and immediately after the Civil War that followed the Bolshevik victory. To the emigrés, the Bolshevik Revolution was not so much a tragedy in the Greek sense as an unexpected, undeserved and essentially unfair disaster. To the Western and especially the American public, it seemed that the Russian people had been cheated of the liberal democracy for which it had so long and nobly struggled. Conspiracy theories explaining the Bolshevik victory gained widespread credence: the most popular of these was that of international Jewish conspiracy, since Trotsky, Zinoviev and a number of other Bolshevik leaders were Jewish; but another theory, recently revived in Solzhenitsyn's *Lenin in Zurich*, pictured the Bolsheviks as pawns of the Germans in a successful plot to take Russia out of the war. Historians, of course, tend to be sceptical of conspiracy theories. But the attitudes that enabled such theories to flourish may also have influenced Western scholarly approaches to the problem. Until quite recently, most historical explanations of the Bolshevik Revolution emphasized its illegitimacy in one way or the other, as if seeking to absolve the Russian people of any responsibility for the event and its consequences.

In the classic Western interpretation of the Bolshevik victory and subsequent evolution of Soviet power, the *deux ex machina* was the Bolsheviks' secret weapon of party organization and discipline. Lenin's pamphlet *What Is To Be Done?* (see above, p. 25), setting out the prerequisites for the successful organization of an illegal, conspiratorial party, was usually cited as the basic text; and it was argued that the ideas of *What Is To Be Done?* moulded the Bolshevik Party in its formative years and continued to determine Bolshevik behaviour even after the final emergence from underground in February 1917. The open, democratic and pluralist politics of the post-February months in Russia were thus subverted, culminating in the Bolsheviks' unlawful seizure of power by a conspiratorially organized coup in October. The Bolshevik tradition of centralized organization and strict party discipline led the new Soviet regime towards repressive authoritarianism and laid the foundations for Stalin's later totalitarian dictatorship.[1]

Yet there have always been problems in applying this general concept of the origins of Soviet totalitarianism to the specific historical situation unfolding between February and October 1917. In the first place, the old underground Bolshevik Party was swamped by an influx of new members, outstripping all other political parties in recruitment, especially in the factories and the armed forces. By the middle of 1917, it had become an open mass party, bearing little resemblance to the disciplined elite organization of full-time revolutionaries described in *What Is To Be Done?* In the second place, neither the party as a whole nor its leadership were united on the most basic policy questions in 1917. In October, for example, disagreements within the party leadership on the desirability of insurrection were so acute that the issue was publicly debated by Bolsheviks in the daily press.

It may well be that the Bolsheviks' greatest strength in 1917 was not strict party organization and discipline (which scarcely existed at this time) but rather the party's stance of intransigent radicalism on the extreme left of the political spectrum. While other socialist and liberal groups jostled for position in the Provisional Government and Petrograd Soviet, the Bolsheviks refused to be co-opted and denounced the politics of coalition and compromise. While other formerly radical politicians called for restraint and responsible, statesmanlike leadership, the Bolsheviks stayed out on the streets with the irresponsible and belligerent revolutionary crowd. As the 'dual power' structure disintegrated, discrediting the coalition parties represented in the Provisional Government and Petrograd Soviet leadership, only the Bolsheviks were in a position to benefit. Among the socialist parties, only the Bolsheviks had overcome Marxist scruples, caught the mood of the crowd and declared their willingness to seize power in the name of the proletarian revolution.

The 'dual power' relationship of the Provisional Government and Petrograd Soviet was usually seen in class terms as an alliance between the bourgeoisie and the proletariat. Its survival depended on continued co-operation between these classes and the politicians claiming to represent them; but it was clear by the summer of 1917 that the shaky consensus of February had been seriously undermined. As urban society became increasingly polarized between a law-and-order right and a revolutionary left, the middle ground of democratic coalition started to crumble. In July, crowds of workers, soldiers and sailors came on to the Petrograd streets demanding that the Soviet take power in the name of the working class and repudiate the 'ten capitalist ministers' of the Provisional Government. In August, the month of General Kornilov's abortive coup, a leading industrialist urged the liberals to be more decisive in defence of their class interests:[2]

We ought to say . . . that the present revolution is a bourgeois revolution, that the bourgeois order which exists at the present time is inevitable, and since it is inevitable, one must draw the completely logical conclusion and insist that those who rule the state think in a bourgeois manner and act in a bourgeois manner.

The 'dual power' was conceived as an interim arrangement pending the summoning of a Constituent Assembly. But its disintegration under attack from left and right and the growing polarization of Russian politics raised disturbing questions about the future as well as the present in mid-1917. Was it still reasonable to hope that Russia's political problems could be resolved by a popularly elected Constituent Assembly and the formal institutionalization of parliamentary democracy on the Western model? The Constituent Assembly solution, like the interim 'dual power', required a degree of political consensus and agreement on the necessity of compromise. The perceived alternatives to consensus and compromise were dictatorship and civil war. It seemed, nevertheless, that these alternatives were likely to be chosen by a turbulent and sharply polarized society which had thrown off the reins of government.

The February Revolution and 'dual power'

In the last week of February, bread shortages, strikes, lock-outs and finally a demonstration in honour of International Women's Day by female workers of the Vyborg district brought a crowd on to the streets of Petrograd that the authorities could not disperse. The Fourth Duma, which had reached the end of its term, petitioned the Emperor once again for a responsible cabinet and asked to remain in session for the duration of the crisis. Both requests were refused; but an unauthorized Duma Committee, dominated by liberals of the Cadet Party and the Progressive Bloc, did in fact remain in session. The Emperor's Ministers held one last, indecisive meeting and then took to their heels, the more cautious of them immediately quitting the capital. Nicholas II himself was absent, visiting Army Headquarters in Mogilev; his response to the crisis was a laconic instruction by telegraph that the disorders should be ended immediately. But the police was disintegrating, and troops from the Petrograd garrison brought into the city to control the crowd had begun to fraternize with it. By the evening of 28 February, Petrograd's Military Commander had to report that the revolutionary crowd had taken over all railway stations, all artillery supplies and, as far as he knew, the whole city; very few reliable troops remained at his disposal, and even his telephones were no longer working.

The Army High Command had two options, either to send in fresh troops who might or might not hold firm, or to seek a political solution with the help of the Duma politicians. It chose the latter alternative. At Pskov, on the return journey from Mogilev, Nicholas's train was met by emissaries from the High Command and the Duma who respectfully suggested that the Emperor should abdicate. After some discussion, Nicholas mildly agreed. But, having initially accepted the suggestion that he should abdicate in favour of his son, he thought further about Tsarevich Aleksei's delicate health and decided instead to abdicate on his own behalf and that of Aleksei in favour of his brother, Grand Duke Michael. Always a family man, he spent the remainder of the journey thinking with remarkable calm and political innocence about his future as a private citizen:

He said he would go abroad for the duration of hostilities [in the war against Germany] and then return to Russia, settle in the Crimea and devote himself completely to the education of his son. Some of his advisors doubted whether he would be allowed to do this, but Nicholas replied that nowhere were parents denied the right to care for their children.[3]

(After reaching the capital, Nicholas was sent to join his family outside Petrograd, and thereafter remained quietly under house arrest while the Provisional Government and the Allies tried to decide what to do with him. No solution was reached. Later, the whole family was sent to Siberia and then to the Urals, still under house arrest but in increasingly difficult circumstances which Nicholas bore with fortitude. In July 1918, after the outbreak of the Civil War, Nicholas and his family were executed on orders of the Bolshevik Urals Soviet. From the time of his abdication to his death, Nicholas did indeed behave as a private citizen, playing no active political role whatsoever.)

In the days following Nicholas's abdication, the politicians of Petrograd were in a state of high excitement and frenetic activity. Their original intention had been to get rid of Nicholas rather than the monarchy. But Nicholas's abdication on behalf of his son had removed the possibility of a regency during Aleksei's minority; and Grand Duke Michael, being a prudent man, declined the invitation to succeed his brother. *De facto*, therefore, Russia was no longer a monarchy. It was decided that the country's future form of government would be determined in due course by a Constituent Assembly, and that in the meantime a self-appointed 'Provisional Government' would take over the responsibilities of the former imperial Council of Ministers. Prince Georgii Lvov, head of the Zemstvo League and a moderate liberal, became head of the new government. His cabinet included Pavel Milyukov, historian and Cadet Party theoretician, as Foreign Minister, two prominent industrialists as Ministers of Finance and Trade and Industry, and the socialist lawyer Aleksandr Kerensky as Minister of Justice.

The Provisional Government had no electoral mandate, deriving its authority from the now defunct Duma, the consent of the Army High Command and informal agreements with public organizations like the Zemstvo League and the War Industries Committee. The old Tsarist bureaucracy provided its executive machinery but, as the result of the earlier dissolution of the Duma, it had no supporting legislative body. Given its fragility and lack of formal legitimacy, the new government's assumption of power seemed remarkably easy. The Allied Powers recognized it immediately. Monarchist sentiment seemed to have disappeared overnight in Russia: in the entire Tenth Army, only two officers refused to swear allegiance to the Provisional Government. As a liberal politician later recalled,

Individuals and organizations expressed their loyalty to the new power. The Stavka [Army Headquarters] as a whole, followed by the entire commanding staff, recognized the Provisional Government. The Tsarist Ministers and some of the assistant Ministers were imprisoned, but all the other officials remained at their posts. Ministries, offices, banks, in fact the entire political mechanism of Russia never ceased working. In that respect, the [February] *coup d'état* passed off so smoothly that even then one felt a vague presentiment that this was not the end, that such a crisis could not pass off so peacefully.[4]

Indeed, from the very beginning there were reasons to doubt the effectiveness of the transfer of power. The most important reason was that the Provisional Government had a competitor: the February Revolution had produced not one but two self-constituted authorities aspiring to a national role. The second was the Petrograd Soviet, formed on the pattern of the 1905 Petersburg Soviet by workers, soldiers and socialist politicians. The Soviet was already in session in the Tauride Palace when the formation of the Provisional Government was announced on 2 March.

The 'dual power' relationship of the Provisional Government and the Petrograd Soviet emerged spontaneously, and the government accepted it largely because it had no choice. In the most immediate practical terms, a dozen Ministers with no force at their disposal could scarcely have cleared the Palace (the initial meeting-place of both the government and the Soviet) of the scruffy throng of workers, soldiers and sailors who were tramping in and out to make speeches, eat, sleep, argue and write proclamations; and the mood of the crowd, intermittently bursting into the Soviet chamber with a captive policeman or former Tsarist Minister to leave at the deputies' feet, must have discouraged the attempt. In broader terms, as War Minister Guchkov explained to the Army's Commander-in-Chief early in March,

The Provisional Government does not possess any real power; and its directives are carried out only to the extent that it is permitted by the Soviet of Workers' and Soldiers' Deputies, which enjoys all the essential elements of real power, since the troops, the railroads, the post and telegraph are all in its hands. One can say flatly that the Provisional Government exists only so long as it is permitted by the Soviet.[5]

In the first months, the Provisional Government consisted mainly of liberals, while the Soviet's Executive Committee was dominated by socialist intellectuals, mainly Mensheviks and SRs by party affiliation. Kerensky, a Provisional Government member but also a socialist, who had been active in setting up both institutions, served as liaison between them. The socialists of the Soviet intended to act as watchdogs over the Provisional Government, protecting the interests of the working class until such time as the bourgeois revolution had run its course. This deference to the bourgeoisie was partly the result of the socialists' good Marxist education and partly a product of caution and uncertainty. As Nikolai Sukhanov, one of the Soviet's Menshevik leaders, noted, there was likely to be trouble ahead, and better that the liberals take the responsibility and, if necessary, the blame:

The Soviet democracy had to entrust the power to the propertied elements, its class enemy, without whose participation it could not now master the technique of administration in the desperate conditions of disintegration, nor deal with the forces of Tsarism and the bourgeoisie, united against it. But the *condition* of this transfer had to assure the democracy of a complete victory over the class enemy in the near future.[6]

But the workers, soldiers and sailors who made up the Soviet's rank and file were not so cautious. On 1 March, before the formal establishment of the Provisional Government or the emergence of 'responsible leadership' in the Soviet, the notorious Order No. 1 was issued in the name of the Petrograd Soviet. Order No. 1 was a revolutionary document and an assertion of the Soviet's power. It called for democratization of the Army by the creation of elected soldiers' committees, reduction of officers' disciplinary powers and, most importantly, recognition of the Soviet's authority on all policy questions involving the armed forces: it stated that no governmental order to the Army was to be considered valid without the counter-signature of the Soviet. While Order No. 1 did not actually mandate the holding of elections to confirm officers in their positions, such elections were in fact being organized in the more unruly units; and there were reports that hundreds of naval officers had been arrested or killed by the sailors of Kronstadt and the Baltic Fleet during the February Days. Order No. 1 therefore had strong overtones of class war, and totally failed to offer reassurance about the prospects for class co-operation. It presaged the most unworkable form of dual power, that is, a situation in which the enlisted men in the armed forces recognized only the authority of the Petrograd Soviet, while the officer corps recognized only the authority of the Provisional Government.

The Executive Committee of the Soviet did its best to retreat from the radical position implied by Order No. 1. But in April Sukhanov commented on the 'isolation from the masses' produced by the Executive Committee's *de facto* alliance with the Provisional Government. It was, of course, only a partial alliance. There were recurrent conflicts between the Soviet Executive Committee and the Provisional Government on labour policy and the problem of peasant land claims. There were also important disagreements about Russia's participation in the European war. The Provisional Government remained firmly committed to the war effort; and Foreign Minister Milyukov's Note of 18 April even implied a continued interest in extending Russian control over Constantinople and the Straits (as agreed in the Secret Treaties signed by the Tsarist government and the Allies), before a public outcry and renewed street demonstrations forced him to resign. The Soviet Executive Committee took the 'defensist' position, favouring continuation of the war as long as Russian territory was under attack but opposing annexationist war aims and the Secret Treaties. But on the floor of the Soviet – and in the streets, the factories and especially the garrisons – the attitude to the war tended to be simpler and more drastic: stop fighting, pull out of the war, bring the troops home.

The relationship that developed between the Soviet Executive Committee and the Provisional Government in the spring and summer of 1917 was intense, intimate and quarrelsome. The Executive Committee guarded its separate identity jealously, but ultimately the two institutions were too closely bound to be indifferent to each other's fate, or to dissociate themselves in the event of disaster. The link was strengthened in May, when the Provisional Government ceased to be a liberal preserve and became a coalition of liberals and socialists, drawing in representatives of the major socialist parties (Mensheviks and SRs) whose influence was predominant in the Soviet Executive Committee. The socialists were not eager to enter the government, but concluded that it was their duty to strengthen a tottering regime at a time of national crisis. They continued to regard the Soviet as their more natural sphere of political action, especially when it became clear that the new socialist Ministers of Agriculture and Labour would be unable to implement their policies because of liberal opposition. Nevertheless, a symbolic choice had been made: in associating themselves more closely with the Provisional Government, the 'responsible' socialists were separating themselves (and, by extension, the Soviet Executive Committee) from the irresponsible popular revolution.

Popular hostility to the 'bourgeois' Provisional Government mounted in the late spring, as war weariness increased and the economic situation in the towns deteriorated. During the street demonstrations that occurred in July (the July Days), demonstrators carried banners calling for 'All power to the soviets', which in effect meant the removal of power from the Provisional Government. Paradoxically – though logically in terms of its commitment to the Government – the Executive Committee of the Petrograd Soviet rejected the slogan of 'All power to the soviets'; and in fact the demonstration was directed as much against the existing Soviet leadership as against the Government itself. 'Take power, you son of a bitch, when it's given you!' shouted one demonstrator, shaking his fist at a socialist politician.[7] But this was an appeal (or perhaps a threat?) to which those who had pledged themselves to 'dual power' could not respond.

The Bolsheviks

At the time of the February Revolution, virtually all leading Bolsheviks were in emigration abroad or in exile in remote regions of the Russian Empire, arrested *en masse* after the outbreak of war because the Bolsheviks not only opposed Russia's participation but also argued that a Russian defeat would be in the interests of the revolution. The Bolshevik leaders who had been exiled in Siberia, including Stalin and Molotov, were among the first to return to the capitals. But those in emigration in Europe found it much more difficult to return, for the simple reason that Europe was at war. To return via the Baltic was dangerous and required Allied co-operation, while the land routes ran across enemy territory. Nevertheless, Lenin and other members of the emigré community in neutral Switzerland were very anxious to return; and, after negotiations conducted by intermediaries, the German government offered them the chance to cross Germany by sealed train. It was clearly in Germany's interest to let Russian revolutionaries opposed to the war return to Russia, but the revolutionaries themselves had to weigh the desirability of returning against the risk of compromising themselves politically. Lenin, together with a small contingent of mainly Bolshevik emigrés, decided to take the risk, and set off towards the end of March. (A much larger group of Russian revolutionaries in Switzerland, including almost all the Mensheviks, decided that it was more prudent to wait – a shrewd move, since they avoided all the controversy and accusations that Lenin's trip provoked. This group followed in a second sealed train, by similar arrangement with the Germans, a month later.)

Before Lenin's return to Petrograd early in April, the former Siberian exiles had already begun to rebuild the Bolshevik organization and publish a newspaper. At this point the Bolsheviks, like other socialist groups, showed signs of drifting into the loose coalition around the Petrograd Soviet. But the Menshevik and SR leaders of the Soviet had not forgotten what a troublemaker Lenin could be, and awaited his arrival with apprehension. It turned out to be justified. On 3 April, when Lenin stepped off the train at the Finland Station in Petrograd, he responded curtly to the Soviet's welcoming committee, addressed a few remarks to the crowd in the rather harsh voice that always grated on his opponents, and departed abruptly for a private celebration and conference with his Bolshevik Party colleagues. Clearly Lenin had not lost his old sectarian habits. He showed no signs of the joyous emotions that, in these early months, often led old political antagonists to embrace as brothers in honour of the revolutionary victory.

Lenin's appraisal of the political situation, known to history as the April Theses, was belligerent, uncompromising and distinctly disconcerting to the Petrograd Bolsheviks who had tentatively accepted the Soviet line of socialist unity and critical support for the new government. Scarcely pausing to acknowledge the achievements of February, Lenin was already looking forward to the second stage of revolution, the overthrow of the bourgeoisie by the proletariat. No support should be given to the Provisional Government, Lenin stated. Socialist illusions of unity and the 'naïve confidence' of the masses in the new regime must be destroyed. The present Soviet leadership, having succumbed to bourgeois influence, was useless (in one speech, Lenin borrowed Rosa Luxemburg's characterization of German Social Democracy and called it 'a stinking corpse').

Nevertheless, Lenin predicted that the soviets – under revitalized revolutionary leadership – would be the key institutions in transferring power from the bourgeoisie to the proletariat. 'All power to the soviets!', one of the slogans of Lenin's April Theses, was in effect a call for class war. 'Peace, land and bread', another of Lenin's April slogans, had similarly revolutionary implications. 'Peace', in Lenin's usage, meant not only withdrawal from the imperialist war but also recognition that such withdrawal '*is impossible* . . . without the overthrow of capital'. 'Land' meant confiscation of the landowners' estates and their redistribution by the peasants themselves – something very close to spontaneous peasant land seizures. No wonder that a Menshevik commentator accused Lenin of 'plant[ing] the banner of civil war in the midst of revolutionary democracy'.[8]

The Bolsheviks, respectful as they were of Lenin's vision and leadership, were shocked by Lenin's April Theses: some were inclined to think that he had lost touch with the realities of Russian life during his years in emigration. But in the following months, under Lenin's exhortations and reproaches, the Bolsheviks did move into a more intransigent position, isolating themselves from the socialist coalition. However, without a Bolshevik majority in the Petrograd Soviet, Lenin's slogan of 'All power to the soviets!' did not provide the Bolsheviks with a practical guide to action. It remained an open question whether Lenin's strategy was that of a master politician or simply that of a cranky extremist – a left-wing counterpart of the old socialist Plekhanov, whose unreserved patriotism on the war issue had taken him out of the mainstream of Russian socialist politics.

The need for socialist unity seemed self-evident to most of the politicians associated with the Soviet, who prided themselves on submerging their old sectarian disagreements. In June, at the First National Congress of Soviets, a speaker asked rhetorically whether any political party was prepared to take on the responsibilities of power alone, assuming that the answer was negative. 'There is such a party!' Lenin interjected. But to most of the delegates, it sounded more like bravado than a serious challenge. It was a serious challenge, however, because the Bolshevik Party was gaining popular support and the coalition socialists losing it.

The Bolsheviks were still in a minority at the June Congress of Soviets, and they had yet to win a major city election. But their growing strength was already evident at the grass-roots level – in the workers' factory committees, in the committees of soldiers and sailors in the armed forces, and in local district soviets in the big towns. Bolshevik Party membership was also increasing spectacularly, although the Bolsheviks never made any formal decision to launch a mass recruitment drive, and seemed almost surprised by the influx. The party's membership figures, shaky and perhaps exaggerated as they are, give some sense of its dimensions: 24,000 Bolshevik Party members at the time of the February Revolution (though this figure is particularly suspect, since the Petrograd party organization could actually identify only about 2,000 members in February, and the

Moscow organization 600); more than 100,000 members by the end of April; and in October 1917 a total of 350,000 members, including 60,000 in Petrograd and the surrounding province and 70,000 in Moscow and the adjacent Central Industrial Region.[9]

The popular revolution

Seven million men were under arms at the beginning of 1917, with two million in the reserve. The armed forces had suffered tremendous losses, and war weariness was evident in the increasing desertion rate and the soldiers' responsiveness to German fraternization at the front. To the soldiers, the February Revolution was an implicit promise that the war would soon end, and they waited impatiently for the Provisional Government to achieve this – if not on its own initiative, then under pressure from the Petrograd Soviet. In the early spring of 1917, the Army, with its new democratic structure of elected committees, its old problems of inadequate supplies and its restless and uncertain mood, was at best a doubtfully effective fighting force. At the front, morale had not totally disintegrated. But the situation in the garrisons around the country, where reserve troops were stationed, was much uglier.

Traditionally, Russia's soldiers and sailors of 1917 have been categorized as 'proletarians', regardless of their occupation out of uniform. In fact most of the enlisted men were peasants, although workers were disproportionately represented in the Baltic Fleet and the armies of the Northern and Western Fronts, since their recruitment area was relatively industrialized. It can be argued in Marxist terms that the men in the armed forces were proletarian by virtue of their current occupation, but the more important thing is that this is evidently how they regarded themselves. As a recent study indicates,[10] front-line soldiers in the spring of 1917 – even when prepared to co-operate with officers who accepted the Revolution and the new norms of behaviour – saw the officers and the Provisional Government as belonging to one class, that of the 'masters', and identified their own interests as those of the workers and the Petrograd Soviet. By May, as the Commander-in-Chief reported with alarm, 'class antagonism' between officers and men had made deep inroads on the Army's spirit of patriotic solidarity.

The Petrograd workers had already demonstrated a revolutionary spirit in February, although they had not then been sufficiently militant or psychologically prepared to resist the creation of a 'bourgeois' Provisional Government. In the first months after the February Revolution, the main grievances expressed by workers in Petrograd and elsewhere were economic, focusing on bread-and-butter issues like the eight-hour day (which the Provisional Government rejected on the grounds of the wartime emergency), wages, overtime and protection against unemployment.[11] But there was no guarantee that this situation would continue, given the tradition of political militancy in the Russian working class. It was true that the war had changed the composition of the working class, greatly increasing the percentage of women as well as somewhat increasing the total number of workers; and it was usually believed that women workers were less revolutionary than men. Yet it was women workers whose strike on International Women's Day had precipitated the February Revolution; and those who had husbands at the front were particularly likely to object strongly to continuation of the war. Petrograd, as a centre of the munitions industry in which many skilled male workers had been exempted from military conscription, retained a comparatively large proportion of its prewar male working class in the factories. Despite the police round-up of Bolsheviks at the beginning of the war, and the subsequent arrest or military drafting of large numbers of other political troublemakers in the factories, Petrograd's major metallurgical and defence plants were employing a surprising number of workers who belonged to the Bolshevik and other revolutionary parties, and even Bolshevik professional revolutionaries who had come to the capital from the Ukraine and other parts of the Empire after the outbreak of war. Other revolutionary workers returned to their factories after the February Revolution, increasing the potential for further political unrest.

The February Revolution had given birth to a formidable array of workers' organizations in all Russia's industrial centres, but especially in Petrograd and Moscow. Workers' soviets were created not only at the city level, like the Petrograd Soviet, but also at the lower level of the urban district, where the leadership usually came from the workers themselves rather than the socialist intelligentsia and the mood was often more radical. New trade unions were established; and at the plant level, workers began to set up factory committees (which were not part of the trade-union structure, and sometimes coexisted with local trade-union branches) to deal with management. The factory committees, closest to the grass roots, tended to be the most radical of all workers' organizations. In the factory committees of Petrograd, the Bolsheviks had assumed a dominant position by the end of May 1917. The factory committees' original function was to be the workers' watchdog over the plant's capitalist management. The term used for this function was 'workers' control' (*rabochii kontrol'*), which implied supervision rather than control in the managerial sense. But in practice the factory committees often went further and started to take over managerial functions. Sometimes this was related to disputes over control of hiring and firing, or was the product of the kind of class hostility that led workers in some plants to tie unpopular foremen and managers into wheelbarrows and dump them in the river. In other instances, the factory committees took over to save the workers from unemployment, when the owner or manager abandoned the plant or threatened to close it because it was losing money. As such events became more common, the definition of 'workers' control' moved closer to something like workers' self-management.

This change took place as the workers' political mood was becoming more militant, and as the Bolsheviks were gaining influence in the factory committees. Militancy meant hostility to the bourgeoisie and assertion of the workers' primacy in the revolution: just as the revised meaning of 'workers' control' was that workers should be masters in their own plants, so there was an emerging sense in the working class that 'soviet power' meant that the workers should be sole masters in the district, the city and perhaps the country as a whole. As political theory, this was closer to anarchism or anarcho-syndicalism than to Bolshevism, and the Bolshevik leaders did not in fact share the view that direct workers' democracy through the factory committees and the soviets was a plausible or desirable alternative to their own concept of a party-led 'proletarian dictatorship'. Nevertheless, the Bolsheviks were realists, and the political reality in Petrograd in the summer of 1917 was that their party had strong support in the factory committees and did not want to lose it. Accordingly, the Bolsheviks were in favour of 'workers' control', without defining too closely what they meant by it.

Rising working-class militancy alarmed the employers: a number of plants were closed down, and one prominent industrialist cautiously expressed his opinion that 'the bony hand of hunger' might ultimately be the means of bringing the urban workers back to order. But in the countryside, the landowners' alarm and fear of the peasantry was much greater. The villages were quiet in February, and many of the young peasant men were absent because of conscription for military service. But by May, it was clear that the countryside was sliding into turmoil as it had done in 1905 in response to urban revolution. As in

1905–6, manor houses were being sacked and burned. In addition, the peasants were seizing private and state land for their own use. During the summer, as the disturbances mounted, many landowners abandoned their estates and fled from the countryside.

Although Nicholas II had clung even after the 1905–6 revolts to the idea that Russian peasants loved the Tsar, whatever their opinion of local officials and landed nobles, the peasants responded to news of the downfall of the monarchy and the February Revolution in a quite different way. It seems to have been assumed throughout peasant Russia that this new revolution meant – or should be made to mean – that the nobles' old illegitimate title to the land was revoked. Land should belong to those who tilled it, peasants wrote in their numerous petitions to the Provisional Government in the spring.[12] What that seems to have meant to the peasants in concrete terms was that they should get the land which they had tilled as serfs for the nobles, and which had been retained by the noble landowners in the Emancipation settlement. (Much of this land was currently leased from the landowners by peasants; in other cases, the landowners cultivated it, using the local peasants as hired labour.)

If the peasants still held assumptions about the land that went back more than half a century to the time of serfdom, it is scarcely surprising that the agrarian reforms carried out by Stolypin in the years before the First World War had made little impact on peasant consciousness. Still, the evident vitality of the peasant *mir* in 1917 came as a shock to many people. The Marxists had been arguing since the 1880s that the *mir* had essentially disintegrated internally, surviving only because the state found it a useful instrument. On paper, the effect of Stolypin's reforms had been to dissolve the *mir* in a high proportion of the villages of European Russia. Yet for all this, the *mir* was clearly a basic factor in peasant thinking about the land in 1917. In their petitions, the peasants asked for an egalitarian redistribution of lands held by the nobility, the state and the Church – that is, the same kind of equal allocation among village households that the *mir* had traditionally organized with regard to the village fields. When unauthorized land seizures began on a large scale in the summer of 1917, the seizures were conducted on behalf of village communities, not individual peasant households, and the general pattern was that the *mir* subsequently divided up the new lands among the villagers as it had traditionally divided up the old ones. Moreover, the *mir* often reasserted its authority over former members in 1917–18: the Stolypin 'separators', who had left the *mir* to set themselves up as independent small farmers in the prewar years, were in many cases forced to return and merge their holdings once again in the common village lands.

Despite the seriousness of the land problem and the reports of land seizures from the early summer of 1917, the Provisional Government procrastinated on the issue of land reform. The liberals were not on principle against expropriation of private lands, and generally seem to have regarded the peasants' demands as just. But any radical land reform would clearly pose formidable problems. In the first place, the Government would have to set up a complicated official mechanism of expropriation and transfer of lands, which was almost certainly beyond its current administrative capacities. In the second place, it could not afford to pay the large compensation to the landowners that most liberals considered necessary. The Provisional Government's conclusion was that it would be best to shelve the problems until they could be properly resolved by the Constituent Assembly. In the meantime, it warned the peasantry (though to little avail) not on any account to take the law into its own hands.

The political crises of the summer

In mid-June, Kerensky, now the Provisional Government's Minister of War, encouraged the Russian Army to mount a major offensive on the Galician Front. It was the first serious military undertaking since the February Revolution, as the Germans had been content to watch the disintegration of the Russian forces without engaging themselves further in the east, and the Russian High Command, fearing disaster, had earlier resisted Allied pressure to take the initiative. The Russians' Galician offensive, conducted in June and early July, failed with an estimated 200,000 casualties. It was a disaster in every sense. Morale in the armed forces disintegrated further, and the Germans began a successful counter-attack that continued throughout the summer and autumn. Russian desertions, already rising as peasant soldiers responded to news of the land seizures, grew to epidemic proportions. The Provisional Government's credit was undermined, and tension between government and military leaders increased. At the beginning of July, a governmental crisis was precipitated by the withdrawal of all the Cadet (liberal) ministers and the resignation of the head of the Provisional Government, Prince Lvov.

In the midst of this crisis, Petrograd erupted once again with the mass demonstrations, street violence and popular disorder of 3–5 July known as the July Days.[13] The crowd, which contemporary witnesses put as high as half a million, included large organized contingents of Kronstadt sailors, soldiers and workers from the Petrograd plants. To the Provisional Government, it looked like a Bolshevik attempt at insurrection. The Kronstadt sailors, whose arrival in Petrograd set off the disorders, had Bolsheviks among their leaders, carried banners with the Bolshevik slogan 'All power to the soviets', and made Bolshevik Party headquarters at the Kseshinskaya Palace their first destination. Yet when the demonstrators reached the Kseshinskaya Palace, Lenin's greeting was subdued, almost curt. He did not encourage them to take violent action against the Provisional Government or the present Soviet leadership; and, although the crowd moved on to the Soviet and milled around in a threatening manner, no such action was taken. Confused and lacking leadership and specific plans, the demonstrators roamed the city, fell to drinking and looting, and finally dispersed.

In one sense, the July Days were a vindication of Lenin's intransigent stand since April, for they indicated strong popular sentiment against the Provisional Government and the dual power, impatience with the coalition socialists and eagerness on the part of the Kronstadt sailors and others for violent confrontation and probably insurrection. But in another sense, the July Days were a disaster for the Bolsheviks. Clearly Lenin and the Bolshevik Central Committee had been caught off balance. They had talked insurrection, in a general way, but not planned it. The Kronstadt Bolsheviks, responding to the sailors' revolutionary mood, had taken an initiative which, in effect, the Bolshevik Central Committee had disowned. The whole affair damaged Bolshevik morale and Lenin's credibility as a revolutionary leader.

The damage was all the greater because the Bolsheviks, despite the leaders' hesitant and uncertain response, were blamed for the July Days by the Provisional Government and the moderate socialists of the Soviet. The Provisional Government decided to crack down, withdrawing the 'parliamentary immunity' that politicians of all parties had enjoyed since the February Revolution. Several prominent Bolsheviks were arrested, along with Trotsky, who had taken a position close to Lenin's on the extreme left since his return to Russia in May and was to become an official Bolshevik Party member in August. Orders were issued for the arrest of Lenin and one of his closest associates in the Bolshevik leaderships, Grigorii Zinoviev. During the July Days, moreover, the Provisional Government had intimated that it had evidence to support the rumours that Lenin was a German agent, and the Bolsheviks were battered by a wave of patriotic denunciations in the press that temporarily eroded their popularity in the armed forces and the factories. The Bolshevik Central Committee (and no doubt Lenin himself) feared for Lenin's life. He went into hiding, and early in August, disguised as a workman, he crossed the border and took refuge in Finland.

If the Bolsheviks were in trouble, however, this was also true of the Provisional Government, headed from early July by Kerensky. The liberal–socialist coalition was in constant turmoil, with the socialists pushed to the left by their Soviet constituency and the liberals moving to the right under pressure from the industrialists, landowners and military commanders, who were all increasingly alarmed by the collapse of authority and the popular disorders. Kerensky, despite an exalted sense of his mission to save Russia, was essentially a go-between and negotiator of political compromises, not greatly trusted or respected, and lacking a political base in any of the major parties. As he sadly complained, 'I struggle with the Bolsheviks of the left and the Bolsheviks of the right, but people demand that I lean on one or the other . . . I want to take a middle road, but nobody will help me.'[14]

It seemed increasingly likely that the Provisional Government would fall one way or the other, but the question was, which? The threat from the left was a popular uprising in Petrograd and/or Bolshevik coup. Such a challenge had failed in July, but German activity on the north-western fronts was heightening tension in the armed forces surrounding Petrograd in a most ominous way, and the influx of deserters who were aggrieved, armed and unemployed presumably increased the danger of street violence in the city itself. The other threat to the Provisional Government was the possibility of a coup from the right to establish a law-and-order dictatorship. By the summer, this course was being discussed in high military circles and had support from some of the industrialists. There were signs that even the Cadets, who would obviously have to oppose such a move before the fact and in public statements, might accept a *fait accompli* with considerable relief.

In August, the coup from the right was finally attempted by General Lavr Kornilov, whom Kerensky had recently appointed Commander-in-Chief with a mandate to restore order and discipline in the Russian Army. Kornilov was evidently not motivated by personal ambition but by his sense of the national interest. He may, in fact, have believed that Kerensky would welcome an Army intervention to create a strong government and deal with left-wing troublemakers, since Kerensky, partially apprised of Kornilov's intentions, dealt with him in a peculiarly devious way. Misunderstandings between the two principal actors confused the situation, and the Germans' unexpected capture of Riga on the eve of Kornilov's move added to the mood of panic, suspicion and despair that was spreading among Russia's civilian and military leaders. In the last week of August, baffled but determined, General Kornilov dispatched troops from the front to Petrograd, ostensibly to quell disorders in the capital and save the Republic.

The attempted coup failed largely because of the unreliability of the troops and the energetic actions of the Petrograd workers. Railwaymen diverted and obstructed the troop trains; printers stopped publication of newspapers supporting Kornilov's move; metalworkers rushed out to meet the oncoming troops and explain that Petrograd was calm and their officers had deceived them. Under this pressure, the troops' morale disintegrated, the coup was aborted outside Petrograd without any serious military engagement, and General Krymov, the commanding officer acting under Kornilov's orders, surrendered to the Provisional Government and then committed suicide. Kornilov himself was arrested at Army Headquarters, offering no resistance and taking full responsibility.

In Petrograd, politicians of the centre and right rushed to reaffirm their loyalty to the Provisional Government, which Kerensky continued to head. But Kerensky's standing had been further damaged by his handling of the Kornilov affair, and the government weakened. The Executive Committee of the Petrograd Soviet also emerged with little credit, since the resistance to Kornilov had been organized largely at the local union and factory level; and this contributed to an upsurge of support for the Bolsheviks which almost immediately enabled them to displace the Soviet's old Menshevik–SR leadership. The Army High Command was hit hardest of all, since the arrest of the Commander-in-Chief and failure of the coup left it demoralized and confused; relations between officers and men deteriorated sharply; and, as if this were not enough, the German advance was continuing, with Petrograd the apparent objective. In mid-September, General Alekseev, Kornilov's successor, abruptly resigned as Commander-in-Chief, prefacing his statement with an emotional tribute to Kornilov's high motives. Alekseev felt he could no longer take responsibility for an army in which discipline had collapsed and 'our officers are martyrs'.

Practically speaking, in this hour of terrible danger, I can state with horror that we have no army (at these words the General's voice trembled and he shed a few tears), while the Germans are prepared, at any moment, to strike the last and most powerful blow against us.[15]

The left gained most from the Kornilov affair, since it gave substance to the previously abstract notion of a counter-revolutionary threat from the right, demonstrated working-class strength, and at the same time convinced many workers that only their armed vigilance could save the revolution from its enemies. The Bolsheviks, with many of their leaders still gaoled or in hiding, played no special role in the actual resistance to Kornilov. But the new swing of popular opinion towards them, already discernible early in August, greatly accelerated after Kornilov's aborted coup; and in a practical sense they were to reap future benefit from the creation of workers' militia units or 'Red Guards' which began in response to the Kornilov threat. The Bolsheviks' strength was that they were the only party uncompromised by association with the bourgeoisie and the February regime, and the party most firmly identified with ideas of workers' power and armed uprising.

The October Revolution

From April to August, the Bolsheviks' slogan 'All power to the soviets' was essentially provocative – a taunt directed at the moderates who controlled the Petrograd Soviet and did not want to take all power. But the situation changed after the Kornilov affair, when the moderates lost control. The Bolsheviks gained a majority in the Petrograd Soviet on 31 August and a majority in the Moscow Soviet on 5 September. If the second national Congress of Soviets, scheduled to meet in October, followed the same political trend as the capitals, what were the implications? Did the Bolsheviks want a quasi-legal transfer of power to the soviets, based on a decision by the Congress that the Provisional Government had no further mandate to rule? Or was their old slogan really a call for insurrection, or an affirmation that the Bolsheviks (unlike the rest) had the courage to take power?

In September, Lenin wrote from his hiding-place in Finland urging the Bolshevik Party to prepare for an armed insurrection. The revolutionary moment had come, he said, and must be seized before it was too late. Delay would be fatal. The Bolsheviks must act *before* the meeting of the Second Congress of Soviets, pre-empting any decision that the Congress might make.

Lenin's advocacy of immediate armed uprising was passionate, but not entirely convincing to his colleagues in the leadership. Why should the Bolsheviks take a desperate gamble, when the tide was so clearly running their way? Moreover, Lenin himself did not return and take charge: surely he would have done this if he were really serious? No doubt the accusations against him in the summer had left him over-wrought. Possibly he had been brooding about his and the Central Committee's hesitation during the July Days, convincing himself that a rare chance to seize power had been lost. In any case, Lenin was temperamental, like all great leaders. This mood might pass.

Lenin's behaviour at this time was certainly contradictory. On the one hand, he insisted on a Bolshevik insurrection. On the other, he remained for some weeks in Finland, despite the fact that the Provisional Government had released the left politicians imprisoned in July, the Bolsheviks now controlled the Soviet, and the time of acute danger to Lenin had surely passed. When he did return to Petrograd, probably at the end of the first week of October, he stayed in hiding, isolated even from the Bolsheviks, and communicated with his Central Committee through a series of angry, exhortatory letters.

On 10 October, the Bolshevik Central Committee agreed that an uprising was desirable in principle. But clearly many of the Bolsheviks were inclined to use their position in the Soviet to achieve a quasi-legal, non-violent transfer of power. According to the later recollections of a member of the Petrograd Bolshevik Committee,

Hardly any of us thought of the beginning as an armed seizure of all the institutions of government at a specific hour . . . We thought of the uprising as the simple seizure of power by the Petrograd Soviet. The Soviet would cease complying with the orders of the Provisional Government, declare itself to be the power, and remove anyone who tried to prevent it from doing this.[16]

Trotsky, recently released from prison and admitted to Bolshevik Party membership, was now the leader of the Bolshevik majority in the Petrograd Soviet. He had also been one of the Soviet's leaders in 1905. Although he did not openly disagree with Lenin (and later claimed that their views had been identical), it seems probable that he too had doubts about insurrection, and thought that the Soviet could and should handle the problem of dislodging the Provisional Government.[17]

Strong objections to a Bolshevik-led insurrection came from two of Lenin's old Bolshevik comrades, Grigorii Zinoviev and Lev Kamenev. They thought it irresponsible for the Bolsheviks to seize power by a coup, and unrealistic to think that they could hold power alone. When Zinoviev and Kamenev published these arguments under their own names in a non-Bolshevik daily newspaper (Maxim Gorky's *Novaya zhizn'*), Lenin's anger and frustration rose to new heights. This was understandable, since it was not only an act of defiance but also a public announcement that the Bolsheviks were secretly planning an insurrection.

It may seem remarkable, under these circumstances, that the Bolsheviks' October coup actually came off. But in fact the advance publicity probably helped Lenin's cause rather than hindered it. It put the Bolsheviks in a position where it would have been difficult *not* to act, unless they had been arrested beforehand, or received strong indications that the workers, soldiers and sailors of the Petrograd area would repudiate any revolutionary action. But Kerensky did not take decisive counter-measures against the Bolsheviks, and their control of the Petrograd Soviet's Military-Revolutionary Committee made it comparatively easy to organize a coup. The Military-Revolutionary Committee's basic purpose was to organize the workers' resistance to counter-revolution *à la* Kornilov, and Kerensky was clearly not in a position to interfere with that. The war situation was also an important factor: the Germans were advancing, and Petrograd was threatened. The workers had already rejected a Provisional Government order to evacuate the major industrial plants from the city: they did not trust the Government's intentions towards the revolution, and for that matter they did not trust its will to fight the Germans. Paradoxically, given the workers' approval of the Bolshevik 'peace' slogan both they and the Bolsheviks reacted belligerently when the German threat was immediate and actual: the old peace slogans were scarcely heard in the autumn and winter of 1917, after the fall of Riga.) Had Kerensky tried to disarm the workers as the Germans approached, he would probably have been lynched as a traitor and capitulationist.

The insurrection began on 24 October, the eve of the meeting of the Second Congress of Soviets, when the forces of the Soviet's Military-Revolutionary Committee began to occupy key governmental institutions, taking over the telegraph offices and the railway stations, setting up roadblocks on the city's bridges and surrounding the Winter Palace, where the Provisional Government was in session. They encountered almost no violent resistance. The streets remained calm, and citizens continued to go about their everyday business. On the night of 24–25 October, Lenin came out of hiding and joined his comrades at the Smolny Institute, a former school for young ladies which was now the headquarters of the Soviet; he too was calm, having apparently recovered from his bout of nervous anxiety, and he resumed his old position of leadership as a matter of course.

By the afternoon of the 25th, the coup was all but accomplished – except, provokingly, for the taking of the Winter Palace, which was still under siege with the Provisional Government members inside. The Palace fell late in the evening, in a rather confused assault against a dwindling body of defenders. It was a less heroic occasion than later Soviet accounts suggest: the battleship Aurora, moored opposite the Palace in the River Neva, did not fire a single live shot, and the occupying forces let Kerensky slip out a side entrance and successfully flee the city by car. It was also slightly unsatisfactory in terms of political drama, since the Congress of Soviets – having delayed its first session for some hours, on Bolshevik insistence – finally began proceedings before the Palace fell, thus frustrating the Bolsheviks' wish to make a dramatic opening announcement. Still, the basic fact remained: the February regime had been overthrown, and power had passed to the victors of October.

Of course, this did leave one question unanswered. Who *were* the victors of October? In urging the Bolsheviks towards insurrection before the Congress of Soviets, Lenin had evidently wanted this title to go to the Bolsheviks. But the Bolsheviks had in fact organized the uprising through the Military-Revolutionary Committee of the Petrograd Soviet; and, by accident or design, the Committee had procrastinated until the eve of the meeting of the national Congress of Soviets. (Trotsky later described this as a brilliant strategy – presumably his own, since it was clearly not Lenin's – of using the soviets to legitimate a Bolshevik seizure of power.[18]) As the news went out to the provinces, the most common version was that the soviets had taken power.

The question was not wholly clarified at the Congress of Soviets which opened in Petrograd on 25 October. As it turned out, a clear majority of the Congress delegates had come with a mandate to support transfer of all power to the soviets. But this was not an exclusively Bolshevik group (300 of the 670 delegates were Bolsheviks, which gave the party a dominant position but not a majority), and such a mandate did not necessarily imply approval of the Bolsheviks' pre-emptive action. That action was violently criticized at the first session by a large group of Mensheviks and SRs, who then quit the Congress in protest. It was questioned in a more conciliatory manner by a Menshevik group headed by Martov, Lenin's old friend; but Trotsky consigned these critics, in a memorable phrase, to 'the dust-heap of history'.

At the Congress, the Bolsheviks called for the transfer of power to workers', soldiers' and peasants' soviets throughout the country. As far as central power was concerned, the logical implication was surely that the place of the old Provisional Government would be taken by the standing Central Executive Committee of the soviets, elected by the Congress and including representatives from a number of political parties. But this was not so. To the surprise of many delegates, it was announced that central governmental functions would be assumed by a new Council of People's Commissars, whose all-Bolshevik membership was read out to the Congress on 26 October by a spokesman for the Bolshevik Party. The head of the new government was Lenin, and Trotsky was People's Commissar (Minister) of Foreign Affairs.

Some historians have recently suggested that the Bolsheviks' one-party rule emerged as the result of historical accident rather than intention[19] – that is, that the Bolsheviks did not mean to take power for themselves alone. But if the intention in question is Lenin's, the argument seems dubious; and Lenin overrode the objections of other leading members of the party. In September and October, Lenin seems clearly to have wanted the Bolsheviks to take power, not the multi-party soviets. He did not even want to use the soviets as camouflage, but would apparently have preferred to stage an unambiguous Bolshevik coup. In the provinces, certainly, the immediate result of the October Revolution was that the soviets took power; and the local soviets were not always dominated by Bolsheviks. Although the Bolsheviks' attitude to the soviets after October is open to different interpretations,[20] it is perhaps fair to say that they had no objection in principle to the soviets exercising power at a local level, as long as the soviets were reliably Bolshevik. But this requirement was difficult to square with democratic elections contested by other political parties.

Certainly Lenin was quite firm on the issue of coalition in the new central government, the Council of People's Commissars. In November 1917, when the Bolshevik Central Committee discussed the possibility of moving from an all-Bolshevik government to a broader socialist coalition, Lenin was adamantly against it, even though several

Bolsheviks resigned from the government in protest. Later a few 'left SRs' (members of a splinter group of the SR Party that had accepted the October coup) were admitted to the Council of People's Commissars, but they were politicians without a strong party base. They were dropped from the government in mid-1918, when the left SRs staged an uprising in protest against the peace treaty recently signed with Germany. The Bolsheviks made no further effort to form a coalition government with other parties.

Had the Bolsheviks a popular mandate to rule alone, or did they believe that they had one? In the elections for the Constituent Assembly (held, as scheduled before the October coup, in November 1917), the Bolsheviks won 25 per cent of the popular vote. This put them second to the SRs, who won 40 per cent of the vote (left SRs, who supported the Bolsheviks on the issue of the coup, were not differentiated in the voting lists). The Bolsheviks had expected to do better, and this is perhaps explicable if one examines the vote in more detail.[21] The Bolsheviks took Petrograd and Moscow, and probably won in urban Russia as a whole. In the armed forces, whose five million votes were counted separately, the Bolsheviks had an absolute majority in the Armies of the Northern and Western Fronts and the Baltic Fleet – the constituencies they knew best, and where they were best known. On the southern fronts and in the Black Sea Fleet, they lost to the SRs and Ukrainian parties. The SRs' overall victory was the result of winning the peasant vote in the villages. But there was a certain ambiguity in this. The peasants were probably single-issue voters, and the SR and Bolshevik programmes on the land were virtually identical. The SRs, however, were much better known to the peasantry, their traditional constituency. Where the peasants knew the Bolshevik programme (usually as a result of proximity to towns, garrisons or railways, where the Bolsheviks had done more campaigning), their votes were split between the Bolsheviks and the SRs.

In democratic electoral politics, nevertheless, a loss is a loss. The Bolsheviks did not take that view of the elections to the Constituent Assembly: they did not abdicate because they had failed to win (and, when the Assembly met and proved hostile, they unceremoniously dispersed it). However, in terms of the mandate to rule, they could and did argue that it was not the population as a whole that they claimed to represent. They had taken power in the name of the working class. The conclusion to be drawn from the elections to the Second Congress of Soviets and the Constituent Assembly was that, as of October –

November 1917, they were drawing more working-class votes than any other party.

But what if at some later time the workers should withdraw their support? The Bolsheviks' claim to represent the will of the proletariat was based on faith as well as observation: it was quite possible, in Lenin's terms, that at some time in the future the workers' proletarian consciousness might prove inferior to that of the Bolshevik Party, without necessarily removing the party's mandate to rule. Probably the Bolsheviks did not expect this to happen. But many of their opponents of 1917 did, and they assumed that Lenin's party would not give up power even if it lost working-class support. Engels had warned that a socialist party taking power prematurely might find itself isolated and forced into repressive dictatorship. Clearly the Bolshevik leaders, and Lenin in particular, were willing to take that risk.

3 The Civil War

The October seizure of power was not the end of the Bolshevik Revolution but the beginning. The Bolsheviks had taken control in Petrograd and, after a week of street-fighting, in Moscow. But the soviets that had sprung up in most provincial centres still had to follow the capitals' lead in overthrowing the bourgeoisie (often, at local level, this meant ousting a 'Committee of Public Safety' set up by the solid citizenry of the town); and, if a local soviet was too weak to take power, support was unlikely to be forthcoming from the capitals. Bolsheviks in the provinces, as well as at the centre, had to work out their attitude to local soviets which successfully asserted their authority but happened to be dominated by Mensheviks and SRs. Rural Russia, moreover, had largely thrown off the yoke of authority imposed from the towns. The outlying and non-Russian areas of the old Empire were in various conditions of complex turmoil. If the Bolsheviks had taken power with the intention of governing the country in any conventional sense, some long and difficult struggles against anarchic, decentralizing and separatist tendencies lay ahead.

In fact, Russia's future form of government remained an open question. Judging by the October coup in Petrograd, the Bolsheviks had reservations about their own slogan of 'All power to the soviets'. On the other hand, the slogan seemed to fit the mood of the provinces in the winter of 1917–18 – but this, perhaps, is only another way of saying that central governmental authority had temporarily collapsed. It remained to be seen just what the Bolsheviks meant by their other slogan of 'dictatorship of the proletariat'. If, as Lenin had strongly suggested in his recent writings, it meant crushing the counter-revolutionary efforts of the old possessing classes, the new dictatorship would have to establish coercive organs comparable in function to the Tsarist secret police; if it meant a dictatorship of the Bolshevik Party, as many of Lenin's political opponents suspected, the continued existence of other political parties raised major problems. Yet could the new regime allow itself to act as repressively as the old Tsarist autocracy, and could it retain popular support if it did? A 'dictatorship of the proletariat', moreover, appeared to imply broad powers and independence for all proletarian institutions, including trade unions and factory committees. What happened if the trade unions and factory committees had different concepts of the workers' interests? If 'workers' control' in the factories meant worker self-management, was this compatible with the centralized planning of economic development that the Bolsheviks saw as a basic socialist objective?

Russia's revolutionary regime had also to consider its position in the wider world. The Bolsheviks considered themselves to be part of an international proletarian revolutionary movement, and hoped that their success in Russia would spark similar revolutions throughout Europe; they did not originally think of the new Soviet Republic as a nation state which would have to have conventional diplomatic relations with other states. When Trotsky was appointed Commissar of Foreign Affairs, he expected to issue a few revolutionary proclamations and then 'close up shop'; as Soviet representative in the Brest-Litovsk peace negotiations with Germany early in 1918, he attempted (unsuccessfully) to subvert the whole diplomatic process by speaking past Germany's official representatives to the German people, particularly the German soldiers on the Eastern Front. Recognition of the need for conventional diplomacy was delayed by the Bolshevik leaders' deep belief in the early years that Russia's revolution could not survive long without the support of workers' revolutions in the more advanced capitalist countries of Europe. Only as the fact of revolutionary Russia's isolation gradually became clear did they begin to reassess their position *vis-à-vis* the outside world, and by that time the habit of combining revolutionary appeals with more conventional state-to-state contacts was firmly entrenched.

The territorial boundaries of the new Soviet Republic and policy towards non-Russian nationalities constituted another major problem. Before the war, Lenin had cautiously endorsed a principle of national self-determination. For Marxists, however, the class question was always more important than the national one; and the Bolsheviks found it very difficult to believe that national separatist movements directed against a 'capitalist' or 'autocratic' state were in any sense comparable to separatist movements which involved repudiation of the internationalist revolutionary cause that the Bolsheviks and the new Soviet Republic represented.

It was as natural for the Bolsheviks in Petrograd to hope for a revolutionary victory of soviet power in Azerbaijan as to hope for it in Hungary – though the Azerbaijanis, as former subjects of Imperial Petersburg, were not very likely to appreciate this. It was also natural for the Bolsheviks to support workers' soviets in the Ukraine and oppose the 'bourgeois' Ukrainian nationalists, regardless of the fact that the soviets (reflecting the ethnic composition of the Ukraine's working class) tended to be dominated by Russians, Jews and Poles who were 'foreigners' not only to the nationalists but also to the Ukrainian peasantry. The Bolsheviks' dilemma – most dramatically illustrated when the Red Army marched into Poland in 1920 and the workers of Warsaw resisted the 'Russian invasion' – was that policies of proletarian internationalism in practice had a disconcerting similarity to the policies of old-style Russian imperialism.

But the Bolsheviks' behaviour and policies after the October Revolution were not formed in a vacuum, and the factor of civil war is almost always crucial in explaining them. The Civil War broke out in the middle of 1918, only a few months after the formal conclusion of the Brest-Litovsk peace between Russia and Germany and Russia's definitive withdrawal from the European war. It was fought on many fronts, against a variety of White (that is, anti-Bolshevik) Armies, which had the support of a number of foreign powers including Russia's former Allies in the European war. The Bolsheviks saw it as a class war, both in domestic and international terms: Russian proletariat against Russian bourgeoisie; international revolution (as exemplified by the Soviet Republic) against international capitalism. The Red (Bolshevik) victory in 1920 was therefore a proletarian triumph, but the bitterness of the struggle had indicated the strength and determination of the proletariat's class enemies. Although the interventionist capitalist powers had withdrawn, the Bolsheviks did not believe that this withdrawal was permanent. They expected that at a more opportune moment the forces of international capitalism would return, and crush the international workers' revolution at its source.

The Civil War undoubtedly had an enormous impact on the Bolsheviks and the young Soviet Republic. It polarized the society, leaving lasting resentments and scars; and foreign intervention created a permanent Soviet fear of 'capitalist encirclement' which had elements of paranoia and xenophobia. The Civil War devastated the economy, bringing industry almost to a standstill and emptying the towns. This had political as well as economic and social implications, since it meant at least a temporary disintegration and dispersal of the industrial proletariat – the class in whose name the Bolsheviks had taken power.

It was in the context of civil war that the Bolsheviks had their first experience of ruling, and this undoubtedly shaped the party's subsequent development in many important respects.[1] Over half a million Communists served in the Red Army at some time during the Civil War (and, of this group, roughly half joined the Red Army before joining the Bolshevik Party). Of all members of the Bolshevik Party in 1927, 33 per cent had joined in the years 1917–20, while only 1 per cent had joined before 1917.[2] Thus the underground life of the prerevolutionary party – the formative experience of the 'old guard' of Bolshevik leaders – was known to most party members in the 1920s only through hearsay. For the cohort that had joined the party during the Civil War, the party was a fighting brotherhood in the most literal sense. The Communists who had served in the Red Army brought military jargon into the language of party politics, and made the army tunic and boots – worn even by those who had stayed in civilian posts or been too young to fight – almost a uniform for party members in the 1920s and early 1930s.

In the judgement of one historian, the Civil War experience 'militarized the revolutionary political culture of the Bolshevik movement', leaving a heritage that included 'readiness to resort to coercion, rule by administrative fiat (*administrirovanie*), centralized administration [and] summary justice'.[3] This view of the origins of Soviet (and Stalinist) authoritarianism is in many ways more satisfactory than the traditional Western interpretation, which stressed the party's prerevolutionary heritage and Lenin's advocacy of centralized party organization and strict discipline. Nevertheless, other factors reinforcing the party's authoritarian tendencies must also be taken into account. In the first place, a minority dictatorship was almost bound to be authoritarian, and those who served as its executants were extremely likely to develop the habits of bossing and bullying that Lenin often criticized in the years after 1917. In the second place, the Bolshevik Party owed its success in 1917 to the support of Russia's workers, soldiers and sailors; and such people were much less inclined than the Old Bolshevik intellectuals to worry about crushing opposition or imposing their authority by force rather than by tactful persuasion.

Finally, in considering the link between the Civil War and authoritarian rule, it must be remembered that there was a two-way relationship between the Bolsheviks and the political environment of 1918–20.

The Civil War was not an unforeseeable act of God for which the Bolsheviks were in no way responsible. On the contrary, the Bolsheviks had associated themselves with armed confrontation and violence in the months between February and October 1917; and, as the Bolshevik leaders knew perfectly well before the event, their October coup was seen by many as an outright provocation to civil war. The Civil War certainly gave the new regime a baptism by fire, and thereby influenced its future development. But it was the kind of baptism the Bolsheviks had risked, and may even have sought.

The Civil War, the Red Army and the Cheka

In the immediate aftermath of the Bolsheviks' October coup, Cadet newspapers issued a call to arms for the salvation of the revolution, General Krasnov's loyalist troops unsuccessfully engaged pro-Bolshevik forces and Red Guards in the battle of Pulkovo Heights outside Petrograd, and there was heavy fighting in Moscow. In this preliminary round, the Bolsheviks were the victors. But almost certainly they were going to have to fight again. In the large Russian armies on the southern fronts of the war against Germany and Austria-Hungary, the Bolsheviks were much less popular than in the north-west. Germany remained at war with Russia and, despite the advantages to the Germans of peace on the Eastern Front, Russia's new regime could no more count on German benevolence than it could on sympathy from the allied powers. As the commander of German forces on the Eastern Front wrote in his diary early in February 1918, on the eve of a renewed German offensive after the breakdown of peace negotiations at Brest-Litovsk,

No other way out is possible, otherwise these brutes [the Bolsheviks] will wipe up the Ukrainians, the Finns and the Balts, and then quietly get together a new revolutionary army and turn the whole of Europe into a pig-sty . . . The whole of Russia is no more than a vast heap of maggots – a squalid, swarming mass.[4]

During the peace negotiations at Brest in January, Trotsky had refused the terms offered by the Germans and attempted a strategy of 'No war, no peace', meaning that the Russians would neither continue the war nor sign a peace on unacceptable terms. This was pure bravado, since the Russian Army at the front was melting away, while the German Army, despite Bolshevik appeals to working-class brotherhood, was not. The Germans called Trotsky's bluff and advanced, occupying large areas of the Ukraine.

Lenin regarded it as imperative that a peace should be concluded. This was very rational, given the state of Russia's fighting forces and the likelihood that the Bolsheviks would soon be fighting a civil war; and, in addition, the Bolsheviks had repeatedly stated before the October Revolution that Russia should withdraw immediately from the European imperialist war. However, it would be rather misleading to see the Bolsheviks as a 'peace party' in any meaningful sense by October. The Petrograd workers who had been ready to fight for the Bolsheviks against Kerensky in October had also been ready to fight for Petrograd against the Germans. This belligerent mood was strongly reflected in the Bolshevik Party in the early months of 1918, and was subsequently to be a great asset to the new regime in fighting the Civil War. At the time of the Brest negotiations, Lenin had the greatest difficulty in persuading even the Bolshevik Central Committee of the need to sign a peace with Germany. The Party's 'left Communists' – a group which included the young Nikolai Bukharin, later to earn a place in history as Stalin's last major opponent in the leadership – advocated a revolutionary war of guerrilla resistance to the German invaders; and the left SRs, who were currently in alliance with the Bolsheviks, took a similar position. Lenin finally forced the decision through the Bolshevik Central Committee by threatening to resign, but it was a hard-fought battle. The terms which the Germans imposed after their successful offensive were considerably harsher than those they had offered in January. (But the Bolsheviks were lucky: Germany subsequently lost the European war, and as a result lost its conquests in the East.)

The Peace of Brest-Litovsk provided only a brief respite from military threat. Officers of the old Russian Army were gathering forces in the south, in the Cossack territory of the Don and the Kuban, while Admiral Kolchak was establishing an anti-Bolshevik government in Siberia. The British had landed troops at Russia's two northern ports, Arkhangelsk and Murmansk, ostensibly to fight the Germans but in fact also with the intention of supporting local opposition to the new Soviet regime.

By a strange fluke of war, there were even non-Russian troops passing through Russian territory – the Czech Legion, numbering about 30,000 men, which was hoping to get to the Western Front before the European war ended, so that they could reinforce their claim to national independency by fighting on the Allied side against their old Austrian masters. Unable to cross the battlelines from the

Russian side, the Czechs were making an improbable journey *east* on the Trans-Siberian Railway, planning to reach Vladivostok and return to Europe by ship. The Bolsheviks had sanctioned the trip, but this did not prevent local soviets from reacting with hostility to the arrival of contingents of armed foreigners at railway stations along the way. In May 1918, the Czechs had their first clash with a Bolshevik-dominated soviet in the Urals town of Chelyabinsk. Other Czech units supported Russian SRs in Samara when they rose up against the Bolsheviks to establish a short-lived Volga Republic. The Czechs ended up more or less fighting their way out of Russia, and it was only after many months that they were all evacuated from Vladivostok and shipped back to Europe.

The Civil War proper – Bolshevik 'Reds' against Russian anti-Bolshevik 'Whites' – began in the summer of 1918.[5] At that time, the Bolsheviks moved their capital to Moscow, since Petrograd had escaped the threat of capture by the Germans only to come under attack by a White Army under General Yudenich. But large areas of the country were not effectively under Moscow's control (these included Siberia, southern Russia, the Caucasus, the Ukraine and even much of the Urals and Volga region, where local Bolsheviks intermittently dominated many of the urban soviets), and White Armies threatened the Soviet Republic from the east, the north-west and the south. Of the Allied Powers, Britain and France were extremely hostile to the new regime in Russia and supported the Whites, though their direct military involvement was on a fairly small scale. Both the US and Japan sent troops to Siberia – the Japanese hoping for territorial gains, the Americans in a muddled effort to restrain the Japanese, police the Trans-Siberian Railway and perhaps support Kolchak's Siberian government if it measured up to American democratic standards.

Although the Bolsheviks' situation seemed desperate indeed in 1919, when the territory firmly under their control was roughly that of Muscovite Russia in the sixteenth century, their opponents also had formidable problems. In the first place, the White Armies operated largely independently of each other, without central direction or co-ordination. In the second place, the Whites' control over their territorial bases was even more tenuous than the Bolsheviks'. Where they set up regional governments, the administrative machinery had to be created almost from scratch, and the results were extremely unsatisfactory. Russia's transport and communications systems, historically highly centralized on Moscow and Petersburg, did not facilitate White operations around the periphery. The White forces were harassed not only by the Reds but also the so-called 'Green Armies' – peasant and Cossack bands that gave allegiance to neither side but were most active in the outlying areas in which the Whites were based. The White Armies, well supplied with officers from the old Tsarist Army, had difficulty keeping up the numbers of recruits and conscripts for them to command.

The Bolsheviks' fighting force was the Red Army, organized under the direction of Trotsky, who became Commissar for War in the spring of 1918. The Red Army had to be built up from the beginning, since the disintegration of the old Russian Army had gone too far to be halted (the Bolsheviks announced its total demobilization shortly after taking power). The nucleus of the Red Army, formed at the beginning of 1918, consisted of Red Guards from the factories and pro-Bolshevik units from the old Army and Fleet. This was expanded by voluntary recruitment and, from the summer of 1918, selective conscription. Workers and Communists were the first to be drafted, and throughout the Civil War provided a high proportion of the combat troops. But by the end of the Civil War, the Red Army was a massive institution with an enlistment of over five million, mainly peasant conscripts. Only about a tenth of these were fighting troops (the forces deployed by either Reds or Whites on a given front rarely exceeded 100,000), while the rest were in supply, transport or administrative work. To a considerable extent, the Red Army had to fill the gap left by the breakdown of civilian administration: it was the largest and best-functioning bureaucracy the Soviet regime possessed in the early years, with first claim on all available resources.

Although many Bolsheviks had an ideological preference for militia-type units like the Red Guards, the Red Army was organized from the first on regular army lines, with the soldiers subject to military discipline and the officers appointed and not elected. Because of the shortage of trained military professionals, Trotsky and Lenin insisted on using officers from the old Tsarist Army, although this policy was much criticized in the Bolshevik Party, and the Military Opposition faction tried to get it reversed at two successive party congresses. By the end of the Civil War, the Red Army had over 50,000 former Tsarist officers, most of them conscripted; and the great majority of its senior military commanders came from this group. To ensure that the old officers remained loyal, they were paired with political commissars, usually Communists, who had to countersign all orders and shared final responsibility with the military commanders.

In addition to its military forces, the Soviet regime quickly created a security force – the All-Russian Extraordinary Commission for Struggle against Counter-Revolution, Sabotage and Speculation, known as the Cheka. When this institution was founded in December 1917, its immediate task was to control the outbreak of banditry, looting and raiding of liquor stores that followed the October seizure of power. But it soon assumed the broader functions of a security police, dealing with anti-regime conspiracies and keeping watch on groups whose loyalty was suspect, including bourgeois 'class enemies', officials of the old regime and Provisional Government and members of the opposition political parties. After the outbreak of the Civil War, the Cheka became an organ of terror, dispensing summary justice including executions, making mass arrests and taking hostages at random in areas that had come under White control or were suspected of leaning towards the Whites. According to Bolshevik figures for twenty provinces of European Russia in 1918 and the first half of 1919, at least 8,389 persons were shot without trial by the Cheka, and 87,000 arrested.[6]

The Bolsheviks' Red terror had its equivalent in the White terror practised by the anti-Bolshevik forces in the areas under their control, and the same kind of atrocities were attributed to each side by the other. However, the Bolsheviks were quite forthright about their own use of terror (which implies not only summary justice but also random punishment, unrelated to individual guilt, whose purpose is the intimidation of a specific group or the population as a whole); and at this point in their history they took some pride in being tough-minded about violence, avoiding the mealy-mouthed hypocrisy of the bourgeoisie and admitting that the rule of any class, including the proletariat, involves the coercion of other classes. All the same, they usually spoke of terror, particularly the use of the death penalty, as a temporary phenomenon, called forth by the exigencies of revolution and civil war.

When the Bolsheviks looked for historical parallels for the activities of the Cheka, they normally referred to the revolutionary terror of 1794 in France. They did not see any parallel to the Tsarist secret police, though Western historians have often drawn one. The Cheka, in fact, operated much more openly and violently than the old police: its style had more in common with the 'class vengeance' of Baltic sailors dealing with their officers in 1917, on the one hand, or Stolypin's armed pacification of the countryside in 1906–7, on the other. The parallel with the Tsarist secret police became more appropriate after the Civil War, when the Cheka was replaced by the GPU (Chief Political Administration) – a move associated with the abandonment of terror and the extension of legality – and the security organs became more routine, bureaucratic and discreet in their methods of operation. In this longer perspective, there clearly were strong elements of continuity (though not continuity of personnel) between the Tsarist and Soviet secret police; and the clearer they became, the more evasive and hypocritical were Soviet discussions of the security function.

The Red Army and the Cheka both made important contributions to the Bolshevik victory in the Civil War. However, it would be inadequate to explain that victory simply in terms of military strength and terror, especially as no one has yet found a way of measuring the balance of force between Reds and Whites. Active support and passive acceptance by the society must also be taken into account, and indeed these factors were probably crucial. The Reds had active support from the urban working class, with the Bolshevik Party providing an organizational nucleus. The Whites had active support from the old middle and upper classes, with part of the Tsarist officer corps serving as the main organizing agent. But it was surely the peasantry, constituting the great majority of the population, that tipped the balance.

Both the Red Army and the White Armies conscripted peasants in the territories they controlled, and both had a substantial desertion rate. As the Civil War progressed, however, the Whites' difficulties with the peasant conscripts became markedly greater than the Reds'. The peasants resented the Bolsheviks' policy of grain requisitioning (see below, p. 74), but the Whites were no different in this respect. The peasants also had no great enthusiasm for serving in anyone's army, as the experience of the Russian Army in 1917 had amply demonstrated. However, the mass desertions of peasants in 1917 had been closely related to the land seizures and redistribution by the villages. This process was largely completed by the end of 1918 (which greatly reduced the peasants' objection to army service), and the Bolsheviks had approved it. The Whites, on the other hand, did not approve of land seizures and supported the former landowners' claims. Thus in the crucial issue of land, the Bolsheviks were the lesser evil.

War Communism

The Bolsheviks took over a war economy in a state of near collapse, and their first and overwhelming problem was to keep it running. This was the pragmatic context of the economic policies of the Civil War that were later labelled 'War Communism'. But there was also an ideological context. In the long term, the Bolsheviks aimed to abolish private property and the free market and distribute products according to need, and in the short term, they might be expected to choose policies that would bring these ideals closer to fulfilment. The balance between pragmatism and ideology in War Communism has long been a subject of debate,[7] the problem being that policies like nationalization and state distribution can plausibly be explained either as a pragmatic response to the exigencies of war or as an ideological imperative of communism. It is a debate in which scholars on both sides can quote the pronouncements of Lenin and other leading Bolsheviks, since the Bolsheviks themselves were not sure of the answer. From a Bolshevik perspective of 1921, when War Communism was jettisoned in favour of the New Economic Policy, the pragmatic interpretation was clearly preferable: once War Communism had failed, the less said about its ideological underpinnings the better. But from an earlier Bolshevik perspective – for example, that of Bukharin and Preobrazhensky in their classic *ABC of Communism* (1919) – the opposite was true. While War Communism policies were in force, it was natural for Bolsheviks to give them an ideological justification – to assert that the party, armed with the scientific ideology of Marxism, was in full control of events rather than simply struggling to keep up.

The question lying behind the debate is how quickly the Bolsheviks thought they could move towards communism; and the answer depends on whether we are talking about 1918 or 1920. The Bolsheviks' first steps were cautious, and so were their pronouncements about the future. However, from the outbreak of the Civil War in mid 1918 the Bolsheviks' earlier caution began to disappear. To cope with a desperate situation, they turned to more radical policies and, in the process, tried to extend the sphere of centralized government control much further and faster than they had originally intended. In 1920, as the Bolsheviks headed towards victory in the Civil War and disaster in the economy, a mood of euphoria and desperation took hold. With the old world disappearing in the flames of Revolution and Civil War, it seemed to many Bolsheviks that a new world was about to arise, phoenix-like, from the ashes.[8] This hope, perhaps, owed more to anarchist ideology than to Marxism, but it was nevertheless expressed in Marxist terms: with the triumph of proletarian revolution, the transition to communism was imminent, possibly only weeks or months away.

This sequence is clearly illustrated in one of the key areas of economic policy, nationalization. As good Marxists, the Bolsheviks nationalized banking and credit very quickly after the October Revolution. But they did *not* immediately embark upon wholesale nationalization of industry: the first nationalization decrees concerned only individual large concerns like the Putilov Works that were already closely involved with the state through defence production and government contracts.

A variety of circumstances, however, were to extend the scope of nationalization far beyond the Bolsheviks' original short-term intentions. Local soviets expropriated plants on their own authority. Some plants were abandoned by their owners and managers; others were nationalized on the petition of their workers, who had driven out the old management, or even on the petition of managers who wanted protection against unruly workers.[9] In the summer of 1918, the government issued a decree nationalizing all large-scale industry, and by the autumn of 1919 it was estimated that over 80 per cent of such enterprises had in fact been nationalized. This far exceeded the organizational capacities of the new Supreme Economic Council: in practice, if the workers themselves could not keep the plants going by organizing the supply of raw materials and distribution of finished products, the plants often just closed down. Yet, having gone so far, the Bolsheviks felt impelled to go further. In November 1920, the government nationalized even small-scale industry, at least on paper. In practice, of course, the Bolsheviks were hard put to name or identify their new acquisitions, let alone direct them. But in theory the whole sphere of production was now in the hands of Soviet power, and even artisan workshops and windmills were part of a centrally directed economy.

A similar sequence led the Bolsheviks towards an almost complete prohibition on free trade and a virtually moneyless economy by the end of the Civil War. From their predecessors they inherited rationing in the towns (introduced in 1916) and a state monopoly on grain which in theory required the peasants to deliver their whole surplus (introduced in the spring of 1917 by the Provisional Government). But the towns were still short of bread and other foodstuffs because the peasants were unwilling to sell when there were almost no manufactured goods on the market to buy. Shortly after the October Revolution, the Bolsheviks tried to increase grain deliveries by offering the peasants manufactured goods instead of money in exchange. They also nationalized wholesale trade and, after the outbreak of the Civil War, prohibited free retail trade in most basic foodstuffs and manufactured products and tried to convert the consumer co-operatives into a state distribution network. These were emergency measures to cope with the food crisis in the towns and the problems of Army supply. But obviously the Bolsheviks could – and did – justify them in ideological terms.

As the food crisis in the towns worsened, barter became a basic form of exchange, and money lost its value.[10] By 1920, wages and salaries were being paid partly in kind (food and goods), and there was even an attempt to construct a budget on a commodity rather than a money basis. Urban services, in so far as they still functioned in the decaying cities, no longer had to be paid for by the individual user. Some Bolsheviks hailed this as an ideological triumph – the 'withering away of money' that indicated how close the society had already come to communism. To less optimistic observers, however, it looked like runaway inflation.

Unfortunately for the Bolsheviks, ideology and practical imperatives did not always converge so neatly. The divergences (together with some Bolshevik uncertainties about what their ideology actually meant in concrete terms) were particularly evident in policies affecting the working class. In regard to wages, for example, the Bolsheviks had egalitarian instincts rather than a strictly egalitarian policy in practice. In the interests of maximizing production, they tried to retain piece-work in industry, though the workers regarded this basis of payment as essentially inegalitarian and unfair. Shortages and rationing probably tended to reduce urban inequalities during the Civil War period, but this could scarcely be counted as a Bolshevik achievement. In fact, the rationing system under War Communism favoured certain categories of the population, including Red Army personnel, skilled workers in key industries, Communist administrators and some groups of the intelligentsia.

Factory organization was another touchy question. Were the factories to be run by the workers themselves (as the Bolsheviks' 1917 endorsement of 'workers' control' seemed to suggest), or by managers appointed by the state, following the directions of central planning and co-ordinating agencies? The Bolsheviks favoured the second, but the effective outcome during War Communism was a compromise, with considerable variation from place to place. Some factories continued to be run by elected workers' committees. Others were run by an appointed director, often a Communist but sometimes the former manager, chief engineer or even owner of the plant. In yet other cases, a worker or group of workers from the factory committee or local trade union was appointed to manage the plant, and this transitional arrangement – halfway between workers' control and appointed management – was often the most successful.

In dealing with the peasantry, the Bolsheviks' first problem was the practical one of getting food. State procurements of grain were not improved either by outlawing private grain trading or by offering manufactured goods instead of money in payment: the state still had too few goods to offer, and the peasants remained unwilling to deliver their produce. Given the urgent necessity of feeding the towns and the Red Army, the state had little choice but to take the peasants' produce by persuasion, cunning, threats or force. The Bolsheviks adopted a policy of grain requisitioning, sending workers' and soldiers' brigades – usually armed, and if possible provided with some goods for barter – to get the hoarded grain out of the peasants' barns. Obviously this produced strained relations between the Soviet regime and the peasantry. But the Whites did the same thing, as had occupying armies throughout the ages. The Bolsheviks' need to live off the land probably surprised themselves more than it surprised the peasants.

But there were other aspects of Bolshevik policy that evidently did surprise and alarm the peasantry. In the first place, they tried to facilitate grain procurements by splitting the village into opposing groups. Believing that the growth of rural capitalism had already produced significant class differentiation among the peasants, the Bolsheviks expected to receive instinctive support from the poor and landless peasants and instinctive opposition from the richer ones. They therefore began to organize village Committees of the Poor, and encouraged them to co-operate with Soviet authorities in extracting grain from the barns of richer peasants. The attempt proved a dismal failure, partly because of the normal village solidarity against outsiders and partly because many formerly landless and poor peasants had improved their position as a result of the land seizures and redistributions of 1917–18. Worse still, it demonstrated to the peasants that the Bolsheviks' understanding of revolution in the countryside was quite different from their own.

For the Bolsheviks, still thinking in terms of the old Marxist debate with the Populists, the *mir* was a decaying institution, corrupted by the Tsarist state and undermined by emergent rural capitalism, lacking any potential for socialist development. Moreover, the Bolsheviks believed, the 'first revolution' in the countryside – land seizures and egalitarian redistribution – was already being followed by a 'second revolution', a class war of poor peasants against rich peasants, which was destroying the unity of the village community and must ultimately break the authority of the *mir*.[11] For the peasants, on the other hand, the *mir* was perceived as a true peasant institution, historically abused and exploited by the state, which had finally thrown off state authority and accomplished a peasant revolution.

Though the Bolsheviks had let the peasants have their way in 1917–18, their long-term plans for the countryside were quite as disruptive as Stolypin's had been. They disapproved of almost every aspect of the traditional rural order, from the *mir* and the strip system of dividing the land to the patriarchal family (*The ABC of Communism* even looked forward to the time when peasant families would give up the 'barbaric' and wasteful custom of eating supper at home, and join their neighbours at a communal village dining-room[12]). They were meddlers in village affairs, like Stolypin; and although they could not in principle share his enthusiasm for a small-farming petty-bourgeoisie, they still had enough ingrained dislike of peasant backwardness to continue the Stolypin policy of consolidating the households' scattered strips into solid blocks suitable for modern small farming.[13]

But the Bolsheviks' real interest was large-scale agriculture, and only the political imperative of winning over the peasantry had led them to condone the breaking up of large estates that took place in 1917–18. On some of the remaining state lands, they set up state farms (*sovkhozy*) – in effect, the socialist equivalent of large-scale capitalist agriculture, with appointed managers supervising the work of agricultural labourers who worked for wages. The Bolsheviks also believed that collective farms (*kolkhozy*) were preferable in political terms to traditional or individual small-holding peasant farming; and some collective farms were established in the Civil War period, usually by demobilized soldiers or workers fleeing hunger in the towns. The collective farms did not divide their land into strips, like the traditional peasant village, but worked the land and marketed produce collectively. Often, the early collective farmers had an ideology similar to the founders of utopian agricultural communities in the United States and elsewhere, pooling almost all their resources and possessions; and, like the utopians, they rarely made a success of farming or even survived long as harmonious communities. The peasants regarded both state and collective farms with suspicion. They were too few and weak to constitute a serious challenge to traditional peasant farming. But their very existence reminded the peasants that the Bolsheviks had strange ideas and were not to be trusted too far.

Visions of the new world

There was a wildly impractical and utopian streak in a great deal of Bolshevik thinking during the Civil War. No doubt all successful revolutions have this characteristic: the revolutionaries must always be driven by enthusiasm and irrational hope, since they would otherwise make the commonsense judgement that the risks and costs of revolution outweigh the possible benefits. The Bolsheviks thought they were immune from utopianism because their socialism was scientific. But, whether or not they were right about the inherently scientific nature of Marxism, even science needs human interpreters, who make subjective judgements and have their own emotional biases. The Bolsheviks were revolutionary enthusiasts, not laboratory assistants.

It was a subjective judgement that Russia was ready for proletarian revolution in 1917, even though the Bolsheviks cited Marxist social-science theory to support it. It was a matter of faith rather than scientific prediction that world revolution was imminent (in Marxist terms, after all, the Bolsheviks might have made a mistake and taken power too soon). The belief, underlying the later economic policies of War Communism, that Russia was on the brink of the definitive transition to communism had scarcely any justification in Marxist theory. The Bolsheviks' perception of the real world had become almost comically distorted in many respects by 1920. They sent the Red Army to advance on Warsaw because, to many Bolsheviks, it seemed obvious that the Poles would recognize the troops as proletarian brothers rather than Russian aggressors. At home, they confused rampant inflation and currency devaluation with the withering away of money under communism. When war and famine produced bands of homeless children during the Civil War, some Bolsheviks saw even this as a blessing in disguise, since the state could give the children a true collectivist upbringing (in orphanages) and they would not be exposed to the bourgeois influence of the old family.

The same spirit was noticeable in the Bolsheviks' early approach to the tasks of government and administration. The utopian texts here were Marx and Engels's dictum that under communism the state would wither away, and the passages in Lenin's *State and Revolution*

(1917) where he suggested that administration would ultimately cease to be the business of full-time professionals and would become a rotating duty of the whole citizenry. In practice, however, Lenin always kept a hard-headed realism about government: he was not among those Bolsheviks who saw the old administrative machinery collapsing in the years 1917–20 and concluded that the state was already withering away as Russia approached communism.

But the Bolshevik authors of *The ABC of Communism* (1919), Bukharin and Preobrazhensky, got much more carried away. They had the kind of vision of a depersonalized, scientifically regulated world that the contemporary Russian writer Evgenii Zamyatin satirized in *We* (written in 1920) and George Orwell later described in *Nineteen Eighty-four*. This world was the antithesis of any actual Russia, past, present or future; and in the chaos of the Civil War that must have made it particularly appealing. In explaining how it would be possible to run a centrally planned economy after the withering away of the state, Bukharin and Preobrazhensky wrote:

The main direction will be entrusted to various kinds of book-keeping offices or statistical bureaux. There, from day to day, account will be kept of production and all its needs; there also it will be decided whither workers must be sent, whence they must be taken, and how much work there is to be done. And inasmuch as, from childhood onwards, all will have been accustomed to social labour, and since all will understand that this work is necessary and that life goes easier when everything is done according to a pre-arranged plan and when the social order is like a well-ordered machine, all will work in accordance with the indications of the statistical bureaux. There will be no need for special ministers of State, for police or prisons, for laws and decrees – nothing of the sort. Just as in an orchestra all the performers watch the conductor's baton and act accordingly, so here all will consult the statistical reports and will direct their work accordingly.[14]

This may have sinister overtones to us, thanks to Orwell's *Nineteen Eighty-four*, but in contemporary terms it was bold, revolutionary thinking that was as excitingly modern (and remote from mundane reality) as Futurist art. The Civil War was a time when intellectual and cultural experimentation flourished, and an iconoclastic attitude to the past was *de rigueur* among young radical intellectuals. Machines – including the 'well-ordered machine' of future society – fascinated artists and intellectuals. Sentiment, spirituality, human drama and undue interest in individual psychology were out of fashion, often denounced as 'petty-bourgeois'. Avant-garde artists like the poet

Vladimir Mayakovsky and the theatre director Vsevolod Meyerhold saw revolutionary art and revolutionary politics as part of the same protest against the old, bourgeois world. They were among the first members of the intelligentsia to accept the October Revolution and offer their services to the new Soviet government, producing propaganda posters in Cubist and Futurist style, painting revolutionary slogans on the walls of former palaces, staging mass re-enactments of revolutionary victories in the streets, bringing acrobatics as well as politically-relevant messages into the conventional theatre, and designing non-representational monuments to revolutionary heroes of the past. If the avant-garde artists had had their way, traditional bourgeois art would have been liquidated even more quickly than the bourgeois political parties. The Bolshevik leaders, however, were not quite convinced that artistic Futurism and Bolshevism were inseparable natural allies, and took a more cautious position on the classics.[15]

The ethos of revolutionary liberation was more wholeheartedly accepted by the Bolsheviks (or at least by the Bolshevik intellectuals) where women and the family were concerned. The Bolsheviks supported the emancipation of women, as most members of the Russian radical intelligentsia had done since the 1860s. Like Friedrich Engels, who had written that in the modern family the husband is the 'bourgeois' and the wife the 'proletarian', they saw women as an exploited group. By the end of the Civil War, laws had been enacted that made divorce easily attainable, removed the formal stigma from illegitimacy, permitted abortion and mandated equal rights and equal pay for women.

While only the most radical Bolshevik thinkers talked about destroying the family, there was a general assumption that women and children were potential victims of oppression within the family, and that the family tended to inculcate bourgeois values. The Bolshevik Party established special women's departments (*zhenotdely*) to organize and educate women, protect their interests and help them to play an independent role. Young Communists had their own separate organizations – the Komsomol for adolescents and young adults, the Young Pioneers (established a few years later) for the ten to fourteen age group – which encouraged their members to watch out for 'bourgeois' tendencies at home and at school, and try to re-educate parents and teachers who looked back nostalgically to the old days, disliked the Bolsheviks and the revolution, or clung to 'religious superstitions'. If one slogan reported during the Civil War, 'Down with the capitalist tyranny of parents!', was a bit on the exuberant side for the older Bolsheviks, the spirit of youthful rebellion was generally prized and respected in the party in the early years.

Sexual liberation, however, was a young-Communist cause that rather embarrassed the Bolshevik leadership. Because of the party's position on abortion and divorce, it was widely assumed that the Bolsheviks advocated 'free love', meaning promiscuous sex. Lenin certainly did not: his generation was against the Philistine morality of the bourgeoisie, but emphasized comradely relations between the sexes and thought promiscuity showed a frivolous nature. Even Aleksandra Kollontai, the Bolshevik leader who wrote most about sexual questions and was something of a feminist, was a believer in love rather than the 'glass of water' theory of sex that was often attributed to her.

But the 'glass of water' approach was popular among young Communists, especially the men who had learnt their ideology in the Red Army and regarded casual sex almost as a Communist rite of passage. Their attitude reflected a general wartime and postwar relaxation of morals that was even more marked in Russia than in other European countries. The older Communists had to put up with it – they assumed that sex was a private matter and, after all, they were revolutionaries and not bourgeois Philistines – as they had to put up with Cubists, advocates of Esperanto and the nudists who, as an act of ideological affirmation, occasionally leapt naked on to crowded Moscow trams. But they felt that such things detracted from the high seriousness of the revolution.

The Bolsheviks in power

Having taken power, the Bolsheviks had to learn to govern. Hardly any of them had administrative experience: by previous occupation, most were professional revolutionaries or workers or free-lance journalists (Lenin listed his own profession as 'man of letters' [*literator*]). They despised bureaucracies and knew very little about how they worked. They knew nothing about budgets. As Anatolii Lunacharsky, head of the People's Commissariat of Enlightenment, wrote of his first finance officer:

[His] face always bore a mark of deepest astonishment when he brought us money from the bank. It still seemed to him that the Revolution and the organization of the new power were a sort of magical play, and that in a magical play it is impossible to receive real money.[16]

During the Civil War, most of the Bolsheviks' organizational talents went into the Red Army, the Food Commissariat and the Cheka. Capable organizers from the local party committees and soviets were continually being mobilized for the Red Army or sent on trouble-shooting missions elsewhere. The old central government ministries (now People's Commissariats) were run by a small group of Bolshe-viks, mainly intellectuals, and staffed largely by officials who had earlier worked for the Tsarist and Provisional Governments. Authority at the centre was confusingly divided between the government (Coun-cil of People's Commissars), the soviets' Central Executive Committee and the Bolshevik Party's Central Committee, with its Secretariat and bureaux for organizational and political affairs, the Orgburo and the Politburo.

The Bolsheviks described their rule as a 'dictatorship of the prole-tariat', a concept which in operational terms had much in common with a dictatorship of the Bolshevik Party. It was clear from the first that this left little room for other political parties: those that were not outlawed for supporting the Whites or (in the case of the left SRs) staging a revolt were harassed and intimidated by arrests during the Civil War and forced into self-liquidation in the early 1920s. But it was much less clear what the dictatorship meant in terms of the form of government. The Bolsheviks did not initially think of their own party organization as a potential instrument of government. They seem to have assumed that the party organization would remain separate from government and free of administrative functions, just as it would have done if the Bolsheviks had become the governing party in a multi-party political system.

The Bolsheviks also described their rule as 'soviet power'. But this was never a very accurate description, in the first place because the October Revolution was essentially a party coup, not a soviet one, and in the second place because the new central government (chosen by the Bolshevik Central Committee) had nothing to do with the soviets. The new government took over control of the various ministerial bureau-cracies from the Provisional Government, which in turn had inherited them from the Tsar's Council of Ministers. But the soviets did acquire a role at local level, where the old administrative machinery had completely collapsed. They (or more precisely their executive commit-tees) became the local organs of the central government, creating their own bureaucratic departments of finance, education, agriculture and so on. This administrative function gave point to the soviets' existence, even after soviet elections had become little more than a formality.

At first, the central government (Council of People's Commissars) seemed the hub of the new political system. But by the end of the Civil War, there were already signs that the Bolshevik Party's Central Committee and Politburo were tending to usurp the government's powers, while at local level the party committees were becoming dominant over the soviets; and this primacy of party over state organs became a permanent feature of the Soviet system. However, it has recently been argued that Lenin (who became seriously ill in 1921 and died in 1924) would have resisted any such tendency if he had not been removed from the scene by illness, and that he intended that the government rather than the party should play the dominant role.[17]

Certainly for a revolutionary and the creator of a revolutionary party, Lenin had an oddly conservative streak when it came to institutions. He wanted a real government, not some kind of improvised directorate, just as he wanted a real army, real laws and perhaps even, in the final analysis, a real Russian Empire. However, it must be remembered that the members of this government were always in effect chosen by the Bolshevik Central Committee and its Politburo. Lenin headed the government, but he was also *de facto* head of the Central Committee and the Politburo; and it was these party organs rather than the government that dealt with the crucial military and foreign-policy questions during the Civil War. From Lenin's point of view, the big advantage of the government side of the system was probably that its bureaucracies included many technical experts (specialists on finance, engineering, law, public health and so on), whose skills Lenin thought it essential to use. The Bolshevik Party was developing a bureaucracy of its own, but it did not employ outsiders who were not party members. In the party, and especially among its working-class members, there was great suspicion of 'bourgeois experts'. This had already been clearly demonstrated in the strong Bolshevik opposition in 1918–19 to the army's use of military professionals (the former Tsarist officers).

The nature of the political system that emerged after the Bolsheviks took power must be explained not only in terms of institutional arrangements but also in terms of the nature of the Bolshevik Party. It was a party with authoritarian tendencies, and one that had always had a strong leader – even, according to Lenin's opponents, a dictatorial one. Party discipline and unity had always been stressed. Before 1917, Bolsheviks who disagreed with Lenin on any important issue usually left the party. In the period 1917–20, Lenin had to deal with dissent and even organized dissident factions within the party, but he seems to have regarded this as an abnormal and irritating situation, and finally took decisive steps to change it (see below pp. 91–3). As to opposition to the Bolsheviks from outside the party, the Bolsheviks responded aggressively before the October Revolution and repressively afterwards. In the latter case, the Civil War was obviously a contributing factor. Nevertheless, it would have been surprising if the Bolsheviks had shown liberal tendencies in power, given that anti-liberalism had previously been so important in the party's self-definition.

The other basic characteristic of the Bolshevik Party was that it was working-class – by its own self-image, by the nature of its support in the society, and to a substantial degree in terms of party membership. For this reason, the issue of the Bolsheviks' 'dictatorship of the proletariat' cannot be dismissed simply by saying that it was really a dictatorship of the party. It was the dictatorship of a more or less proletarian party, and that had consequences. Among the consequences, perhaps, was reinforcement of the party's authoritarian, illiberal, rough and repressive traits. In the folk wisdom of the party, working-class Bolsheviks were 'tough' and sometimes 'crude', while Bolsheviks from the intelligentsia were 'mild' and sometimes lapsed into a furtive liberalism betraying their class origins. These images were surely not totally unfounded.

The Bolsheviks' political thinking revolved around class and the relationship of the working class to power. They believed that society was divided into antagonistic classes, and that the political struggle was a reflection of the social one. They assumed that their own social support could only come from the urban proletariat and groups like agricultural labourers and poor peasants that had been similarly exploited. They had no doubt that the political threat to Bolshevik rule came from the bourgeoisie, the kulaks (prosperous peasants) and other groups that had been privileged or wealthy under the old regime, and that the Bolsheviks' enemies would be backed by the forces of international capitalism.

For the Bolsheviks, therefore, it was crucial not so much to eliminate the old patterns of exploitation as to reverse them, and thereby consolidate the proletarian victory. One way of reversing them was to apply principles of 'class justice':

In the old law-courts, the class minority of exploiters passed judgement upon the working majority. The law-courts of the proletarian dictatorship are places where the working majority passes judgement upon the exploiting minority. They are specially constructed for the purpose. The judges are elected by the workers alone. The judges are elected solely from among the workers. For the exploiters, the only right that remains is the right of being judged.[18]

These principles were obviously not egalitarian. But the Bolsheviks never claimed to be egalitarian in the period of revolution and transition to socialism. From the Bolshevik standpoint, it was impossible to regard all citizens as equal when some of them were class enemies of the regime. Thus the 1918 Constitution of the Russian Republic gave the vote to all 'toilers' (regardless of sex and nationality), but removed it from members of the exploiting classes and other identifiable enemies of Soviet power – employers of hired labour, persons living on unearned income or from rent, kulaks, priests, former gendarmes and some other categories of Tsarist official, and officers in the White Armies.

The question 'Who rules?' may be posed in abstract terms, but it also has the concrete meaning of 'Which people get the jobs?' Political power had changed hands, and (as a temporary expedient, the Bolsheviks thought) new bosses had to be found to replace the old ones. Given the Bolshevik cast of mind, class was inevitably a criterion in the selection. Some Bolshevik intellectuals, including Lenin, might argue that education was important as well as class, while a few others worried that workers departing for long periods from the factory bench would lost their proletarian identity. But in the party as a whole, the firm consensus was that the only people who could really be trusted with power by the new regime were proletarians who had been victims of exploitation under the old one.[19]

By the end of the Civil War, tens of thousands of workers, soldiers and sailors – Bolsheviks and those who had fought with them in 1917, in the first instance, but later those who had distinguished themselves in the Red Army or the factory committees, those who were young and comparatively well-educated, or simply those who showed an ambition to rise in the world – had become 'cadres', that is, persons holding responsible, usually adminstrative, jobs. They were in the Red Army command, the Cheka, the food administration and the party and soviet bureaucracy. Many were appointed factory managers, usually after working in the local factory committee or trade union. In 1920–1, it was not absolutely clear to the party leaders if and how this process of 'worker promotion' could continue on a large scale, since the party's original pool of worker members had been much depleted, and industrial collapse and urban food shortages during the Civil War had dispersed and demoralized the industrial working class of 1917. Nevertheless, the Bolsheviks had found out by experience what they meant by 'dictatorship of the proletariat'. It was not a collective class dictatorship exercised by workers who remained in their old jobs at the factory bench. It was a dictatorship run by full-time 'cadres' or bosses, in which as many as possible of the new bosses were former proletarians.

4 NEP and the Future of the Revolution

The Bolsheviks' victory in the Civil War brought them face to face with the country's internal problems of administrative chaos and economic devastation. The towns were hungry and half empty. Coal production had dropped catastrophically, the railways were breaking down and industry was almost at a standstill. The peasants were mutinously resentful about food requisitioning. Crop sowings had dropped, and two consecutive years of drought had brought the Volga and other agricultural regions to the brink of famine. Deaths from hunger and epidemics in 1921–2 would exceed the combined total of casualties in the First World War and Civil War. In addition, the emigration of about two million persons during the years of revolution and war had removed much of Russia's educated elite.

There were over five million men in the Red Army, and the ending of the Civil War meant that most of them had to be demobilized. This was a much more difficult operation than the Bolsheviks had anticipated: it meant dismantling a large part of what the new regime had managed to build since the October Revolution. The Red Army had been the backbone of Bolshevik administration during the Civil War and of the economy of War Communism. Moreover, the Red Army soldiers constituted the largest body of 'proletarians' in the land. The proletariat was the Bolsheviks' chosen base of social support, and since 1917 they had defined the proletariat for all practical purposes as Russia's workers, soldiers, sailors and poor peasants. Now a large part of the soldier-and-sailor group was about to disappear; and, worse still, the demobilized soldiers – unemployed, hungry, armed, often stranded far from home by transport breakdowns – were causing turmoil. With over two million demobilized by the early months of 1921, the Bolsheviks had discovered that fighters for the revolution could be transformed overnight into bandits.

The fate of the core proletariat of industrial workers was equally alarming. Industrial closures, military conscription, promotion to administrative work and, above all, flight from the towns because of hunger had reduced the number of industrial workers from 3.6 million in 1917 to 1.5 million in 1920.[1] A substantial proportion of these workers had returned to the villages, where they still had family, and received plots of land as members of the village communities. The Bolsheviks did not know how many workers were in the villages, or how long they would remain there. Perhaps they had simply been reabsorbed into the peasantry and would never come back to the towns. But, whatever the long-term prospects, the immediate situation was clear: over half of Russia's 'dictator class' had vanished.

The Bolsheviks had originally counted on support for the Russian Revolution from the European proletariat, which seemed poised on the brink of revolution at the end of the First World War. But the postwar revolutionary wave in Europe had subsided, leaving the Soviet regime without any European counterparts that could be regarded as permanent allies. Lenin concluded that the lack of support from abroad made it imperative for the Bolsheviks to obtain support from Russia's peasantry. Yet requisitions and the collapse of the market under War Communism had alienated the peasants, and in some regions they were in open revolt. In the Ukraine, a peasant army headed by Nestor Makhno was fighting the Bolsheviks. In Tambov, an important agricultural region of central Russia, a peasant revolt was suppressed only after the dispatch of 50,000 Red Army troops.[2]

The worst blow to the new regime came in March 1921 when, after an outbreak of workers' strikes in Petrograd, the sailors at the nearby Kronstadt naval base rebelled.[3] The Kronstadters, heroes of the July Days of 1917 and supporters of the Bolsheviks in the October Revolution, had become almost legendary figures in Bolshevik mythology. Now they were repudiating the Bolsheviks' revolution, denouncing 'the arbitrary rule of the commissars' and calling for a true soviet republic of workers and peasants. The Kronstadt revolt occurred while the Tenth Party Congress was in session, and a number of delegates had to leave abruptly to join the elite units of Red Army and Cheka troops that were sent over the ice to fight the rebels. The occasion could scarcely have been more dramatic, or more calculated to imprint itself on Bolshevik consciousness. The Soviet press, in what seems to have been its first major effort to conceal unpleasant truths, claimed that the revolt was inspired by emigrés and led by a mysterious White general. But the rumours circulating at the Tenth Party Congress said otherwise.

The Kronstadt revolt seemed a symbolic parting of the ways between the working class and the Bolshevik Party. It was a tragedy, both to those who thought that the workers had been betrayed, and to those who thought that the party had been betrayed by the workers. The Soviet regime, for the first time, had turned its guns on the revolutionary proletariat. Moreover, the trauma of Kronstadt occurred almost simultaneously with another disaster for the revolution. German Communists, encouraged by Comintern leaders in Moscow, attempted a revolutionary uprising that failed miserably. Their defeat meant that even the most optimistic Bolsheviks lost hope that European revolution was imminent. The Russian Revolution would have to survive by its own, unaided efforts.

The Kronstadt and Tambov revolts, both fuelled by economic as well as political grievances, drove home the need for a new economic policy to replace the policy of War Communism. The first step, taken in the spring of 1921, was to end requisitioning of peasant produce and introduce a tax in kind. What this meant in practice was that the state took only a fixed quota instead of everything it could lay hands on (later, after the restabilization of the currency in the first half of the 1920s, the tax in kind became a more conventional money tax).

Since the tax in kind presumably left the peasant with a marketable surplus, the next logical step was to permit a revival of legal private trade and try to close down the flourishing black market. In the spring of 1921, Lenin was still strongly opposed to the legalization of trade, regarding it as a repudiation of Communist principles, but subsequently the spontaneous revival of private trade (often sanctioned by local authorities) presented the Bolshevik leadership with a *fait accompli*, which it accepted. These steps were the beginning of the New Economic Policy, known by the acronym NEP. It was an improvised response to desperate economic circumstances, undertaken initially with very little discussion and debate (and little evident dissent) in the party and the leadership. The beneficial impact on the economy was swift and dramatic.

Further economic changes followed, amounting to a wholesale abandonment of the system that in retrospect began to be called 'War Communism'. In industry, the drive for complete nationalization was abandoned and the private sector was allowed to re-form, though the state retained control of the economy's 'commanding heights', including large-scale industry and banking. Foreign investors were invited to take out concessions for industrial and mining enterprises and development projects. The Finance Commissariat and State Bank began to heed the advice of the old 'bourgeois' financial experts, pushing for stabilization of the currency and limitations on government and public spending. The central government budget was severely cut, and efforts were made to increase state revenue from taxation. Services like schools and medical care, previously free, now had to be paid for by the individual user; access to old-age pensions ánd sickness and unemployment benefits was restricted by putting them on a contributory basis.

From the Communist standpoint NEP was a retreat, and a partial admission of failure. Many Communists felt deeply disillusioned: it seemed that the revolution had changed so little. Moscow, the Soviet capital since 1918 and headquarters of the Comintern, became a bustling city again in the early years of NEP, although to all outward appearances it was still the Moscow of 1913, with peasant women selling potatoes in the markets, churchbells and bearded priests summoning the faithful, prostitutes, beggars and pickpockets working the streets and railway stations, gypsy songs in the nightclubs, uniformed doormen doffing their caps to the gentry, theatre-goers in furs and silk stockings. In this Moscow, the leather-jacketed Communist seemed a sombre outsider, and the Red Army veteran was likely to be standing in line at the Labour Exchange. The revolutionary leaders, quartered incongruously in the Kremlin or the Hotel Luxe, looked to the future with foreboding.

The discipline of retreat

The strategic retreat of NEP, Lenin said, was forced on the Bolsheviks by desperate economic circumstances, and by the need to consolidate the victories that the revolution had already won. Its purpose was to restore the shattered economy and to calm the fears of the non-proletarian population. NEP meant concessions to the peasantry, the intelligentsia and the urban petty-bourgeoisie; relaxation of controls over economic, social and cultural life; the substitution of conciliation for coercion in the Communists' dealings with society as a whole. But Lenin made it very clear that the relaxation should not extend into the political sphere. Within the Communist Party, 'the slightest violation of discipline must be punished severely, sternly, ruthlessly':

When an army is in retreat, a hundred times more discipline is required than when the army is advancing, because during an advance everybody presses forward. If everybody started rushing back now, it would spell immediate and inevitable disaster . . . When a real army is in retreat, machine-guns are kept ready, and when an orderly retreat degenerates into a disorderly one, the command to fire is given, and quite rightly, too.

As for other political parties, their freedom to express their views publicly should be even more strictly curtailed than during the Civil War, particularly if they tried to claim the Bolsheviks' new moderate positions as their own.

When a Menshevik says, 'You are now retreating; I have been advocating retreat all the time; I agree with you, I am your man, let us retreat together,' we say in reply, 'For public manifestations of Menshevism our revolutionary courts must pass the death sentence, otherwise they are not our courts, but God knows what.'[4]

There was some hyperbole in this, since in practice Lenin's normal method of dealing with prominent political opponents was not the firing squad. But he certainly had no scruples about annihilating them politically. The introduction of NEP was accompanied by the arrest of a couple of thousand Mensheviks, including all the members of the Menshevik Central Committee. In 1922, a group of right SRs was put on public trial for crimes against the state: some were given death sentences, although the death sentences were apparently not carried out. In 1922 and 1923, some hundreds of prominent Cadets and Mensheviks were forcibly deported from the Soviet Republic.

Former members of opposition parties who remained were tolerated as long as they abstained totally from all oppositionist political activity. Throughout the 1920s, in fact, some of them held quite responsible positions in the universities, the Academy of Sciences, the state economic and planning organs and (in the case of former left SRs) the GPU, which was the Cheka's successor. But all political parties other than the ruling Communist Party (as the Bolshevik Party was now usually called) were effectively outlawed shortly after the introduction of NEP.

At the same time, the question of discipline *within* the Communist Party was being re-examined. The Bolsheviks, of course, had always put a strong theoretical emphasis on party discipline, going back to Lenin's 1902 pamphlet *What Is To Be Done?* All Bolsheviks accepted the principle of democratic centralism, which meant that party members could freely debate issues before a policy decision was reached, but were bound to accept the decision once a final vote had been taken at a party congress or in the Central Committee. But the principle of democratic centralism did not in itself determine the party's conventions regarding internal debate – how much debate was acceptable, how sharply the party's leaders could be criticized, whether the critics could organize 'factions' or pressure groups on specific issues, and so on.

Before 1917, internal party debate meant for all practical purposes debate within the emigré community of Bolshevik intellectuals. Because of Lenin's dominant position, the Bolshevik emigrés were a more unified and homogeneous group than their Menshevik and SR counterparts, who tended to cluster in a number of small circles with their own individual leaders and political identities. Lenin strongly resisted any such development among the Bolsheviks. When another powerful Bolshevik personality, Aleksandr Bogdanov, started to build a group of disciples who shared his philosophical and cultural approach in the post-1905 emigration, Lenin forced Bogdanov and his group to leave the Bolshevik Party, even though the group did not really constitute a political faction or an internal party opposition.

The situation changed radically after the February Revolution, with the merging of the emigré and underground Bolshevik contingents in a larger and more diverse party leadership, and the enormous increase in total party membership. In 1917, the Bolsheviks were more concerned with riding the wave of popular revolution than with party discipline. Many individuals and groups within the party disagreed with Lenin on major policy issues, both before and after October, and Lenin's opinion did not always prevail. Some groups solidified into semipermanent factions, even after their platform had been rejected by a majority on the Central Committee or at a party congress. The minority factions (consisting largely of Old Bolshevik intellectuals) did not usually leave the party, as they would have done before 1917. Their party was now in power in a virtually one-party state; and leaving the party therefore meant quitting political life altogether.

Despite these changes, however, Lenin's old theoretical premisses on party discipline and organization were still part of Bolshevik ideology at the end of the Civil War, as was clear from the Bolsheviks' handling of the new, Moscow-based international communist organization, the Comintern. In 1920, when the Second Comintern Congress discussed the prerequisites for admission to the Comintern, the Bolshevik leaders insisted on imposing conditions that were clearly based on the model of the pre-1917 Bolshevik Party in Russia, even though this meant excluding the large and popular Italian Socialist Party (which wanted to join the Comintern without first purging itself of its right wing and centrist groups) and weakening the Comintern as a competitor with the revived Socialist International in Europe. The '21 Conditions' for admission adopted by the Comintern required, in effect, that the member parties should be minorities of the far left, recruiting only highly-committed revolutionaries, and preferably formed by a split (comparable with the split between Bolsheviks and Mensheviks in 1903) in which the party left had demonstratively separated itself from the 'reformist' centre and right wing. Unity, discipline, intransigence and revolutionary professionalism were the essential qualities of any Communist party operating in a hostile environment.

Of course, the same rules did not necessarily apply to the Bolsheviks themselves, since they had already taken power. It could be argued that a ruling party in a one-party state must, in the first place, become a mass party, and, in the second place, accommodate and even institutionalize diversity of opinion. This was, in fact, what had been happening in the Bolshevik Party since 1917. Factions had developed within the leadership on specific policy issues and (in violation of the principle of democratic centralism) tended to remain in existence even after losing the final vote. By 1920, the factions participating in the current debate on the status of trade unions had become well-organized groups that not only offered competing policy platforms but also lobbied for support in the local party committees during the discussions and selection of delegates that preceded the Tenth Party Congress. The Bolshevik Party, in other words, was developing its own version of 'parliamentary' politics, with the factions playing the role of political parties in a multi-party system.

From the standpoint of later Western historians – and indeed any outside observer with liberal-democratic values – this was obviously an admirable development and a change for the better. But the Bolsheviks were not liberal democrats; and there was considerable uneasiness within the Bolshevik ranks that the party was becoming fragmented, losing its old purposeful unity and sense of direction. Lenin certainly did not approve of the new style of party politics. In the first place, the trade-union debate – which was quite peripheral to the urgent and immediate problems facing the Bolsheviks in the aftermath of the Civil War – was taking up an enormous amount of the leaders' time and energy. In the second place, the factions were implicitly challenging Lenin's personal leadership in the party. One faction in the trade-union debate was led by Trotsky, the biggest man in the party next to Lenin despite his relatively recent admission to membership. Another faction, the 'Workers' Opposition' led by Aleksandr Shlyapnikov, claimed a special relationship with the party's working-class members which was potentially very damaging to the old core leadership of emigré intellectuals headed by Lenin.

Lenin therefore set out to destroy the factions and factionalism within the Bolshevik Party. To do this, he did not use 'parliamentary' tactics. When the Tenth Party Congress met early in 1921, he quietly organized a small, trusted group to work on the non-aligned delegates and split the big delegations that had previously pledged themselves to one of the opposition factions. According to Anastas Mikoyan, a young Armenian Communist who was working for Lenin in this operation, Lenin thoroughly enjoyed this nostalgic excursion into the old conspiratorial politics of his youth, and even wanted to call in 'an old Communist comrade from the underground who has type and a hand printing press' to run off leaflets for secret distribution among the delegations. However Stalin, Lenin's chief operations man, thought that this might offend some democratic sensibilities in the party leadership and give ammunition to the opposition factions.[5]

Lenin defeated Trotsky's faction and the Workers' Opposition in the vote on the trade union issue. But this was not all, by any means. Lenin's group went on to push through its list for the new Central Committee elected by the Congress, ensuring both a Leninist majority and (according to Mikoyan) just enough representation of the defeated factions to avoid scandalizing the party's rank-and-file. Two of Trotsky's supporters were voted off the Central Committee's Secretariat, and a close associate of Lenin and Stalin (Vyacheslav Molotov) was voted on. Finally, in a surprise move which stunned the factional leaders, Lenin's group introduced and the Tenth Party Congress approved a resolution 'On party unity', which ordered the existing factions to disband and forbade any further factional activity within the party.

Lenin described this ban on factions as temporary. This may have been sincere, although Lenin clearly disliked organized opposition and preferred that any dissenting opinions be expressed by individuals rather than by factions. But it is also possible that Lenin was simply giving himself room to back off if the ban on factions turned out to be basically unacceptable to party opinion. As it turned out, this was not the case: the party as a whole seemed quite prepared to sacrifice factions in the interests of unity, probably because the factions had not sunk deep roots in the party rank-and-file and were regarded by many as a diversion of intellectuals in the party leadership. Strong objections within the party leadership, however, made it virtually impossible in Lenin's lifetime to implement a secret clause in the resolution 'On party unity' allowing the party to expel persistent factionalists, and the Central Committee to remove any of its own elected members who were judged guilty of factionalism.

Nevertheless, members of the opposition factions of 1920–1 did not all escape without punishment. The Central Committee's Secretariat, now headed by one of Lenin's men, had charge of appointments and distribution of party personnel; and it proceeded to send a number of prominent Workers' Oppositionists on assignments that kept them far from Moscow and thus effectively excluded them from active participation in leadership politics. The practice of using such 'administrative methods' to reinforce unity in the leadership was later greatly developed by Stalin, after he became General Secretary of the party (that is, head of the Central Committee's Secretariat) in 1922; and scholars have often regarded it as the real death-knell of internal democracy within the Soviet Communist Party. But it was a practice that originated with Lenin and arose out of the conflicts at the Tenth Party Congress, when Lenin was still the master strategist and Stalin and Molotov were his faithful henchmen.

The problem of bureaucracy

As revolutionaries, all Bolsheviks were against 'bureaucracy'. They could happily see themselves as party leaders or military commanders, but what true revolutionary could admit to becoming a bureaucrat, a *chinovnik* of the new regime? When they discussed administrative functions, their language became full of euphemisms: Communist officials were 'cadres' and Communist bureaucracies were 'apparats' and 'organs of Soviet power'. The word 'bureaucracy' was always pejorative: 'bureaucratic methods' and 'bureaucratic solutions' were to be avoided at all costs, and the revolution must be protected from 'bureaucratic degeneration'.

But all this should not obscure the fact that the Bolsheviks had established a dictatorship with the intention of ruling over the society and also transforming it. They could not achieve these objectives without administrative machinery, since they rejected from the start the idea that the society was capable of self-rule or spontaneous transformation. Thus the question was, what kind of administrative machinery did they need? They had inherited a large central government bureaucracy whose roots in the provinces had crumbled. They had soviets, which had partly taken over the functions of local government in 1917. Finally, they had the Bolshevik Party itself – an institution whose previous function of preparing and carrying out a revolution was clearly inappropriate to the situation after October.

The old government bureaucracy, now under Soviet control, still employed many officials and experts inherited from the Tsarist regime, and the Bolsheviks feared its capacity to undermine and sabotage their revolutionary policies. Lenin wrote in 1922 that the 'conquered nation' of old Russia was already in the process of imposing its values on the Communist 'conquerors':

If we take Moscow, with its 4,700 Communists in responsible positions, and if we take that huge bureaucratic machine, that gigantic heap, we must ask: Who is directing whom? I doubt very much whether it can truthfully be said that the Communists are directing that heap. To tell the truth, they are not directing, they are being directed . . . [The] culture [of the old bureaucracy] is miserable, insignificant, but it is still on a higher level than ours. Miserable and low as it is, it is higher than that of our responsible Communist administrators, for the latter lack administrative ability.[6]

Although Lenin saw the danger that Communist values would be swamped by the old bureaucracy, he believed that the Communists had no alternative to working with it. They needed the technical expertise of the old bureaucracy – not just administrative expertise, but also specialized knowledge in fields like government finance, railway administration, weights and measures or geological surveying which the Communists themselves could not hope to supply. In Lenin's view, any party member who did not appreciate the new regime's need for 'bourgeois experts' – including those who had worked as officials or consultants to the old regime – was guilty of 'Communist conceit', meaning an ignorant and childish belief that Communists could solve all the problems for themselves. It would be a long time before the party could hope to train a sufficient number of Communist experts. Until then, Communists had to learn to work with the bourgeois experts and, at the same time, keep them under firm control.

Lenin's views on the experts were generally accepted by other party leaders, but they were less popular with the Communist rank-and-file. Most Communists had very little concept of the kind of expertise required at the higher levels of government. But they had a clear idea of what it meant at local level if minor officials from the old regime had managed to work their way into similar jobs with the soviet, or if a chief accountant happened to disapprove of the local Communist activists at his plant, or even if the village schoolteacher was a religious believer who made trouble for the Komsomol and taught catechism in school.

To most Communists it seemed obvious that if something important had to be done, it was best to do it through the party. Of course, the party's central apparat could not compete with the huge government bureaucracy on a day-to-day administrative level – it was far too small. But at local level, where the party committees and the soviets were both building from scratch, the situation was different. The party committee began to emerge as the dominant local authority after the Civil War, with the soviet falling into a secondary role not unlike that of the old zemstvo. Policy transmitted through the party chain of command (from the Politburo, Orgburo or Central Committee to the local party committees) had a much better chance of being implemented than the mass of decrees and instructions that came down from the central government to the uncooperative and often chaotic soviets. The government had no hiring and firing powers over soviet personnel, and it did not have much effective budgetary control either. The party committees, on the other hand, were staffed by Communists who were obliged by party discipline to obey instructions from higher party organs. The party secretaries who headed the committees, though formally elected by their local party organizations, could in practice be removed and replaced by the Secretariat of the party's Central Committee.

But there was one problem. The party's apparat – a hierarchy of committees and 'cadres' (who were really appointed officials), topped by the Central Committee's Secretariat – was to all intents and purposes a bureaucracy; and bureaucracy was something that Communists disliked on principle. In the succession struggle of the mid-1920s (see below, pp. 97–102), Trotsky tried to discredit Stalin, the party's General Secretary, by pointing out that he had built a party bureaucracy and was manipulating it for his own political ends. However, this criticism seemed to make little impact on the party as a whole. One reason was that the appointment (rather than election) of party secretaries was much less of a departure from Bolshevik tradition than Trotsky claimed: in the old days of the pre-1917 underground party, the committees had always relied heavily on the leadership of professional revolutionaries sent out by the Bolshevik Centre; and, even when the committees came above ground in 1917, it was more common for them to forward urgent requests for 'cadres from the Centre' than to insist on their democratic right to choose their own local leadership.

In more general terms, however, it seems that most Communists simply did not regard the party apparat as a bureaucracy in the pejorative sense. To them (as to Max Weber), a bureaucracy operated by applying a clearly defined body of law and precedent, and was also characterized by a high degree of specialization and deference to professional expertise. But the party apparat of the 1920s was not specialized to any significant degree, and (except on security and military matters) it did not defer to professional experts. Its officials were not encouraged to 'go by the book': in the early years, there were no compilations of party decrees to fall back on, and later, any secretary who stuck to the letter of an old Central Committee instruction rather than responding to the spirit of the current party line was likely to be rebuked for 'bureaucratic tendencies'.

When Communists said that they did not want a bureaucracy, they meant that they did not want an administrative structure that would not or could not respond to revolutionary commands. But, by the same token, they wanted very much to have an administrative structure that *would* respond to revolutionary commands – one whose officials were willing to accept orders from the revolution's leaders and eager to carry out policies of radical social change. That was the revolutionary function that the party apparat (or bureaucracy) could perform, and most Communists instinctively recognized it.

Most Communists also believed that the organs of the 'proletarian dictatorship' ought to be proletarian, meaning by this that former workers should hold the responsible administrative jobs. This may not have been quite what Marx meant by proletarian dictatorship, and it was not quite what Lenin intended either. (The workers 'would like to build a better apparatus for us,' Lenin wrote in 1923, 'but they do not know how. They cannot build one. They have not yet developed the culture required for this; and it is culture that is required.'[7]) Nevertheless, it was taken for granted in all the party's debates that an institution's political soundness, revolutionary fervour and freedom from 'bureaucratic degeneration' were directly correlated with the percentage of its cadres that came from the working class. The class criterion was applied to all the bureaucracies, including the party apparat. It was also applied in the party's own recruitment of members, which would necessarily affect the composition of the Soviet administrative elite in the future.

In 1921, the industrial working class was in a shambles and the regime's relationship with it was in a state of crisis. But by 1924, economic revival had eased some of the difficulties, and the working class was beginning to recover and grow. It was in that year that the party reaffirmed its commitment to a proletarian identity by announcing the Lenin Levy, a campaign to recruit hundreds of thousands of workers as party members. Implicit in this decision was a commitment to continue creating a 'proletarian dictatorship' by encouraging workers to move into administrative jobs.

By 1927, after three years of heavy working-class recruitment, the Communist Party had a total of over a million full members and candidates, of whom 39 per cent were currently workers by occupation and 56 per cent had been workers by occupation when they joined the party.[8] The difference between these two percentages indicates the approximate size of the group of worker-Communists who had moved permanently into administrative and other white-collar jobs. For workers who joined the party in the first decade of Soviet power, the odds on subsequent promotion into administrative work (even excluding promotions after 1927) were at least 50:50.

The party apparat was a more popular destination for rising working-class Communists than the government bureaucracy, partly because the workers felt more at home in a party environment and partly because educational deficiencies were less of a problem for a local party secretary than, say, a department head in the government's Commissariat of Finance. In 1927, 49 per cent of the Communists in responsible positions in the party apparat were former workers, whereas the corresponding figure for Communists in the government and soviet bureaucracy was 35 per cent. The discrepancy was even more marked at the highest levels of the administrative hierarchy. Very few of the Communists in the top government jobs were working-class, while almost half the regional party secretaries (heads of *oblast'*, *guberniya* and *krai* organizations) were former workers.[9]

The leadership struggle

While Lenin lived, the Bolsheviks acknowledged him as the party's leader. Nevertheless, the party did not formally have a Leader, and it offended Bolsheviks to think that it necessarily required one. In moments of political turbulence, it was not unheard of for party comrades to rebuke Lenin for trading too much on his personal authority; and, while Lenin usually insisted on having his way, he did not require flattery or any particular show of respect. The Bolsheviks had nothing but contempt for Mussolini and his Italian Fascists, regarding them as political primitives for dressing up in comic-opera uniforms and swearing loyalty to *Il Duce*. Furthermore, they had learned the lessons of history, and had no intention of letting the Russian Revolution degenerate as the French Revolution had done when Napoleon Bonaparte declared himself Emperor. Bonapartism – the transformation of a revolutionary war leader into a dictator – was a danger that was often discussed in the Bolshevik Party, usually with implicit reference to Trotsky, the creator of the Red Army and hero of Communist youth during the Civil War. It was assumed that any potential Bonaparte would be a charismatic figure, capable of stirring oratory and grandiose visions, and probably wearing military uniform.

Lenin died in January 1924. But his health had been in serious decline since the middle of 1921, and thereafter he was only intermittently active in political life. A stroke in May 1922 left him partially paralysed, and a second stroke in March 1923 caused further paralysis and loss of speech. His political death, therefore, was a gradual process, and Lenin himself was able to observe its first results. His responsibilities as head of the government were taken over by three deputies, of whom Aleksei Rykov, who became Lenin's successor as Chairman of the Council of People's Commissars in 1924, was the most important. But it was clear that the main locus of power was not in the government but in the party's Politburo, which had seven full members including Lenin. The other Politburo members were Trotsky (Commissar for War), Stalin (General Secretary of the party), Zinoviev (head of the Leningrad party organization and also head of the Comintern), Kamenev (head of the Moscow party organization), Rykov (first deputy Chairman of the Council of People's Commissars) and Mikhail Tomsky (head of the Central Council of Trade Unions).

During Lenin's illness – and indeed after his death – the Politburo pledged itself to act as a collective leadership, and all its members vehemently denied that any one of them could replace Lenin or aspire to a similar position of authority. Nevertheless, a fierce though rather furtive succession struggle was in progress in 1923, with the triumvirate of Zinoviev, Kamenev and Stalin pitted against Trotsky. Trotsky

– the odd man out in the leadership, both because of his late entry into the Bolshevik Party and his spectacular performance since – was perceived as an ambitious contender for the top position, though he strongly denied it. In *The New Course*, written late in 1923, Trotsky retaliated with the warning that the old guard of the Bolshevik Party was losing its revolutionary spirit, succumbing to 'conservative, bureaucratic factionalism', and behaving more and more like a small ruling elite whose only concern was to stay in power.

Lenin, removed from active leadership by his illness but still able to observe the manoeuvring of his would-be successors, was developing a similarly jaundiced view of the Politburo, which he began to describe as an 'oligarchy'. In the so-called 'testament' of December 1922, Lenin surveyed the qualities of various party leaders – including the two he identified as outstanding, Stalin and Trotsky – and, in effect, damned them all with faint praise. His comment on Stalin was that he had accumulated enormous powers as General Secretary of the party, but might not always use those powers with sufficient caution. A week later, after a clash between Stalin and Lenin's wife, Nadezhda Krupskaya, over Lenin's sickbed regime, Lenin added a postscript to the Testament saying that Stalin was 'too rude' and should be removed from his position as General Secretary.[10]

At the time, many Bolsheviks would have been surprised to find Stalin ranked as Trotsky's equal in political stature. Stalin had none of the attributes that the Bolsheviks normally associated with outstanding leadership. He was not a charismatic figure, a fine orator or a distinguished Marxist theoretician like Lenin or Trotsky. He was not a war hero, an upstanding son of the working class or even much of an intellectual. He was 'a grey blur', in Nikolai Sukhanov's words – a good backroom politician, an expert on the internal working of the party, but a man without personal distinction. It was generally assumed that Zinoviev rather than Stalin was the dominant member of the Politburo triumvirate. Lenin, however, was in a better position than most to appreciate Stalin's capacities, for Stalin had been his right-hand man in the internal party struggle of 1920–1.

The triumvirate's battle with Trotsky came to a head in the winter of 1923–4. Despite the existence of a formal ban on party factions, the situation was in many ways comparable with that of 1920–1, and Stalin followed much the same strategy as Lenin had done. In the party discussions and election of delegates preceding the Thirteenth Party Conference, Trotsky's supporters campaigned as an opposition, while the party apparat was mobilized in support of 'the Central Committee majority', that is, the triumvirate. The 'Central Committee majority' won, though there were pockets of support for Trotsky in the party cells of the central government bureaucracy, the universities and the Red Army.[11] After the initial voting, an intensive assault on the pro-Trotsky cells induced many of them to defect to the majority. Only a few months later, when delegates were elected in the spring of 1924 for the forthcoming Party Congress, Trotsky's support seemed to have evaporated almost completely.

This was essentially a victory for the party machine – that is, a victory for Stalin, the General Secretary. The General Secretary was in a position to manipulate what one scholar has labelled a 'circular flow of power'.[12] The Secretariat appointed the secretaries who headed local party organizations, and could also dismiss them if they showed undesirable factional leanings. The local party organizations elected delegates to the national party conferences and congresses, and it was increasingly common for the secretaries to be routinely elected at the top of the local delegate list. The national party congresses, in turn, elected the members of the party's Central Committee, Politburo and Orgburo – and, of course, the Secretariat. In short, the General Secretary could not only punish political opponents but also stack the congresses which confirmed his tenure in office.

With the crucial battle of 1923–4 behind him, Stalin proceeded systematically to consolidate his gains. In 1925, he broke with Zinoviev and Kamenev, forcing them into a defensive opposition in which they looked like the aggressors. Later, Zinoviev and Kamenev joined Trotsky in a united opposition, which Stalin defeated with ease: their supporters found themselves appointed to jobs in distant provinces; and, while the opposition leaders could still take the floor at party congresses, there were so few oppositionist delegates present that the leaders seemed irresponsible *frondistes* who had totally lost touch with the mood of the party. In 1927, the opposition leaders and many of their supporters were finally expelled from the party for breaking the rule against factionalism. (Trotsky and others were then sent into internal exile, and in 1929 Trotsky was stripped of Soviet citizenship and deported from the country.)

Issues were argued in the conflict between Stalin and Trotsky, particularly with relation to industrialization strategy and policy towards the peasants. But Stalin and Trotsky were not deeply divided on these substantive issues (see below, pp. 104–6): both were industrializers without any special tenderness towards the peasantry, though Stalin's public stance in the mid-1920s was more moderate than Trotsky's; and a few years later, Stalin was to be accused of stealing Trotsky's policies in the First Five-Year Plan drive for rapid industrialization. For rank-and-file party members, the contenders' disagreements on issues were much less clearly perceived than some of their personal characteristics. Trotsky was widely (though not necessarily favourably) known to be a Jewish intellectual who had shown ruthlessness and a flamboyant, charismatic style of leadership during the Civil War; Stalin, a more neutral and shadowy figure, was known to be not charismatic, intellectual or Jewish.

In a sense, the real issue in a conflict between a party machine and its challengers is the machine itself. Thus, whatever their original disagreements with the dominant faction, all the oppositions of the 1920s ended up with the same central grievance: the party had become 'bureaucratized', and Stalin had killed the tradition of internal party democracy.[13] This 'oppositionist' viewpoint has even been attributed to Lenin in his last years[14] – and perhaps with some justice, since Lenin too had been forced out of the inner circle of leaders, though in his case the cause was illness rather than political defeat. But it would be hard to see Lenin, Stalin's political mentor in so many ways, as a real convert on principle to the cause of party democracy against the party machine. In the past, it had not been concentration of power *per se* that worried Lenin, but the question in whose hands power was concentrated. Similarly, in the Testament of December 1922, Lenin did not propose reducing the powers of the party Secretariat. He simply said that someone other than Stalin should be appointed General Secretary.

Still, whatever the elements of continuity between Lenin and the Stalin of the 1920s, Lenin's death and the succession struggle constituted a political turning-point. In seeking power, Stalin used Leninist methods against his opponents, but used them with a thoroughness and ruthlessness that Lenin – whose personal authority in the party was long established – never contemplated. Once in power, Stalin began by taking Lenin's old role: first among equals in the Politburo. But Lenin, meanwhile, had been transformed by death into the Leader, endowed with almost godlike qualities, beyond error or reproach, his body embalmed and reverently placed in the Lenin Mausoleum for the inspiration of the people.[15] The posthumous Lenin cult had destroyed the old Bolshevik myth of a leaderless party. If the new leader wished to become more than first among equals, he had a foundation on which to build.

Building socialism in one country

The Bolsheviks summarized their objectives in power as 'the building of socialism'. However vague their concept of socialism may have been, they had a clear idea that the key to 'building socialism' was economic development and modernization. As prerequisites of socialism, Russia needed more factories, railways, machinery and technology. It needed urbanization, a shift of population from the countryside to the towns, and a much larger, permanent urban working class. It needed greater popular literacy, more schools, more skilled workers and engineers. Building socialism meant transforming Russia into a modern industrial society.

The Bolsheviks had a clear image of this transformation because it was essentially the transformation wrought by capitalism in the more advanced countries of the West. But the Bolsheviks had taken power 'prematurely' – that is, they had undertaken to do the capitalists' work for them in Russia. The Mensheviks thought this risky in practice and highly dubious in theory. The Bolsheviks themselves did not really know how it was going to be accomplished. In the first years after the October Revolution, they often implied that Russia would need the help of industrialized Western Europe (once Europe had followed Russia's revolutionary example) in order to move forward to socialism. But the revolutionary movement in Europe collapsed, leaving the Bolsheviks still uncertain how to proceed, but determined to make their way somehow. Looking back at the old argument about premature revolution in 1923, Lenin continued to find the Mensheviks' objections 'infinitely commonplace'. In a revolutionary situation, as Napoleon said of war, *'on s'engage et puis on voit'*. The Bolsheviks had taken the risk and, Lenin concluded, there could now – six years later – be no doubt that 'on the whole' they had been successful.[16]

This was perhaps putting a brave face on it, for even the most optimistic Bolsheviks had been shaken by the economic situation that confronted them at the end of the Civil War. It was as if, in mockery of all the Bolsheviks' aspirations, Russia had shrugged off the twentieth century and regressed from comparative to total backwardness. Towns had withered, machinery was rusting in deserted factories, mines were flooded and half the industrial working class had apparently been reabsorbed into the peasantry. As the 1926 census would reveal, European Russia was actually *less* urbanized in the years immediately after the Civil War than it had been in 1897. The peasants had reverted to traditional subsidence agriculture, seemingly intent on recapturing that golden age in the past before the advent of serfdom.

The introduction of the New Economic Policy (NEP) in 1921 was an admission that the Bolsheviks could perhaps do the work of the big capitalists, but for the time being could not get along without the small ones. In the towns, private trade and small-scale private industry were allowed to revive. In the countryside, the Bolsheviks had already let the peasants have their way over the land, and were now anxious to ensure that they played their role as reliable 'petty-bourgeois' producers for the urban market, as well as consumers of urban manufactured goods. The policy of assisting peasants to consolidate their holdings (begun under Stolypin) was continued by Soviet authorities in the 1920s, though without any frontal attack on the authority of the *mir*. From the Bolshevik standpoint, small-capitalist peasant farming was preferable to the traditional communal and near-subsistence cultivation of the village, and they did their best to encourage it.

But the Bolsheviks' attitude to the private sector during NEP was always ambivalent. They needed it to restore the shattered economy after the Civil War, and they assumed that they would probably need it for the early stages of subsequent economic development. However, even a partial revival of capitalism was offensive and frightening to most party members. When 'concessions' for manufacturing and mining were granted to foreign companies, Soviet authorities hovered anxiously, waiting for the moment when the enterprise looked solid enough for them to withdraw the concession and buy the foreign company out. Local private entrepreneurs ('Nepmen') were treated with great suspicion, and the restrictions on their activities became so onerous by the second half of the 1920s that many businesses went into liquidation, and the remaining Nepmen acquired the shady look of profiteers operating on the fringes of the law.

The Bolsheviks' approach to the peasantry during NEP was even more contradictory. Collective and large-scale farming was their long-term objective, but the conventional wisdom of the mid-1920s held that this was a prospect only for the distant future. In the meantime, the peasantry must be conciliated and allowed to follow its own petty-bourgeois path; and it was in the state's economic interest to encourage the peasants to improve their agricultural methods and increase production. This implied that the regime tolerated and even approved of peasants who worked hard and made a success of their individual farming.

In practice, however, the Bolsheviks were extremely suspicious of peasants who became more prosperous than their neighbours. They regarded such peasants as potential exploiters and rural capitalists, often classifying them as 'kulaks', which meant that they suffered various forms of discrimination including loss of voting rights. For all their talk of forging an alliance with the 'middle' peasant (the category between 'prosperous' and 'poor', into which the great majority of all peasants fell), the Bolsheviks were continually on the watch for signs of class differentiation within the peasantry, hoping for a chance to throw themselves into a class struggle and support the poor peasants against the richer ones.[17]

But it was the town, not the village, that the Bolsheviks saw as the key to economic development. When they spoke of building socialism, the main process that they had in mind was industrialization, which would ultimately transform not only the urban economy but also the rural one. In the immediate aftermath of the Civil War, it seemed a gigantic task just to restore industrial production to the levels of 1913: Lenin's electrification plan was virtually the only long-range development scheme of the first half of the 1920s, and, for all the publicity given to it, the original goals were quite modest. But in 1924-5, an unexpectedly rapid industrial and general economic recovery caused an upsurge of optimism among the Bolshevik leaders, and a reassessment of the possibilities of major industrial development in the near future. Feliks Dzerzhinsky, head of the Cheka during the Civil War and one of the party's best organizers, took over the chairmanship of the Supreme Economic Council (Vesenkha) in 1924 and began to mould it into a powerful ministry of industry which, like its Tsarist predecessors, focused largely on the development of the metallurgical, metalworking and machine-building industries. The new optimism about rapid industrial development was reflected in Dzerzhinsky's confident statement at the end of 1925:

These new tasks [of industrialization] are not just tasks of the kind we were considering in abstract terms ten, fifteen or even twenty years ago, when we said that it is impossible to build socialism without setting a course for the industrialization of the country. Now we are not posing the question on a general theoretical level, but as a definite, concrete objective of all our present economic activity.[18]

There was no real disagreement among the party leaders on the desirability of rapid industrialization, although inevitably the issue was bandied around in the factional struggles of the mid-1920s. Trotsky, one of the few Bolsheviks who had actively supported state economic planning even in the dismal early years of NEP, would have been happy to champion the cause of industrialization against his political opponents. But in 1925 Stalin made it clear that industrialization was now *his* issue and one of his highest priorities. On the eighth anniversary of the October Revolution, Stalin compared the party's recent decision to press forward with industrialization on the basis of a Five-Year Plan with Lenin's momentous decision to seize political power in 1917.[19] This was a bold comparison, suggesting not only the stature Stalin hoped for himself but also the importance he attached to the industrialization policy. Already, it appeared, he was staking out his place in history as Lenin's successor: he was to be Stalin the Industrializer.

The party's new orientation was expressed in Stalin's slogan 'Socialism in One Country'. What this meant was that Russia was preparing to industrialize, to become strong and powerful, and to create the preconditions of socialism by its own unaided efforts. National modernization, not international revolution, was the primary objective of the Soviet Communist Party. The Bolsheviks did not need revolutions in Europe as a prop for their own proletarian revolution. They did not need the goodwill of foreigners – whether revolutionaries or capitalists – to build Soviet power. Their own forces were sufficient, as they had been in October 1917, to win the fight.

Given the undeniable fact of Soviet isolation in the world and Stalin's intention to industrialize no matter what the cost, 'Socialism in One Country' was a useful rallying cry and good politically strategy. But it was the kind of strategy that Old Bolsheviks, trained in a strict school of Marxist theory, often felt compelled to dispute even when they had no major practical objections. There were, after all, *theoretical* problems to be ironed out, disturbing undertones of national chauvinism, as if the party were pandering to the politically backward masses of the Soviet population. First Zinoviev (leader of the Comintern until 1926) and then Trotsky took the bait, raising objections to 'Socialism in One Country' that were ideologically impeccable and politically disastrous. The objections enabled Stalin to smear his opponents, while at the same time underlining the politically advantageous fact that Stalin had taken a stand for nation-building and Russian national strength.[20]

When Trotsky, a Jewish intellectual, pointed out that the Bolsheviks had always been true internationalists, Stalin's supporters portrayed him as a cosmopolitan who cared less about Russia than about Europe. When Trotsky correctly asserted that he was no less an industrializer than Stalin, Stalin's men recalled that he had advocated labour conscription in 1920 and thus, unlike Stalin, was probably an industrializer who was prepared to sacrifice the interests of the Russian working class. Yet, when the financing of industrialization became an issue and Trotsky argued that foreign trade and credits were essential if the Russian population were not to be squeezed beyond endurance, this was only further proof of Trotsky's 'internationalism' – not to mention his lack of realism, since it appeared increasingly unlikely that large-scale foreign trade and credits would be obtainable. Stalin, by contrast, took the position that was simultaneously patriotic and practical: the Soviet Union had no need or desire to beg favours from the capitalist West.

However, the financing of the industrialization drive was a serious issue, not to be dismissed by rhetorical flourishes. The Bolsheviks knew that capital accumulation had been a prerequisite for bourgeois industrial revolution, and that, as Marx had vividly described, this process had meant suffering for the population. The Soviet regime must also accumulate capital in order to industrialize. The old Russian bourgeoisie had already been expropriated, and the new bourgeoisie of Nepmen and kulaks had not had time or opportunity to accumulate much. If, being politically isolated as a result of the revolution, Russia could no longer follow Witte's example and obtain capital from the West, the regime must draw on its own resources and those of the population, still predominantly peasant. Did Soviet industrialization therefore mean 'squeezing the peasantry'? If it did, could the regime survive the political confrontation that was likely to follow?

In the mid-1920s, this issue was the subject of a debate between Preobrazhensky, an Oppositionist, and Bukharin, then a Stalinist. These two, who had earlier co-authored *The ABC of Communism*, were both noted Marxist theoreticians, specializing respectively in economic and political theory. In their debate, Preobrazhensky – arguing as an economist – said that it would be necessary to exact 'tribute' from the peasantry to pay for industrialization, largely by turning the terms of trade against the rural sector. Bukharin found this unacceptable in political terms, objecting that it was likely to alienate the peasants, and that the regime could not afford to risk breaking the worker-peasant alliance that Lenin had described as the political basis of NEP. The result of the debate was inconclusive, since Bukharin agreed that it was necessary to industrialize and therefore to accumulate capital somehow, and Preobrazhensky agreed that coercion and violent confrontation with the peasantry were undesirable.

Stalin did not participate in the debate, which led many to assume that he shared the position of his ally, Bukharin. However, there were already some indications that Stalin's attitude to the peasantry was less conciliatory than Bukharin's: he had taken a tougher line on the kulak threat, and in 1925 he explicitly dissociated himself from Bukharin's cheerful exhortation to the peasantry to 'Get rich' with the blessing of the regime. Moreover, Stalin had committed himself very firmly to an industrialization drive; and the conclusion to be drawn from the Preobrazhensky–Bukharin debate was that Russia should either postpone its industrialization or risk a major confrontation with the peasantry. Stalin was not a man to announce unpopular policies in advance, but with hindsight it is not hard to guess which conclusion he preferred. As he noted in 1927, the economic recovery of NEP, which had brought industrial output and the size of the industrial proletariat almost up to prewar levels, had changed the balance of power between town and countryside in favour of the town. Stalin intended to industrialize, and if this meant a political confrontation with the countryside, Stalin thought that 'the town' – that is, the urban proletariat and the Soviet regime – would win.

In introducing the New Economic Policy in 1921, Lenin described it as a strategic retreat, a time for the Bolsheviks to rally their forces and gather strength before renewing the revolutionary assault. Less than a decade later, Stalin abandoned most of the NEP policies and initiated a new phase of revolutionary change with the First Five-Year Plan industrialization drive and the collectivization of peasant agriculture. Stalin said, and no doubt believed, that this was the true Leninist course, the path that Lenin himself would have followed had he lived. Other party leaders including Bukharin and Rykov disagreed, as will be discussed in the next chapter, pointing out that Lenin had said that the moderate and conciliatory policies of NEP must be followed 'seriously and for a long time' before the regime could hope to take further decisive steps towards socialism.

Lenin's political legacy remains a live issue for many historians, both Soviet and Western. Some accept Stalin as Lenin's true heir, whether for good or ill, while others see Stalin as essentially the betrayer of Lenin's revolution. Trotsky, of course, took the latter view and saw himself as the rival heir, but he had no real disagreements in principle with Stalin's abandonment of NEP and his drive for economic and social transformation during the First Five-Year Plan. More recently, it is the 'Bukharin alternative' to Stalin that has attracted scholars who see a fundamental divergence between Leninism (or 'original Bolshevism') and Stalinism.[22] The Bukharin alternative was, in effect, a continuation of NEP for the foreseeable future, implying at least the possibility that, having gained power, the Bolsheviks could achieve their revolutionary economic and social goals by evolutionary means.

Whether Lenin would have abandoned NEP at the end of the 1920s had he lived is one of the 'if' questions of history that can never be definitively answered. In his last years, 1921–3, he was pessimistic about the prospects for radical change – as were all the Bolshevik leaders at that time – and anxious to discourage any lingering regrets in the party for the policies of War Communism that had just been jettisoned. But he was an exceptionally volatile thinker and politician, whose mood – like that of other Bolshevik leaders – might have changed sharply in response to the unexpectedly rapid economic recovery of 1924–5. In January 1917, after all, Lenin had thought it possible that 'the decisive battles of this revolution' would not come in his lifetime, but by September of the same year he was insisting on the absolute necessity of seizing power in the name of the proletariat. Lenin in general did not care to be a passive victim of circumstance, which was essentially the Bolsheviks' understanding of their position under NEP. He was a revolutionary by temperament, and NEP was by no means a realization of his revolutionary objectives in economic and social terms.

Beyond the debate about Lenin, however, lies the broader question of whether the Bolshevik Party as a whole was ready to accept NEP as the end and outcome of the October Revolution. After Khrushchev's denunciation of the abuses of the Stalin era at the Twentieth Party Congress in 1956, many Soviet intellectuals of the older generation wrote memoirs of their youth in the 1920s in which NEP seemed almost like a golden age; and Western historians have often taken a similar view. But the virtues of NEP in retrospect – relative relaxation and diversity within the society, a comparatively *laissez-faire* attitude on the part of the regime – were not qualities that were much appreciated by Communist revolutionaries at the time. Communists of the

1920s were afraid of class enemies, intolerant of cultural pluralism and uneasy about the lack of unity in the party leadership and the loss of a sense of direction and purpose. They wanted their revolution to transform the world, but it was very clear during NEP how much of the old world had survived.

To Communists, NEP had the smell of Thermidor, the period of degeneration of the great French Revolution. In 1926–7, a debate between representatives of the party leadership and the Opposition on 'Thermidorian degeneration' showed that both sides shared the belief that the revolution was stagnating and that many party members and young people were becoming disillusioned. Workers (including Communist workers) were resentful of the privileges of 'bourgeois experts' and Soviet officials, the profits of sharp-dealing Nepmen, high unemployment and the perpetuation of inequality of opportunity and living standards. Party agitators and propagandists frequently had to respond to the angry question 'What did we fight for?' The mood in the party was not one of satisfaction that finally the young Soviet Republic had entered a quiet harbour. It was a mood of restlessness, dissatisfaction and barely-subdued belligerence and, especially among party youth, nostalgia for the old heroic days of the Civil War. For the Communist Party – a young party in the 1920s, moulded by the experiences of revolution and Civil War, still perceiving itself as (in Lenin's phrase in 1917) 'the working class in arms' – peace had perhaps come too soon.

5 Stalin's Revolution

The industrialization drive of the First Five-Year Plan (1929–32) and the forced collectivization of agriculture that accompanied it have often been described as a 'revolution from above'. But the imagery of war was equally appropriate, and at the time – 'in the heat of the battle', as Soviet commentators liked to put it – war metaphors were even more common than revolutionary ones. Communists were 'fighters'; Soviet forces had to be 'mobilized' to the 'fronts' of industrialization and collectivization; 'counter-attacks' and 'ambushes' were to be expected from the bourgeois and kulak class enemy. It was a war against Russia's backwardness, and at the same time a war against the proletariat's class enemies inside and outside the country. In the view of some later historians, indeed, this was the period of Stalin's 'war against the nation'.[1]

The war imagery was clearly meant to symbolize a return to the spirit of the Civil War and War Communism, and a repudiation of unheroic compromises of NEP. But Stalin was not simply playing with symbols, for in many ways the Soviet Union during the First Five-Year Plan did resemble a country at war. Political opposition and resistance to the regime's policies were denounced as treachery and often punished with almost wartime severity. The need for vigilance against spies and saboteurs became a constant theme in the Soviet press. The population was exhorted to patriotic solidarity and had to make many sacrifices for the 'war effort' of industrialization: as a further (if unintentional) re-creation of wartime conditions, rationing was reintroduced in the towns.

Although the wartime crisis atmosphere is sometimes seen purely as a response to the strains of crash industrialization and collectivization, it actually predated them. The psychological state of war emergency began with the great war scare of 1927, when it was widely believed in the party and the country as a whole that a renewed military intervention by the capitalist powers was imminent. The Soviet Union had recently suffered a series of rebuffs in its foreign and Comintern policy

– a British raid on the Soviet trade mission (ARCOS) in London, the nationalist Kuomintang's attack on its Communist allies in China, the assassination of a Soviet diplomatic plenipotentiary in Poland – and a number of Soviet and Comintern leaders publicly interpreted these rebuffs as evidence of an active anti-Soviet conspiracy, led by Britain, which was likely to end in a concerted military onslaught on the Soviet Union. Domestic tension was increased when the GPU (successor to the Cheka) began rounding up suspected enemies of the regime, and the press reported incidents of anti-Soviet terrorism and the discovery of internal conspiracies against the regime. In expectation of a war, peasants began to withhold grain from the market; and there was panic buying of basic consumer goods by both the rural and urban population.

Most Western historians conclude that there was no actual, immediate danger of intervention, which suggests that the crisis may have been at least partly invented and manipulated by the party leadership.[2] Some party leaders, like the excitable Bukharin (currently head of the Comintern, where alarmist rumours flourished and hard information on the intentions of foreign governments was scarce), may genuinely have believed in the immediate danger, although the diplomats and Communist leaders of the Soviet Commissariat of Foreign Affairs clearly did not. Other party leaders, who may or may not have thought there was real danger of war, saw it as an issue that could be exploited for factional purposes. Trotsky and other Oppositionists took the lead, blaming Stalin for the foreign policy disasters, especially China, that had allegedly produced a crisis in the Soviet Union's relations with the outside world.

Stalin remained silent during some months of anxious discussion of the war danger. Then, in the middle of 1927, he very skilfully turned the issue back on the Opposition. Denying that war was immediately imminent, he nevertheless pilloried Trotsky for his statement that, like Clemenceau during the First World War, he would continue active opposition to the country's leadership even with the enemy at the gates of the capital. To loyal Communists and Soviet patriots, this sounded close to treason; and it was probably decisive in enabling Stalin's group to deliver the final blow against the Opposition a few months later, when Trotsky and other Opposition leaders were expelled from the party. Subsequently, however, it became clear that for Stalin the war scare was not just a weapon to be used in the party's internal factional struggles. Throughout the First Five-Year Plan period, the threat of war – never imminent in the next weeks or months, but always looming on the horizon 'within the next few years' – was constantly emphasized by the party leadership, as a justification for the extraordinary demands made on party cadres and the sacrifices that the industrialization drive imposed on the population.[3] By the second half of the 1930s, when the threat of war with Germany and/or Japan became alarmingly real, the 'country-in-danger' mentality was already firmly embedded in Soviet political culture.

The crisis atmosphere generated by the 1927 war scare was kept alive in the early months of 1928 by the beginning of a real confrontation between the regime and the peasantry (see below, pp. 114–15) and an artificially induced alarm about the disloyalty of the old 'bourgeois' intelligentsia. In March 1928, the State Prosecutor announced that a group of engineers in the Shakhty region of the Donbass was to be tried for deliberate sabotage of the mining industry and conspiracy with foreign powers.[4] This was the first in a series of show trials of bourgeois experts, in which the prosecution linked the internal threat from class enemies with the threat of intervention by foreign capitalist powers, and the accused confessed their guilt and offered exciting (though largely fictional) accounts of their cloak-and-dagger activities.

The trials (large portions of which were reported verbatim in the daily newspapers) were circuses for the masses, bearing the political message that the old bourgeoisie was not to be trusted, and even the new elite of Soviet and Communist officials might become dupes and unwitting collaborators of the bourgeois experts with whom they worked. For the secret police and the party committees, the trials signalled a new, tough policy in dealing with class enemies and provided models that were followed at local level in a wave of smaller trials and arrests of engineers suspected of wrecking and sabotage.

Intimidation of the experts could be rationalized in terms of the senior government experts' tendency to see the First Five-Year Plan targets approved by the leadership as unrealistically ambitious. But most 'bourgeois technical experts' were just ordinary engineers, and they were almost the only engineers the country possessed in 1928. The new policy therefore had enormous costs for a regime that was preparing to embark on a crash programme of industrialization, just as the 1928–9 campaign against 'kulak' enemies did in the agricultural realm. Rapid economic development was the goal of the First Five-Year Plan; and it appeared that the goal was to be achieved at any cost, but not by any means. Like Lenin in 1917, Stalin wanted the means to be revolutionary – violent confrontation, class war and a bloody defeat for the class enemy. To many people, including the modernization-minded bourgeois engineers whom Stalin himself had described as natural allies of the Soviet regime only a few months before the Shakhty trial, it seemed an unreasonable strategy for modernization. But the means, as well as the end, were an integral part of Stalin's Revolution.

Stalin versus the Right

In the winter of 1927–8, the party leadership found itself divided on policy towards the peasantry, with Stalin on one side and a group later known as the Right Opposition on the other. The immediate problem was grain procurement. Despite a good harvest in the autumn of 1927, peasant marketing and state procurement of grain fell far below expectations. The war scare was a factor, but so also was the low price that the state was offering for grain. With the industrialization drive already in prospect, the question was whether the regime should run the political risk of squeezing the peasants harder, or take the economic consequences of buying them off.

During NEP, it was part of the regime's economic philosophy to further state capital accumulation by paying relatively low prices for the peasants' agricultural produce, while at the same time charging relatively high prices for the manufactured goods produced by nationalized industry. But in practice this had always been mitigated by the existence of a free market in grain, which kept state prices close to the market level. The state had not wanted confrontation with the peasantry, and had therefore made concessions when, as happened in the 'scissors crisis' of 1923–4, the discrepancy between agricultural and industrial prices became too great.

In 1927, however, the impending industrialization drive changed the equation in a number of ways. Unreliable grain procurements jeopardized plans for large-scale grain export to balance the import of foreign machinery. Higher grain prices would reduce the funds available for industrial expansion, and perhaps make it impossible to fulfil the First Five-Year Plan. Moreover, since it was surmised that a very large proportion of all marketed grain came from only a small proportion of Russia's peasant farmers, it seemed likely that the benefit from higher grain prices would go to 'kulaks' – the regime's enemies – rather than the peasantry as a whole.

At the Fifteenth Party Congress, which met in December 1927, the main topics on the public agenda were the First Five-Year Plan and the excommunication of the Left (Trotskyite–Zinovievite) Opposition. But behind the scenes, the grain procurements issue was very much on the leaders' minds, and anxious discussions were held with delegates from the main grain-producing regions of the country. Shortly after the Congress, a number of Politburo and Central Committee members departed on urgent investigative missions to these regions. Stalin himself, in one of his few trips to the provinces since the Civil War, went to investigate the situation in Siberia. The Siberian party committee, led by one of the party's rising stars, the well-educated and efficient Sergei Syrtsov, had been attempting to avoid confrontation with the peasantry over procurements, and had recently been assured by Rykov (head of the Soviet government and a Politburo member) that this was the correct line to follow. Stalin, however, thought otherwise. On his return from Siberia early in 1928, he made his views known to the Politburo and the Central Committee.[5]

The basic problem, Stalin concluded, was that kulaks were hoarding grain and attempting to hold the Soviet state to ransom. Conciliatory measures like raising grain prices or increasing the supply of manufactured goods to the countryside were pointless, since the kulaks' demands would only escalate. In any case, the state could not afford to meet their demands, because industrial investment had priority. The short-term solution (sometimes referred to as the 'Urals-Siberian method' of dealing with the peasantry) was coercion: peasant 'hoarders' should be prosecuted under Article 107 of the Criminal Code, originally designed to deal with urban speculators.

The long-term solution, Stalin suggested, was to press forward with agricultural collectivization, which would ensure a reliable source of grain for the needs of the towns, the Red Army and export, and would also break the kulaks' dominance in the grain market. Stalin denied that this policy implied radical measures against the kulaks ('dekulakization') or a return to the Civil War practice of forced requisitioning of grain. But the denial itself had a sinister ring: for Communists looking for guidelines, the reference to Civil War policies coupled with the absence of any catchwords associated with NEP amounted to a signal to attack.

Stalin's policy – confrontation rather than conciliation, prosecutions, barn searches, road-blocks to prevent peasants taking their grain to traders offering a higher price than the state's – was put into effect in the spring of 1928, and produced a temporary improvement in the level of grain procurements, together with a sharp increase in tension in the countryside. But there was also a great deal of tension within the party about the new policy. In January, local party organizations had received a variety of often contradictory instructions from the Politburo's and Central Committee's visiting firemen. While Stalin was telling the Siberian Communists to be tough, Moshe Frumkin (deputy Commissar of Finance) was touring the neighbouring region of the southern Urals and advising conciliation and the offer of manufactured goods in direct exchange for grain; and Nikolai Uglanov (head of the Moscow party organization and a candidate member of the Politburo) was giving similar advice in the lower Volga area, and moreover noting that excessive pressure from the centre had led some local party officials to use undesirable 'War Communist methods' to get in the grain.[6] Whether by accident or design, Stalin had made the Uglanovs and Frumkins look foolish. Within the Politburo, he had departed from his earlier practice of building a consensus and, in the most arbitrary and provocative manner, simply forced his policy through.

A Right Opposition to Stalin began to coalesce in the party leadership early in 1928, only a few months after the final defeat of the Left Opposition. The essence of the Right's position was that the political framework and basic social policies of NEP should remain unchanged, and that they represented the true Leninist approach to the building of socialism. The Right opposed coercion of the peasantry, undue emphasis on the kulak danger and policies intended to stimulate class war in the countryside by playing the poor peasants against the more prosperous ones. To the argument that coercion of the peasantry was necessary to guarantee grain deliveries (and hence grain exports and the financing of the industrialization drive), the Right responded with the suggestion that the First Five-Year Plan targets for industrial output and development should be kept 'realistic', that is, relatively low. The Right also opposed the new policy of aggressive class war against the old intelligentsia exemplified by the Shakhty trial, and attempted to defuse the crisis atmosphere engendered by constant discussion of the imminence of war and the danger from spies and saboteurs.

The Politburo's two major Rightists were Rykov, head of the Soviet government, and Bukharin, chief editor of *Pravda*, head of the Comintern and distinguished Marxist theoretician. Behind their specific policy disagreements with Stalin lay the sense that Stalin had unilaterally changed the rules of the political game as it had been played since Lenin's death, brusquely discarding the conventions of collective leadership at the same time as he seemed to be abandoning many of the basic policy assumptions of NEP. Bukharin, a fiery polemicist for Stalin in the battles with the Trotskyite and Zinovievite Oppositions, had a particular sense of personal betrayal. Stalin had treated him as a political equal and assured him that they were the two 'Himalayas' of the party,[7] but his actions now suggested that he had little genuine political or personal respect for Bukharin. Reacting impetuously to his disappointment, Bukharin took the politically disastrous step of opening secret discussions with some of the defeated Left Opposition leaders in the summer of 1928. His private characterization of Stalin as a 'Genghis Khan' who would destroy the Revolution quickly became known to Stalin, but did not increase his credibility with those whom he had so recently attacked on Stalin's behalf.

Despite this private initiative of Bukharin's, the Politburo Rightists made no real attempt to organize an opposition faction (having observed the penalties for 'factionalism' that the Left had incurred), and conducted their arguments with Stalin and his Politburo supporters behind closed doors. However, this tactic also turned out to have severe disadvantages, since the Politburo's closet Rightists were forced to participate in public attacks on a vague and anonymous 'rightist danger' – meaning a tendency to faintheartedness, indecisive leadership and lack of revolutionary confidence – within the party. It was clear to those outside the closed circle of the party leadership that some sort of power struggle was going on, but neither the issues nor the identity of those under attack for rightism were clearly defined for many months. The Politburo Rightists could not seek broad support in the party, and their platform was publicized only in distorted paraphrase by their opponents, and in occasional hints and Aesopian references by the Rightists themselves.

The Right's two main power bases were the Moscow Party organization, headed by Uglanov, and the Central Council of Trade Unions, headed by a Rightist member of the Politburo, Mikhail Tomsky. The first fell to the Stalinists in the autumn of 1928, and subsequently underwent a thorough purge directed by Stalin's old associate, Vyacheslav Molotov. The second fell a few months later, the guiding hand in this case being that of a rising Stalinist supporter, Lazar Kaganovich, still only a candidate member of the Politburo but already renowned for his toughness and political skill on a previous assignment to the notoriously troublesome Ukrainian party organization. Isolated and outmanœuvred, the Politburo Rightists were finally identified by name and brought to judgement early in 1929. Tomsky lost the leadership of the trade unions, and Bukharin was removed from his positions in the Comintern and *Pravda* editorial board. Rykov – the senior member of the Politburo Right, a more cautious and pragmatic politician than Bukharin but perhaps also more of a force to be reckoned with in the party leadership – remained head of the Soviet government for almost two years after the collapse of the Right, but was replaced by Molotov at the end of 1930.

The Right's real strength in the party and the administrative elite is difficult to assess, given the absence of an open conflict or an organized faction. Since an intensive purge of the party and government bureaucracy followed the defeat of the Right, it might seem that the Right had (or was believed to have) substantial support.[8] However, the officials demoted for rightism were not necessarily ideological Rightists. The label of rightism was applied both to ideological deviationists and bureaucratic deadwood – that is, officials who were judged too incompetent, apathetic or corrupt to rise to the challenge of implementing Stalin's aggressive policies of revolution from above. These categories were clearly not identical: the common label was simply one of the Stalinists' ways of discrediting the ideological Right.

Like previous oppositions to Stalin, the Right was defeated by the party machine which Stalin controlled. But, in contrast to the earlier leadership struggles, this one involved clear-cut issues of principle and policy. Since these issues were not put to a vote, we can only speculate on the attitude of the party as a whole. The Right's platform involved less danger of social and political upheaval, and did not require party cadres to change the habits and orientation of NEP. On the debit side, the Right was promising much less in the way of achievement than Stalin; and the party in the late 1920s was hungry for achievement, and did not have our retrospective knowledge of what it was going to cost. The Right, after all, was proposing a moderate, small-gains, low-conflict programme to a party that was belligerently revolutionary, felt itself threatened by an array of foreign and domestic enemies, and continued to believe that society could and should be transformed. Lenin had won acceptance for such a programme in 1921. But the Right in 1928–9 had no Lenin to lead it; and the NEP policies of retreat could no longer be justified (as in 1921) by the imminence of total economic collapse and popular revolt.

If the leaders of the Right did not seek to publicize their platform or force a broad party debate on the issues, they may have had good reasons that went beyond their expressed scruples about party unity. The Right's platform was rational and perhaps also (as they claimed) Leninist, but it was not a good platform to campaign on within the Communist Party. In political terms, the Rightists had the kind of problem that would, for example, confront British Conservative leaders who had decided to offer major concessions to the trade unions, or US Republicans who planned to extend Federal controls and increase government regulation of business. Such policies may, for pragmatic reasons, prevail in the closed councils of government (which was the hope and basic strategy of the Right in 1928). But they do not provide good slogans for rallying the party stalwarts.

While the Right, like earlier oppositions, also took up the cause of greater democracy within the party, this had dubious value as a way of winning Communist votes. Local party officials complained that it undermined their authority. In a particularly sharp exchange in the Urals, Rykov was told that the Right seemed to be out to 'get the [party] secretaries'[9] – that is, blame them for anything that went wrong and, on top of that, pretend they had no right to their jobs because they were not properly elected. From the standpoint of a middle-level provincial official, the Rightists were elitists rather than democrats, men who had perhaps served too long in Moscow and lost touch with the party's grass roots.

The industrialization drive

To Stalin, as to the foremost modernizer of the late Tsarist period, Count Witte, rapid development of Russia's heavy industry was a prerequisite of national strength and military might. 'In the past,' Stalin said in February 1931,

we had no fatherland, nor could we have had one. But now that we have overthrown capitalism and power is in our hands, in the hands of the people, we have a fatherland, and we must uphold its independence. Do you want our socialist fatherland to be beaten and to lose its independence? If you do not want this, you must put an end to its backwardness in the shortest possible time and develop a genuine Bolshevik tempo in building up its socialist economy.

This was a matter of absolute urgency, for the pace of Soviet industrialization would determine whether the socialist fatherland survived or crumbled before its enemies.

To slacken the tempo would mean falling behind. And those who fall behind get beaten. But we do not want to be beaten. No, we refuse to be beaten! One feature of the history of old Russia was the continual beatings she suffered because of her backwardness. She was beaten by the Mongol khans. She was beaten by the Turkish beys. She was beaten by the Swedish feudal rulers. She was beaten by the Polish and Lithuanian gentry. She was beaten by British and French capitalists. She was beaten by Japanese barons. All beat her – because of her backwardness, because of her military backwardness, cultural backwardness, political backwardness, industrial backwardness, agricultural backwardness . . . We are fifty or a hundred years behind the advanced countries. We must make good this distance in ten years. Either we do it or we shall go under.[10]

The First Five-Year Plan (1929–32) focused on iron and steel, pushing the established metallurgical plants of the Ukraine to maximum output and constructing massive new complexes like Magnitogorsk in the southern Urals from scratch. Tractor plants also had high priority, not only because of the immediate requirements of collectivized agriculture (made more urgent by the peasants' slaughter of draught animals during the collectivization process) but also because they could be relatively easily converted to tank production in the future. The machine-tool industry was rapidly expanded in order to free the country from dependence on machinery imports from abroad. The textile industry languished, despite the fact that the state had invested quite heavily in its development during NEP and it possessed a large and experienced workforce. As Stalin is said to have remarked, the Red Army would not fight with leather and textiles but with metal.[11]

The metal priority was inextricably linked with national security and defence considerations but, as far as Stalin was concerned, it seemed to have a significance that went beyond this. Stalin, after all, was the Bolshevik revolutionary who had taken his party name from the Russian word for steel (*stal'*); and in the early 1930s the cult of steel and pig-iron production exceeded even the emerging cult of Stalin. Everything was sacrificed for metal in the First Five-Year Plan. Indeed, investment in coal, electric power and railways was so inadequate that fuel and power shortages and transport breakdowns often threatened to bring the metallurgical plants to a standstill. In the view of Gleb Krzhizhanovsky, the Old Bolshevik who headed the State Planning Commission until 1930, Stalin and Molotov were so obsessed with metal production that they tended to forget that the plants were dependent on rail shipments of raw materials and reliable supplies of fuel, water and electricity.

Yet the organization of supply and distribution was possibly the most formidable task assumed by the state during the First Five-Year Plan. As it had done (unsuccessfully and temporarily) under War Communism a decade earlier, the state took over almost total control of the urban economy, distribution and trade; and this time the takeover was to be permanent. Curtailment of private manufacturing and trading began in the latter years of NEP, and the process gathered speed with a drive against Nepmen – combining vilification in the press, legal and financial harassment, and numerous arrests of private entrepreneurs for 'speculation' – in 1928–9. By the early 1930s, even the artisans and small shopkeepers had been put out of business or forced into state-supervised co-operatives. With the simultaneous collectivization of a substantial part of peasant agriculture, the old mixed economy of NEP was fast disappearing.

To the Bolsheviks, the principle of centralized planning and state control of the economy had great significance, and the introduction of the First Five-Year Plan in 1929 was a milestone on the road to socialism. Certainly it was in these years that the institutional foundations of the Soviet planned economy were laid, although it was a period of transition and experimentation in which the 'planning' component of economic growth cannot always be taken too literally. The First Five-Year Plan had a much more tenuous relationship to the actual functioning of the economy than later Five-Year Plans: in fact, it was a hybrid of genuine economic planning and political exhortation. One of the paradoxes of the time was that at the height of the Plan, in the years 1929–31, the state planning agencies were being so ruthlessly purged of rightists, ex-Mensheviks and bourgeois economists that they were scarcely able to function at all.

Both before and after its introduction in 1929, the First Five-Year Plan went through many versions and revisions, with competing sets of planners responding in different degrees to pressure from the politicians.[12] The basic version adopted in 1929 failed to anticipate mass collectivization of agriculture, vastly underestimated industry's need for labour, and dealt extremely fuzzily with issues like artisan production and trade, where the regime's policy remained ambiguous or unarticulated. The Plan set out production targets – though in key areas like metal these were repeatedly raised after the Plan had gone into operation – but gave only the vaguest indication of where the resources for increased production were to come from. Neither the successive versions of the Plan nor the final statement of the Plan's achievements bore much relation to reality. Even the title of the Plan turned out to be inaccurate, since it was ultimately decided to complete (or conclude) the First Five-Year Plan in its fourth year.

Industry was exhorted to 'overfulfil' the Plan rather than simply to carry it out. This Plan, in other words, was not meant to allocate resources or balance demands but to drive the economy forward pell-mell. The Stalingrad tractor factory, for example, could best carry out the Plan by producing *more* tractors than planned, even if this threw the schedules of plants supplying Stalingrad with metal, electrical parts and tyres into total disarray. Supply priorities were not determined by the written Plan but by a series of *ad hoc* decisions from the Commissariat of Heavy Industry, the government's Council of Labour and Defence and even the party's Politburo. Fierce competition surrounded the official list of top-priority (*udarnye*) enterprises and construction projects, since inclusion meant that suppliers were required to ignore all previous contracts and obligations until the top-priority orders were filled.

But the top priorities were constantly changing in response to crisis, impending disaster or a new raising of targets in one of the key industrial sectors. 'Breaks in the industrialization front', requiring that fresh reserves of men and materials be rushed in, provided an element of drama to the coverage in the Soviet press, and indeed to the everyday life of Soviet industrialists. The successful Soviet manager during the First Five-Year Plan was less like an obedient functionary than a wheeling-and-dealing entrepreneur, ready to cut corners and seize any opportunity to outdo his competitors. The end – fulfilling and overfulfilling the Plan – was more important than the means; and there were cases when plants desperate for supplies ambushed freight trains and commandeered their contents, suffering no worse consequences than an aggrieved note of complaint from the authorities in charge of transport.

However, despite the emphasis on immediate increase in industrial output, the real purpose of the First Five-Year Plan was to build. The giant new construction projects – Nizhny Novgorod (Gorky) Auto, Stalingrad and Kharkov Tractor, Kuznetsk and Magnitogorsk Metallurgical, Dnieper (Zaporozhe) Steel, and many others – swallowed up enormous resources during the First Five-Year Plan, but came into full production only after 1932, under the Second Five-Year

Plan (1933–7). They were an investment for the future. Because of the magnitude of the investment, decisions made during the First Five-Year Plan on the location of the new industrial giants were in effect redrawing the economic map of the Soviet Union.

As early as 1925, during Stalin's conflict with the Zinovievite Opposition, the investment issue had played some part in internal party politics, as Stalin's campaigners had made sure that regional party leaders understood the benefits that his industrialization plans would bring to their particular regions. But it was in the last years of the 1920s, with the final First Five-Year Plan decisions imminent, that the Bolsheviks' eyes were really opened to a whole new dimension of politics – regional competition for development allocations. At the Sixteenth Party Conference in 1929, speakers had difficulty keeping their minds on the ideological struggle with the Right because of their intense concern with more practical questions: as one Old Bolshevik wryly noted, 'Every speech ends. . . "Give us a factory in the Urals, and to hell with the Rights! Give us a power station, and to hell with the Rights!"' [13]

The party organizations of the Ukraine and the Urals were at daggers drawn over the distribution of investment monies for mining and metallurgical complexes and machine-building plants; and their rivalry – which drew in major national politicians like Lazar Kaganovich, formerly party secretary in the Ukraine, and Nikolai Shvernik, who headed the Urals party organization before taking over national leadership of the trade unions – was to continue throughout the 1930s. Intense rivalries also sprung up over the location of specific plants scheduled for construction during the First Five-Year Plan. Half a dozen Russian and Ukrainian cities put in bids for the tractor plant ultimately built in Kharkov. A similar battle, probably the first of its kind, had raged from 1926 over the site of the Urals Machine-Building Plant (Uralmash): Sverdlovsk, the ultimate victor, began construction on local funds and without central authorization in order to force Moscow's hand on the location decision.

Strong regional competition (for example, that between the Ukraine and the Urals) often resulted in a double victory – the authorization of two separate plants, one in each region, where the planners' original intention had been to build only a single plant. This was one factor behind the soaring targets and ever-increasing costs that were characteristic of the First Five-Year Plan. But it was not the only factor, for Moscow's central politicians and planners were clearly in the grip of 'gigantomania', the obsession with hugeness. The Soviet Union must build more and produce more than any other country. Its plants must be the newest and the biggest in the world. It must not only catch up with the West in economic development, but surpass it.

Modern technology, as Stalin never tired of pointing out, was essential to the process of catching up and surpassing. The new auto and tractor factories were built for assembly-line production, although many experts had advised against it, because the legendary capitalist Ford must be beaten at his own game. In practice, the new conveyor belts often stood idle during the First Five-Year Plan, while workers painstakingly assembled a single tractor by traditional methods on the shop floor. But even an idle conveyor-belt had a function. In substantive terms, it was part of the First Five-Year Plan investment in future production. In symbolic terms, photographed by the Soviet press and admired by official and foreign visitors, it passed on the message that Stalin wanted the Soviet people and the world to receive: backward Russia would soon become 'Soviet America'; its great breakthrough in economic development was under way.

Collectivization

The Bolsheviks had always believed that collectivized agriculture was superior to individual peasant small-farming, but it was assumed during NEP that converting the peasants to this point of view would be a long and arduous process. In 1928, collective farms (*kolkhozy*) accounted for only 1.2 per cent of the total sown area, with 1.5 per cent in state farms, and the remaining 97.3 per cent under individual peasant cultivation.[14] The First Five-Year Plan did not anticipate any large-scale transition to collectivized agriculture during its term; and indeed the formidable problems of rapid industrialization seemed quite enough for the regime to handle for the next few years, without adding a basic reorganization of agriculture.

However, as Stalin recognized – and as both Preobrazhensky and Bukharin had done in their debates a few years earlier (see above, pp. 106–7) – the question of industrialization was closely linked to the question of peasant agriculture. For the industrialization drive to succeed, the state needed reliable grain deliveries and low grain prices. The procurements crisis of 1927–8 underlined the fact that the peasants – or the small minority of relatively prosperous peasants who provided most of the marketed grain – could 'hold the state to ransom' as long as a free market existed and the state's grain prices were effectively negotiable, as they had been during NEP.

As early as January 1928, Stalin had indicated that he saw the kulak hoarder as the villain in the procurements crisis, and believed that collectivization of peasant agriculture would provide the lever of control that the state needed to guarantee adequate deliveries at the state's time and price. But encouragement of voluntary collectivization in 1928 and the first half of 1929 produced only modest results; and procurements remained an acute problem, preoccupying the regime not only because of the food shortages in the towns but also because of the commitment to grain export as a means of financing industrial purchases abroad. With the coercive procurement methods favoured by Stalin generally in the ascendant, hostility mounted between the regime and the peasantry: despite intensive efforts to discredit kulaks and stimulate class antagonism within the peasantry, village unity seemed rather to have been reinforced by outside pressure than to be crumbling from within.

In the summer of 1929, having largely eliminated the free market in grain, the regime imposed procurement quotas with penalties for non-delivery. In the autumn, attacks on the kulaks became more strident, and the party leaders began to speak of an irresistible peasant movement towards mass collectivization. This no doubt reflected their sense that the regime's confrontation with the peasantry had gone so far that there was no drawing back, since few can have deceived themselves that the process could be accomplished without a bitter struggle. In the words of Yurii Pyatakov, a former Trotskyite who had become an enthusiastic supporter of the First Five-Year Plan:

There is no solution to the problem of agriculture within the framework of individual farming, and therefore *we are obliged to adopt extreme rates of collectivisation of agriculture* . . . In our work we must adopt the rates of the Civil War. Of course I am not saying we must adopt the methods of the Civil War, but that each of us . . . is obliged to work with the same tension with which we worked in the time of armed struggle with our class enemy. *The heroic period of our socialist construction has arrived.*[15]

By the end of 1929, the party had committed itself to an all-out drive to collectivize peasant agriculture. But the kulaks, class enemies of the soviet regime, were not to be admitted to the new collectives. Their exploitative tendencies could no longer be tolerated, Stalin announced in December. The kulaks must be 'liquidated as a class'.

The winter of 1929–30 was a time of frenzy, when the party's apocalyptic mood and wildly revolutionary rhetoric did indeed recall that of an earlier 'heroic period' – the desperate climax of the Civil War and War Communism in 1920. But in 1930 it was not just rhetorical revolution that the Communists were bringing to the countryside, and they were not simply raiding the villages for food and departing, as they had done during the Civil War. Collectivization was an attempt to reorganize peasant life, and at the same time establish administrative controls that would reach down to village level. The exact nature of the required reorganization must have been unclear to many Communists in the provinces, since instructions from the centre were both fervent and imprecise. But it was clear that control was one of the objectives, and that the method of reorganization was belligerent confrontation.

In practical terms, the new policy required officials in the country-side to force an immediate showdown with the kulaks. That meant that local Communists went into the villages, collected a small band of poor or greedy peasants, and proceeded to intimidate a handful of 'kulak' families (usually the richest peasants, but sometimes peasants who were simply unpopular in the village, or disliked by the local authorities for some other reason), drive them from their homes and confiscate their property.

At the same time, local officials were supposed to be encouraging the rest of the peasants to organize themselves voluntarily into collectives – and it was clear from the tone of central instructions in the winter of 1929–30 that this 'voluntary' movement had to produce quick and impressive results. What this usually meant in practice was that the officials called a village meeting, announced the organization of a kolkhoz, and lectured and browbeat the villagers until a sufficient number agreed to inscribe their names as voluntary kolkhoz members. Once this had been achieved, the initiators of the new kolkhoz would attempt to take possession of the villagers' animals – the main movea-ble item of peasant property – and declare them the property of the collective. For good measure, Communist (and particularly Komso-mol) collectivizers were likely to desecrate the church or insult local 'class enemies' like the priest and the schoolteacher.

These actions produced immediate outrage and chaos in the coun-tryside. Rather than hand over their animals, many peasants slaugh-tered them on the spot or rushed to the nearest town to sell them. Some expropriated kulaks fled to the towns, but others hid in the woods by day and returned to terrorize the village by night. Wailing peasant women, often in the company of the priest, hurled insults at the collectivizers. Officials were often beaten, stoned or shot at by unseen assailants as they approached or departed from the villages. Many new kolkhoz members hastily left the villages to find work in the towns or on the new construction projects.

To this manifest disaster, the regime reacted in two ways. In the first place, the OGPU (successor to the Cheka and the GPU) came in to arrest the expropriated kulaks and other troublemakers, and subsequently organized mass deportations to Siberia, the Urals and the north. In the second place the party leadership backed a few steps away from extreme confrontation with the peasantry as the time for spring sowing approached. In March, Stalin published the famous article entitled 'Dizzy with success', in which he blamed local authorities for exceeding their instructions and ordered that most of the collectivized animals (except those of kulaks) be returned to their original owners.[16] Seizing the moment, peasants hastened to withdraw their names from the lists of kolkhoz members, causing the proportion of peasant households officially collectivized throughout the USSR to drop from over half to under a quarter between 1 March and 1 June 1930.

Some Communist collectivizers, betrayed and humiliated by 'Dizzy with success', were reported to have turned Stalin's portrait to the wall and succumbed to melancholy thoughts. Nevertheless, the collapse of the collectivization drive was only temporary. Tens of thousands of Communists and urban workers (including the well-known '25,000-ers', mainly recruited from the big plants of Moscow, Leningrad and the Ukraine) were urgently mobilized to work in the countryside as kolkhoz organizers and chairmen. Villagers were steadily persuaded or coerced to sign up for the kolkhoz once again, this time keeping their cows and chickens. By 1932, according to official Soviet figures, 62 per cent of peasant households had been collectivized. By 1937, the figure had risen to 93 per cent.[17]

Collectivization was undoubtedly a real 'revolution from above' in the countryside. But it was not quite the kind of revolution described in the contemporary Soviet press, which greatly exaggerated the scope of the changes that had taken place; and in some respects it was actually a less radical reorganization of peasant life than that attempted in the Stolypin reforms of the late Tsarist period (see above, pp. 30–1). As portrayed in the Soviet press, the kolkhoz was a much larger unit than the old village, and its agricultural methods had been transformed by mechanization and the introduction of tractors. In fact, the tractors were largely imaginary in the early 1930s; and the highly-publicized 'kolkhoz giants' of 1930–1 quickly collapsed, or were simply eliminated by the same kind of paper transaction that had created them.[18] The typical kolkhoz was the old village, with the peasants – actually somewhat fewer peasants than before, as a result of migration and deportations, and considerably fewer draught animals – living in the same wooden huts and tilling the same village fields as they had done before. The main things that had changed in the village were its management and its marketing procedures.

The village *mir* was abolished in 1930, and the kolkhoz administration that took its place was headed by an appointed chairman (in the early years, usually a worker or Communist from the towns). Within the village/kolkhoz, the peasants' traditional leadership had been intimidated, and in part removed by the deportation of the kulaks. According to the estimate of Soviet historians, over a million peasants were deported as kulaks in the years 1930–3, an average of about one household per village.[19] (More than half the deported kulaks were put to work in industry and construction; and, while most of them were working as free rather than convict labourers within a few years, they were still forbidden to move out of the region to which they had been deported and could not return to their native villages.)

The kolkhozy had to deliver set amounts of grain and technical crops to the state, with payment divided among the kolkhoz members according to their work contribution. Only the produce of the peasants' small private plots was still individually marketed, and this concession was not formalized until a few years after the original collectivization drive. For the general kolkhoz produce, delivery quotas were very high – up to 40 per cent of the crops, or two to three times the percentage that the peasants had previously marketed – and prices were low. The state's squeeze on the peasants put them at subsistence level, and in 1932–3 peasants in some key grain-producing areas dropped below subsistence into famine. Details on the famine are scarce, since news of it was rigorously suppressed, but the disorders and challenge to soviet control in the countryside at this time may well have exceeded those of 1930. Some millions of peasants are thought to have died in the famine, and there was a fresh wave of arrests of 'kulaks' and 'kulak hirelings'.

One of the immediate consequences of the famine was that in December 1932 the regime reintroduced internal passports, issuing them automatically to the urban population but not to the rural one: for the duration of the crisis, every effort was made to keep starving peasants from leaving the countryside and seeking refuge and rations in the towns. This undoubtedly reinforced peasants' belief that collectivization was a second serfdom; and it also left some Western observers with the mistaken impression that one of the purposes of collectivization was to keep peasants locked up on the farm. The regime had no such intention (except under the special circumstances created by the famine), since its main objective during the 1930s was rapid industrialization, which meant a rapidly expanding urban labour force. It had long been an accepted truth that Russia's countryside was greatly overpopulated, and the Soviet leaders expected that collectivization and mechanization would rationalize agricultural production and thus further reduce the number of working hands that agriculture required. In functional terms, the relationship between collectivization and the Soviet industrialization drive had much in common with that between the enclosure movement and Britain's industrial revolution more than a century earlier.

Of course this was not an analogy that Soviet leaders were likely to draw: Marx, after all, had emphasized the suffering caused by enclosures and peasant uprooting in Britain, even though the same process rescued peasants from 'the idiocy of rural life' and raised them to a higher level of social existence in the long term by transforming them into urban proletarians. Soviet Communists may have felt some similar ambivalence about collectivization and the accompanying peasant out-migration, which was a bewildering mixture of voluntary departure to the newly created jobs in industry, flight from the kolkhoz and involuntary departure *via* deportation. But they also clearly felt defensive and embarrassed about the disasters associated with collectivization, and tried to hide the whole subject in a smokescreen of evasions, implausible assertions and false optimism. Thus in 1931, a year in which two and a half million peasants migrated permanently to the towns, Stalin made the incredible statement that the kolkhoz had proved so attractive to peasants that they no longer felt the traditional urge to flee from the miseries of rural life.[20] But this was only by way of preamble to his main point – that organized recruitment of labour from the kolkhozy should replace spontaneous and unpredictable peasant departures.

During the First Five-Year Plan, no fewer than nine million peasants left the villages and entered the urban and industrial labour force; and for the whole inter-census period 1926–39 the number of permanent migrants was around nineteen million.[21] These were enormous figures, a demographic upheaval unprecedented in Russia's experience and, it has been claimed, in that of any other country over so short a period. Young and able-bodied peasants were disproportionately represented in the migration, and this surely contributed to the subsequent weakness of collectivized agriculture and demoralization of the peasantry. But, by the same token, the migration was part of the dynamics of Russia's industrialization. For every three peasants joining kolkhozy during the First Five-Year Plan, one peasant left the village to become a blue- or white-collar wage-earner elsewhere. The departures were as much a part of Stalin's revolution in the countryside as collectivization itself.

Cultural Revolution

The struggle against class enemies was a major preoccupation of Communists during the First Five-Year Plan, as it had been during the Civil War. In the collectivization campaign, 'liquidation of the kulaks as a class' was a focal point of Communist activity. In the reorganization of the urban economy, private entrepreneurs (Nepmen) were the class enemies that had to be eliminated. At the same period, the international communist movement adopted a new belligerent policy of 'class against class'. These policies – all involving repudiation of a more conciliatory approach that had prevailed during NEP – had their counterpart in the cultural and intellectual sphere, where the class enemy was the bourgeois intelligentsia. Struggle against the old intelligentsia, bourgeois cultural values, elitism, privilege and bureaucratic routine constituted the phenomenon which contemporaries labelled 'Cultural Revolution'.[22] The purpose of Cultural Revolution was to establish Communist and proletarian 'hegemony', which in practical terms meant both asserting party control over cultural life and opening up the administrative and professional elite to a new cohort of young Communists and workers.

The Cultural Revolution was initiated by the party leadership – or, more precisely, Stalin's faction of the leadership – in the spring of 1928, when the announcement of the forthcoming Shakhty trial (see above, p. 112) was coupled with a call for Communist vigilance in the cultural sphere, re-examination of the role of bourgeois experts, and rejection of the old intelligentsia's pretensions to cultural superiority and leadership. This campaign was closely linked with Stalin's struggle against the Right. The Rightists were depicted as protectors of the bourgeois intelligentsia, over-reliant on the advice of non-party experts, complacent about the influence of experts and former Tsarist officials within the government bureaucracy, and prone to infection by 'rotten liberalism' and bourgeois values. They were likely to choose bureaucratic methods rather than revolutionary ones, and favour the government apparat over that of the party. Moreover, they were probably Europeanized intellectuals who had lost touch with the party's proletarian rank-and-file.

But there was more to the Cultural Revolution than a factional struggle within the leadership. The fight against bourgeois cultural dominance appealed very much to Communist youth, as well as to a number of militant Communist organizations whose drive had been thwarted by the party leadership during NEP, and even to groups of non-Communist intellectuals in various fields who were at odds with the established leadership of their professions. Groups like the Russian Association of Proletarian Writers (RAPP) and the League of Militant Atheists had been agitating throughout the 1920s for more aggressive policies of cultural confrontation. Young scholars in the Communist Academy and the Institute of Red Professors had been itching for a fight with the entrenched senior scholars, mainly non-Communist, who still dominated many academic fields. The Komsomol Central Committee and its secretariat, always tending towards revolutionary 'avantgardism' and aspiring to a larger policy-making role, had long suspected that the numerous institutions with which the Komsomol had policy disagreements had succumbed to bureaucratic degeneration. For the young radicals, Cultural Revolution was a vindication and, as one observer put it, an unleashing.

Seen from this perspective, Cultural Revolution was an iconoclastic and belligerent youth movement, whose activists, like the Red Guards of the Chinese Cultural Revolution in the 1960s, were by no means a docile tool of the party leadership. They were intensely party-minded, asserting their own right as Communists to lead and dictate to others, but at the same time they were instinctively hostile to most existing authorities and institutions, which they suspected of bureaucratic and 'objectively counter-revolutionary' tendencies. They were self-consciously proletarian (although most of the activists were white-collar by social origin as well as by occupation), scornful of the bourgeoisie and, in particular, of middle-aged, respectable 'bourgeois Philistines'. The Civil War was their revolutionary touchstone and the source of much of their rhetorical imagery. Sworn enemies of capitalism, they nevertheless tended to admire America because its capitalism was modern and on the grand scale. Radical innovation in any field had an enormous appeal to them.

Because many of the initiatives taken in the name of Cultural Revolution were spontaneous, they produced some unexpected results. The militant atheists carried their campaign to the villages at the height of collectivization, confirming peasant suspicions that the kolkhoz was the work of Antichrist. Raids by the Komsomol 'Light Cavalry' disrupted work in government offices; and the Komsomol's 'Cultural Army' (created primarily to fight illiteracy) almost succeeded in abolishing local education departments – which was certainly not an objective of the party leadership – on the grounds that they were bureaucratic.

Young enthusiasts broke up performances of 'bourgeois' plays in state theatres by whistling and booing. In literature, the militants of RAPP launched a campaign against the respected (though not strictly proletarian) writer Maxim Gorky just at the time when Stalin and other party leaders were trying to persuade him to return from his exile in Italy. Even in the realm of political theory, the radicals followed their own path. They believed, as many Communist enthusiasts had done during the Civil War, that apocalyptic change was imminent: the state would wither away, taking with it familiar institutions like law and the school. In mid-1930, Stalin stated quite clearly that this belief was mistaken. But his pronouncement was almost ignored until, more than a year later, the party leadership began a serious attempt to discipline the activists of Cultural Revolution and put an end to their 'hare-brained scheming'.

In fields like social science and philosophy, young Cultural Revolutionaries were sometimes used by Stalin and the party leadership to discredit theories associated with Trotsky or Bukharin, attack former Mensheviks or facilitate the subordination of respected 'bourgeois' cultural institutions to party control.[23] But this aspect of Cultural Revolution coexisted with a brief flowering of visionary utopianism which was far from the world of practical politics and factional intrigue. The visionaries – often outsiders in their own professions, whose ideas had previously seemed eccentric and unrealizable – were busy with plans for new 'socialist cities', projects for communal living, speculations on the transformation of nature and the image of the 'new Soviet man'. They took seriously the First Five-Year Plan slogan 'We are building a new world'; and for a few years at the end of the 1920s and the beginning of the 1930s, their ideas were also taken seriously, receiving wide publicity and also, in many cases, substantial funding from various government agencies and other official bodies.[24]

Although the Cultural Revolution was described as proletarian, this should not be taken literally in the realm of high culture and scholarship. In literature, for example, the young activists of RAPP used 'proletarian' as a synonym for 'Communist': when they spoke of establishing 'proletarian hegemony', they were expressing their own desire to dominate the literary field and to be acknowledged as the Communist Party's only accredited representative among literary organizations. To be sure, the RAPPists were not totally cynical in invoking the name of the proletariat, for they did their best to encourage cultural activities in the factories and open channels of communication between professional writers and the working class. But this was all very much in the spirit of the Populists' 'going to the people' in the 1870s [25] (see above, pp. 19–20). RAPP's intelligentsia leaders were for the proletariat rather than of it.

In political terms, however, there was some real substance to the class aspect of proletarian Cultural Revolution. In the first place, Cultural Revolution was an incitement to class war against the old intelligentsia – and, while the aggressor in this war was clearly the Communist Party rather than the working class, the policy was one that had always appealed to Communists of working-class and peasant origin rather than to the Old Bolshevik intellectuals in the party leadership. During NEP, the party leaders had recognized that anti-intellectualism – closely linked with a more general resentment of privilege, and also associated with xenophobia and antisemitism – was endemic in the working class, and lay behind much of the grass-roots pressure within the party for tougher policies towards the bourgeois experts. But there was a kind of gentlemen's agreement within the NEP leadership not to appeal to working-class prejudices or, in Bukharin's phrase, unduly 'fan the flames of class war'. It was not until 1928, when the staging of the Shakhty trial broke this agreement, that it became clear that Stalin saw working-class prejudices and resentments as a political resource, which could be used both against his opponents in the leadership and as a means of re-creating the revolutionary atmosphere of crisis and struggle after the lull of NEP.

Violence based on class resentment and prejudice was not an officially sanctioned part of the Cultural Revolution, but it was surely an anticipated consequence. In the factories, where workers received detailed reports of the unmasking of bourgeois wreckers and conspiracies by the OGPU, they often reacted by denouncing or defying unpopular engineers, or simply by beating them up. In the society as a whole, antisemitic incidents increased and were less frequently punished. Among working-class Communists, the view that the Jewish people was innately 'bourgeois' gained respectability; and, in borderline cases where, for example, the expropriation of Jewish Nepmen acquired strong antisemitic overtones, Communists who objected or filed complaints against the officials concerned found the central authorities unresponsive.[26] In the countryside, there was a reported upsurge of rape of female teachers – especially those who were daughters of priests or well-to-do peasants – by Communists and other local officials. As in the Civil War, the courts were operating on the principle of 'class justice', which meant that a proletarian or Communist offender was likely to escape punishment, while a victim from the wrong social background was unlikely to obtain redress.

But there was also a second substantive class aspect to proletarian Cultural Revolution – the appeal to the ambition of young workers (and, to a lesser extent, peasants) to rise into the intelligentsia. The treachery of the bourgeois intelligentsia, Stalin said apropos of the Shakhty trial, had made it imperative to train proletarian replacements with all possible speed. The old dichotomy of Reds and experts must be abolished. It was time that the Soviet regime acquired its own intelligentsia (a term which in Stalin's usage covered both the administrative and specialist elite), and this new intelligentsia must be recruited from the lower classes, especially the urban working class.[27]

The policy of 'promoting' workers into administrative jobs and sending young workers to higher education was not new, but it had never been implemented with such urgency or on such a massive scale as during the Cultural Revolution. Enormous numbers of workers were promoted directly into industrial management, became soviet or party officials, or were appointed as replacements for the 'class enemies' purged from the central government and trade-union bureaucracy. Of the 861,000 jobs in the elite category of 'leading cadres and specialists' in November 1933, over 140,000 were filled by persons who had been workers at the bench in 1928. But these were only the most dramatic examples of the mass phenomenon of upward mobility – in large part, a natural consequence of rapid industrialization, but one which the regime energetically fostered and proclaimed as a fulfilment of the promises of the Revolution. More than half a million Communist workers moved from manual to white-collar occupations in 1930–3 alone, and their numbers were matched by workers who were not (at the time of their 'promotion') party members. The total

number of workers moving into white-collar jobs during the First
Five-Year Plan was probably at least one and a half million.[28]

At the same time, Stalin launched an intensive campaign to send
young workers and Communists to higher education, producing a
major upheaval in the universities and technical schools, outraging the
'bourgeois' professors and, for the duration of the First Five-Year
Plan, making it extremely difficult for white-collar high-school gradu-
ates and other middle-class applicants to obtain a higher education.
Most of the favoured proletarian and Communist group went to
engineering schools, since technical expertise rather than Marxist
social science was now regarded as the best qualification for leadership
of an industrializing society.

About 150,000 workers and Communists entered higher education
during the First Five-Year Plan[29] – among them Nikita Khrushchev,
Leonid Brezhnev, Aleksei Kosygin and a whole cohort of future
political leaders, most of whom trained and worked briefly as engineers before transferring to administrative and political work. The
150,000, later to become the core of the Stalinist elite after the Great
Purge of 1937–8, were young men (and a much smaller number of
women) with a sense of purpose and, in the Calvinist meaning of the
term, election. They were the chosen builders of socialism, sons of the
working class whom the Revolution had rewarded and trusted with
great responsibilities. The utopian, iconoclastic and eccentric aspects
of Cultural Revolution meant little to them; they experienced class war
mainly in the classroom, where political vigilance often took second
place to an earnest desire to learn even from bourgeois professors;
most were indifferent to the factional struggles in the party; and the
group as a whole was too busy studying to see much of the collectivization campaign in the countryside at first hand. They were the beneficiaries of Cultural Revolution, not its enthusiasts; and their personal
commitment was not so much to the fighting party of the Civil War as
to the industrializing party which, under Comrade Stalin's leadership,
had broken with Russia's historic backwardness and accomplished its
first Five-Year Plan.

6 The End of the Revolutionary Era

In Crane Brinton's terms, a revolution is like a fever which grips the patient, rises to a climax and finally subsides, leaving the patient to resume his normal life – 'perhaps in some respects actually strengthened by the experience, immunized at least for a while from a similar attack, but certainly not wholly made over into a new man'.[1] This concept of revolution is, of course, quite different from the classical Marxist one, in which the political revolution *does* produce substantive change, though that change in the superstructure has been made possible and necessary by previous changes in the economic base. It is different, too, from the assumption made by all revolutionaries that their revolution, if successful, will change the world.

Using Crane Brinton's metaphor, the Russian Revolution went through two bouts of fever, the first bout starting in 1917 and abating at the end of the Civil War, and the second occurring during the period of the First Five-Year Plan. In this scheme, the NEP interlude was a time of convalescence followed by a relapse or, some might argue, a new injection of the virus into the hapless patient. A second period of convalescence began in the early 1930s, with the stabilization policies that Timasheff labelled 'the great retreat'.[2] After another partial relapse during the Great Purge of 1937–8, the fever appeared to be cured and the patient ready to return to a more or less normal routine.

But was the patient really the same man as before his bouts of revolutionary fever? Certainly the 'convalescence' of NEP meant in many respects a resumption of the kind of life that had been interrupted by the outbreak of war in 1914, the revolutionary upheavals of 1917 and the Civil War. But the 'convalescence' of the 1930s had a different character. There were many signs that life was returning to normal, with orderly routine gradually replacing revolutionary ferment. Yet the return to normalcy was not so much the resumption of the old life as the beginning of a new one.

Soviet propagandists of the time expressed this idea in terms that were both grandiose and misleading, leaving the capitalist West –

deeply shaken by the Great Depression, which lent plausibility to the Marxists' predictions that capitalism was heading towards inevitable collapse – fearful and uneasy about the Soviet challenge and alarmed by Soviet *hubris*. According to Soviet claims, the First Five-Year Plan and the move towards a planned economy represented a giant step forward in man's mastery of the world. Socialist theory had made it possible to transform the social and economic environment. Even the physical environment would ultimately be brought under human control, as Soviet scientists and engineers applied themselves to 'the conquest of nature'. Man himself could be transformed or 'remade' in the process of building socialism. Already, Soviet writers claimed, a 'new Soviet man' was emerging. It seemed that there were no limits to Soviet aspirations and power.

The reality, of course, was very different from the rhetoric. Yet, in the most prosaic terms of everyday life, Russia had been changed by the First Five-Year Plan upheavals in a way that it had not been changed by the earlier revolutionary experience of 1917–20. In 1924, during the NEP interlude, a Muscovite returning after ten years' absence could have picked up his city directory (immediately recognizable, because its old design and format had scarcely changed since the prewar years) and still had a good chance of finding listings for his old doctor, lawyer and even stockbroker, his favourite confectioner (still discreetly advertising the best imported chocolate), the local tavern and the parish priest, and the firms which had formerly repaired his clocks and supplied him with building materials or cash registers. Ten years later, in the mid 1930s, almost all these listings would have disappeared, and the returning traveller would have been further disoriented by the renaming of many Moscow streets and squares. If he looked hard enough, he might perhaps have discovered his old clock-repairer working for a co-operative or state trust, and his old doctor employed in a municipal health department or medical research institute. But only a part of prerevolutionary Moscow and old Russia remained by the mid 1930s, either visible or hidden behind a Soviet façade. Another part had disappeared forever.

Stalin's First Five-Year Plan revolution had produced economic, demographic and institutional changes of staggering dimensions, some planned and desired by the regime, but others unanticipated and alarming. Over half the peasant population had become kolkhoz members; and in addition a sizeable group of peasants had been deported as kulaks, and a much larger group had voluntarily left the village to work in industry and the towns. In the towns, unemployment had disappeared (though the Plan had not anticipated this), and over-crowding in housing had reached crisis proportions. Together with the influx of peasants into the urban labour force had come an influx of women: in a working-class family, it was now customary for the wife as well as the husband to work full-time in the factory, partly because demand for labour now exceeded supply and partly to offset the decline in real wages. There were more public and institutional dining-rooms, fewer shops and a chronic shortage of all kinds of consumer goods.

The old industrial centres had vastly expanded, and at the same time new ones were arising in the empty steppe and in formerly quiet provincial towns. Massive new metallurgical and machine-building plants were under construction or already in operation. The first of the great canal and hydroelectric projects were under way. Yet the con-struction industry was experiencing an acute shortage of nails and bricks, items formerly produced by artisan and peasant industry; and all branches of industry were adversely affected by the collapse of peasant haulage and cartage, an unanticipated consequence of collec-tivization and the slaughter of draught animals.

Collectivization was the Achilles' heel of the First Five-Year Plan, source of a series of major crises, confrontations and improvised solutions. As intended, it provided a mechanism for increasing state procurements of grain. But it left the peasantry resentful and demoral-ized, and caused the state to make much heavier investment of cadres and capital in the agricultural sector than was compatible with the original implicit strategy of 'squeezing the peasantry'.[3] A sharp drop in peasant food consumption, related to high procurement quotas and Stalin's determination to keep up grain exports, led to the disastrous famine of 1932–3, in which peasant deaths are estimated at three to five million. The legacy of collectivization was bitterness, low productivity and a high level of mutual mistrust in the relationship of the peasantry and the regime.

In the urban sector, growth was the watchword of the period, with a doubling of gross industrial production between 1927–8 and 1932 and a similar increase in output of basics like hard coal, oil, iron ore and pig iron.[4] But the shock tactics used in the First Five-Year Plan were costly: real wages and living standards fell, rationing had to be intro-duced in the towns, and even then the Plan targets were not met in some important areas like steel production. Stalin's approach to the industrialization drive generated a sense of urgency and purpose, especially among Communists and the young, and made it possible to celebrate economic achievements like national war victories. Nevertheless, it is by no means clear that this was the optimal strategy for growth in purely economic terms. Using input–output analysis, one Western scholar has recently argued that similar levels of growth could have been achieved by the mid 1930s without any basic departure from the NEP framework.[5]

Still, in a whole series of areas not directly connected with production, rapid growth seemed to become epidemic during the First Five-Year Plan. As often as not, it was unplanned growth, but important in the general context of social modernization. The education system suddenly began to expand wildly at every level at the end of the 1920s – though, ironically, the party's longtime supporters of increased investment in education had just suffered a resounding political defeat.[6] Scientific research institutes proliferated, despite the cloud of suspicion that hung over the heads of the bourgeois experts. Urban population soared; and the total number of wage- and salary-earners jumped from 11.6 million in 1928 to 22.9 million in 1932, well above the increase projected by the Plan.[7] Bureaucracies mushroomed, regardless of the anti-bureaucratic campaigns of the Cultural Revolution and the purging of officials whose political or class allegiance was suspect. The Communist Party – one of whose functions was to provide cadres for the bureaucracies – recruited new working-class and peasant members on an unprecedented scale, and equally energetically 'promoted' them into white-collar and administrative jobs or sent them off to school. The party's total membership increased from 1.3 million in 1928 to 3.6 million at the beginning of 1933; and in the years 1930–3 alone, more than half a million Communists moved from manual to white-collar employment.[8]

The cult of Stalin had begun in earnest with the celebration of his fiftieth birthday at the end of 1929. In the same year, the last real opposition to Stalin in the party leadership was defeated, marking the end of more than a decade of intense factional struggle and the real implementation of the ban on factions formally imposed in 1921. Overt disagreements on policy were now a rarity in party congresses: the party, it was often emphasized, was not a debating club for intellectuals but an instrument of proletarian rule. Regional party organizations had become heavily involved in the practical tasks of supervising industrial development and agriculture.

The party leadership was increasingly secretive about its own deliberations, and the minutes of Central Committee meetings were no longer routinely circulated and accessible to rank-and-file party members. The Soviet press had also changed, becoming far less lively and informative about internal affairs than it had been in the 1920s. Economic achievements were stressed, often in a way that involved considerable distortion of reality and manipulation of statistics; disasters like those associated with collectivization and the 1932–3 famine were usually suppressed altogether. The newspapers no longer carried Western-style advertisements for the latest Mary Pickford film nor reported trivia like street accidents, rapes and robberies.

Soviet politics was acquiring an increasingly monolithic façade. But behind that façade, and despite official insistence that the party's interest was one and indivisible, bureaucratic and regional rivalries persisted and – as in most other political systems – provided much of the everyday substance of political life. More importantly, the institutional balance changed during and as a result of the First Five-Year Plan. Certain institutions were remarkably successful in asserting their prerogatives and building bureaucratic empires. One notable example was the Commissariat of Heavy Industry (successor to the Supreme Economic Council), which was headed from 1930 to 1937 by an energetic Politburo member, Sergo Ordzhonikidze, and took full advantage of its position as chief executant of the state's industrialization policy.

Another institution that prospered during this period was the OGPU or secret police. Its expansion and growing stature was related to the regime's increased reliance on coercion in carrying out policies like the liquidation of the urban private sector, the hunt for spies and saboteurs, collectivization and dekulakization. As a result of the mass arrests at the end of the 1920s, the OGPU had a large convict labour force at its disposal just at the time when industry was experiencing unforeseen shortages of free labour in critical areas. Some convict labour and even arrested engineers were made available to regular industrial enterprises like Magnitogorsk. But the OGPU also established its own industrial empire during the First Five-Year Plan, mainly in timber, mining and remote construction projects. Much of this was kept secret, but in the early 1930s a few OGPU enterprises like the building of the White Sea Canal were widely publicized as socialist experiments in the rehabilitation of former class enemies. The OGPU also set up communes for juvenile delinquents which were highly praised: one of them was celebrated in the first Soviet sound film, *Road to Life* (1931).

After the frenzy and turmoil of the First Five-Year Plan, the Soviet Union entered a phase which had many Thermidorian characteristics. Policies of consolidation and stabilization began to replace policies of upheaval. Systematic and orderly procedures were encouraged, and the calls for emergency mobilization and all-out attack became less frequent. But it would be an over-simplification to describe this only in terms of a 'great retreat' and a repudiation of revolutionary objectives. Some aspects of the revolution were being repudiated, but others were being incorporated into a new political and social order, often labelled 'Stalinism', though in many respects it was to outlast the Stalin era. In the following pages, I shall examine the nature of the revolutionary settlement – what revolutionary objectives were attained, what objectives forgotten and ideals betrayed, and what legacy the revolution left behind it.

Revolution accomplished

Socialism was the Bolsheviks' revolutionary goal,[9] and in 1936 the new Soviet Constitution implied that it had been achieved. The phase of class war and the 'building of socialism' had ended, and (according to the new Constitution) all Soviet citizens now possessed the equal rights and guaranteed civil liberties that were appropriate to a socialist state. These claims have infuriated many non-Soviet commentators over the years: socialists have denied that the Stalinist system was true socialism; others have pointed out that the Constitution's promise of freedom and equality were a sham. Of course the claims were untenable in many ways, and untestable (given the elusive nature of socialism) in others. But they embodied two judgements by Stalin and the party leadership that deserve to be taken seriously. The first was that the revolution was over. The second was that some important revolutionary objectives had been realized.

Like almost all revolutionaries, the Bolsheviks in 1917 had a utopian vision (the future communist society) and an immediate desire to emancipate society from oppressive authority and tradition. But they also had some more specific ideas about the measures that would be necessary to move Russia from capitalism to socialism. They had to create a dictatorship of the proletariat to direct the process of transition. Since the revolution had been premature in Marxist terms, they had to industrialize and eliminate Russia's historic backwardness. At some point during the transitional period – shortly after the political revolution, according to the prevailing view during the Civil War; at some unspecified later time, according to the more pessimistic assessments of the early years of NEP – they would have to establish the economic prerequisites of socialism, notably complete nationalization of industry and trade and collective or state-capitalist organization of agriculture.

The degree to which these different objectives had been realized by the mid 1930s varied considerably. Many of the emancipation objectives were dropped altogether, either in the 1920s or in the period of 'great retreat' following Stalin's First Five-Year Plan revolution. The proletarian dictatorship became the dictatorship of a party recruiting primarily from the working class, while at the same time evolving towards a personal dictatorship exercised through the party. In formal terms, however, the proletarian dictatorship was only a transitional institution: its historic mission was fulfilled with the completion of the building of socialism.

It was in the sphere of economic objectives that most had been achieved; and the transformation associated with the First Five-Year Plan was the real basis for Stalin's claim to have completed the building of socialism. It was not a wholly unreasonable claim in Marxist terms. According to Marxist theory, the level of economic development and the mode of production are the base upon which the political, social and cultural superstructure rests. When the base changes, the superstructure can be expected to adapt itself accordingly. Once the economic prerequisites existed, the obvious inference for Marxists was that the political prerequisites would follow.

The accomplishment of the Revolution's economic objectives during the First Five-Year Plan may be summarized as follows. The industrialization drive had greatly expanded the country's heavy industrial base and produced a large population shift from village to town. Outside the agricultural sector, production had been almost completely nationalized; in the countryside, over half of peasant agriculture had been collectivized, and the process was continuing. The framework for centralized state planning of the economy had been established, and its efficacy demonstrated by the economic breakthrough of the First Five-Year Plan. Since the kulaks had been expropriated and the urban private sector eliminated, the Bolsheviks no longer had to fear an internal capitalist *revanche* of the type that had seemed possible during NEP.

Of course, it was arguable (within the context of Bolshevik assumptions) how close the country had come to socialism as a result of these changes. Of Stalin's old Bolshevik opponents, many former Trotskyites had left the opposition because of their enthusiasm for the First Five-Year Plan, and even Trotsky himself, in the bitterness of exile, conceded that the new economic structure was compatible with future socialist development. The Right Opposition had hinted in 1928–9 that Stalin was following the letter of the socialist law while violating the spirit by his coercive methods and personal dictatorship; but its leaders had recanted and, whatever their inward reservations, continued to hold responsible positions under Stalin's regime. Clearly many Communists in the early 1930s must have had private doubts about forced collectivization and its socialist potential, but these were offset by satisfaction with the achievements of the industrialization drive. If the Soviet Union still lagged behind the advanced capitalist nations of the West, despite some public bragging to the contrary, this at least provided an acceptable explanation for any deficiencies or lapses from the socialist ideal: 'We still pay the penalty for past backwardness,' Communists would argue, 'but we are moving forward, and we have found the right road.'

Right or not, it was the road that the Soviet Union would continue to follow. There was to be no subsequent retreat from state economic planning, nationalization of industry, prohibition of private trade and collectivization of agriculture: unlike the temporary and abortive transformation under War Communism, the First Five-Year Plan changes proved to be permanent and were to become an integral part of the Stalinist system. Moreover, industrialization – with a continued emphasis on heavy industry, large-scale projects and geographical dispersion – remained a primary policy objective throughout the Stalin period. In this sphere, the Revolution was not betrayed, but rather accomplished, consolidated and institutionalized under Stalin's regime.

However, consolidation and institutionalization – the whole process of making the changes stick and finding ways to make the new system work – meant abandonment of revolutionary methods, as well as repudiation of other revolutionary objectives that were now seen as peripheral or incompatible with social stability and economic efficiency. Class war and the revolutionary spirit of 'storming the fortresses' fell out of favour. The working class lost its special position, and the regime firmly dissociated itself from the egalitarianism which had traditionally been a part of the workers' (and, to a lesser degree, the

Bolsheviks') revolution. The managerial values of discipline, order and cost-effectiveness came to the fore, and were now described as socialist values.

As far as industry was concerned, the new approach could literally be called managerial, since it not only represented the interests of Soviet industrialists but also originated in Orzhonikidze's Commissariat of Heavy Industry[10] – an institution which, as has already been noted, was a major political beneficiary of Stalin's industrialization drive. The industrialists wanted a restoration of order and discipline in the factories. In particular, they wanted an end to the harassment of 'bourgeois' engineers, which was extremely disruptive of plant discipline; and they were publicly advocating this as early as the winter of 1930–1. They wanted greater wage differentials and more material incentives for skilled workers and engineering-technical personnel. They wanted (and had already in large part obtained) increased authority for the plant manager, with the factory's party and trade-union committees taking subordinate roles. By the end of the First Five-Year Plan, the leaders of the Commissariat of Heavy Industry were ready to abandon assault tactics, unrealistically high Plan targets and financial non-accountability in favour of sober economic planning and cost accounting.

Stalin took up many, though not all, of these points in his famous 'Six Conditions' speech of 23 June 1931,[11] which set the agenda for the 1930s and foreshadowed the 'post-revolutionary' approach to industrialization. In this speech, he denounced vulgar egalitarianism (*uravnilovka*) in wages policy – a statement that was less remarkable for its substantive content (since the levelling tendencies of the First Five-Year Plan were largely spontaneous, not the product of any earlier official endorsement of the principle of wage egalitarianism) than for its casual disrespect for one of the sacred cows of workers' revolution. At the same time, with equal lack of ceremony, Stalin sloughed off part of his own policy of class war and proletarian vigilance in the face of the class enemy. It turned out, he said baldly, that the old technical intelligentsia had largely abandoned its attempt to sabotage the Soviet economy, realizing that the penalties were too great and that the success of the industrialization drive was already assured. Industry needed the engineers' skills, and they should be fully utilized. Bourgeois experts should no longer be harassed as a group.

In 1932, during the drafting discussion of the Second Five-Year Plan, the question of high targets and the 'storming the fortress' approach to economic growth became a focus of controversy within the party leadership. This was one question on which Stalin had not yet become a convert to moderation: he and Molotov (who had replaced Rykov as head of the Soviet government) favoured continuation of the revolutionary strategy of the First Five-Year Plan. But the industrialists, headed by Ordzhonikidze, and the State Planning Commission, also headed by a Politburo member, wanted lower targets, less wild exhortation and more real economic planning. The attitudes of Communist leaders directly involved in economic work were no doubt influenced by the advice of their scientific consultants, many of them recently rehabilitated bourgeois experts. But there were also pragmatic reasons for following a more sober and moderate line, notably famine in the countryside, acute transport problems, and repeated industrial breakdowns caused by overuse of the old plant and starting-up difficulties with the new. The debate continued through 1933, ending in a victory for the moderates. But in a sense this was also a victory for the principle of rational planning – a revolutionary objective which the First Five-Year Plan had honoured in the breach rather than the observance.

In industry, the watchwords of the 1930s were raising productivity and acquiring skills. The principle of material incentives became firmly established, with increased piecework and differentiation of workers' wages according to skill and bonuses for output above the norm. Specialists' salaries were raised, and in 1932 the average salary of engineers and technicians stood higher in relation to the average worker's wage than at any time in the Soviet period before or after. These were logical policies, given the state's priority of rapid industrial growth, but they accentuated the regime's movement away from the original revolutionary identification with the working class. The Stakhanovite movement (named for a record-breaking coalminer from the Donbass) was perhaps the most curious example of the Soviet post-revolutionary ethos and the regime's ambivalent attitude towards workers. The Stakhanovite was a norm-buster, lavishly rewarded for his achievements and fêted by the media, but in the real world almost inevitably resented and shunned by his fellow workers. He was also an innovator and rationalizer of production, encouraged to challenge the conservative wisdom of the experts and expose the unspoken agreement between factory management, engineers and trade-union branches to resist the constant pressure from above to raise norms. The Stakhanovite movement glorified individual workers, while being at the same time essentially anti-labour and in some respects also anti-management.

Agriculture also had its Stakhanovites in the 1930s, but in this sphere the official celebration of kolkhoz achievements and the glories of collectivization had a much hollower ring. The problem of the 1930s was to make collectivization work, but it was only partially solved: productivity remained dangerously low and the peasants remained deeply resentful, even as the percentage of peasant households rose steadily to reach almost 100 per cent by 1937, the last year of the Second Five-Year Plan. The peasants had some reason to see collectivization as a second serfdom, since as a group they did not enjoy the same rights as the rest of the population: they were not automatically entitled to internal passports (which were reintroduced at the end of 1932) and were thus in principle restricted in their movements. In practice, to be sure, peasants continued to migrate to the towns in very large numbers: industrial demand for labour remained high, education gave young peasants an opportunity and excuse for moving, and it was only in the famine years 1933–4 that the regime made serious efforts to keep peasant migrants out of the towns. But the legal barrier remained, a source of grievance for the peasantry and shame for the regime. The deported kulaks, moreover, were forbidden to leave the region to which they had been deported, even after the majority recovered the right to vote in 1935 and those working in industry had attained the status of free workers in almost all respects but that of freedom to move outside the region. With regard to children of deported kulaks, the ban was lifted in 1938; but for the kulaks themselves it remained in force until some years after the Second World War.[12]

The regime now governed the countryside in a sense that it had not done in the 1920s, when the villages had been left largely to their own devices because of the weakness of the rural administrative structure. Although most of the Communists and urban workers sent out to the countryside to serve as kolkhoz chairmen had left by the end of 1932, kolkhoz chairmen were still appointed and kolkhoz democracy remained largely a sham. In 1933–4, control over the kolkhozy was exercised by the political departments of the Machine-Tractor Stations (MTS), which provided mechanized services on a contract basis to all the kolkhozy in a given area (tractors, naturally, were still in short supply, despite the popularity of the girl-meets-boy-meets-tractor motif in Soviet films and novels). After the dissolution of the political departments, the kolkhozy came under the jurisdiction of the district party committees and the agricultural departments of district soviets.

In one important respect, however, collectivization turned out to be a less radical change in the mode of agricultural production than appeared at first glance. The peasant became a collective producer, but the land which the kolkhoz collectively cultivated was mainly devoted to grain, and grain (harvested by the MTS, which retained a high proportion of the crop as payment for its services) was also the main item of state procurement. In other respects, the kolkhoz peasant was able to remain a private producer, cultivating his private plot (usually the yard around his house) and entitled to raise a limited number of animals outside the collective framework. Although the private plots were small, they were of great importance to the peasants, and indeed to the national economy as a whole. Produce from the private plots could be sold in kolkhoz markets in the towns, and the proceeds went directly to the individual peasant, not to the kolkhoz. From 50 to 70 per cent of total production of vegetables, fruit, milk and meat came from the private plots in 1937, and a substantial proportion of this was sold on the kolkhoz market rather than to state procurement agencies.[13]

In reality, therefore, the rural economy remained mixed even after collectivization, with the kolkhoz peasant straddling the boundary between the collective and private sector. When he was working on kolkhoz land, the peasant was a collective farmer, albeit often a lazy and recalcitrant one who regarded himself as working under orders of the new masters. But when he was working on his own private plot or marketing its produce, he was still an individual cultivator and his own man: not surprisingly, it was the private plot that absorbed much of the kolkhoz peasant's time and effort.

Revolution betrayed

The pledge of *liberté, égalité, fraternité* is a part of almost all revolutions, but it is a pledge that the victorious revolutionaries almost inevitably dishonour. The Bolsheviks knew this in advance because they had read Marx. They did their best, even in the euphoria of October, to be hard-headed scientific revolutionaries and not utopian dreamers. They hedged their promises of *liberté, égalité* and *fraternité* with references to class war and the dictatorship of the proletariat. But it was as difficult to repudiate the classic revolutionary slogans as it would have been to conduct a successful revolution without enthusiasm. Emotionally, the Old Bolshevik leaders could not help being somewhat egalitarian and libertarian; and they were somewhat utopian too, for all their Marxist theory. The new Bolsheviks of 1917 and Civil War vintage had the same emotional response without the intellectual inhibitions. While the Bolsheviks did not exactly set out to make an egalitarian, libertarian and utopian revolution, the Revolution made the Bolsheviks at least intermittently egalitarian, libertarian and utopian.

The ultra-revolutionary strain in post-October Bolshevism came to the fore during the Civil War, and again during the First Five-Year Plan Cultural Revolution. It was manifested in class-war militancy, aggressive rejection of social privilege, anti-elitism, wage egalitarianism, cultural iconoclasm, hostility to the family and experimentation in everything from organizational methods to education. In Lenin's time, such tendencies were often pejoratively labelled 'leftist' or 'avant-gardist'; but the leaders also viewed them with a certain indulgence, as products of youthful revolutionary exuberance or untutored proletarian instinct. When Stalin repudiated them sharply in the 'great retreat' policies of the 1930s, Trotsky, commenting from exile, saw this as part of an overall betrayal of revolution.[14] It was true, though coming from Trotsky as a 'Leninist' criticism it was also rather unfair. The paradox of Stalin's retreat from revolutionary enthusiasm was that it was so well grounded in Leninist tradition and Bolshevik ideology.

With the 'great retreat' of the 1930s, the Stalinist party shed the iconoclasm and anti-bourgeois fervour of the Cultural Revolution and became, as it were, respectable. Respectability meant new cultural and moral values, reflecting the metaphorical transition from proletarian youth to middle-class middle age; a striving for order and manageable routine; and acceptance of a social hierarchy based on education, occupation and status. Authority was to be obeyed rather than challenged. Tradition was to be respected rather than flouted. The regime was still described as 'revolutionary', but that increasingly meant revolutionary in origin and legitimacy rather than revolutionary in practice.

The change was reflected in the manners and style of leadership. In the 1920s, proletarian manners were cultivated even by Bolshevik intellectuals: when Stalin told a party audience that he was a 'crude' man, it sounded more like self-promotion than self-deprecation. But in the 1930s, Stalin began to present himself to Soviet Communists and foreign interviewers as a man of culture, like Lenin. Among his colleagues in the party leadership, the newly-risen Khrushchevs, confident of their proletarian origins but afraid of behaving like peasants, were beginning to outnumber the Bukharins, who were confident of their culture but afraid of behaving like bourgeois intellectuals. At a lower level of officialdom, Communists tried to learn the rules of polite behaviour and put away their Army boots and cloth caps, not wishing to be mistaken for members of the non-upwardly-mobile proletariat. A new schoolmistressly tone of rather smug didacticism, later familiar to generations of Intourist visitors, could be detected in the pages of *Pravda*.

Discipline was stressed – not just party discipline, a separate concept to which Communists had long attached an aura of heroic dedication and mystery like a priest's vow of celibacy, but the more mundane types of discipline required of ordinary citizens in everyday life. There was particular concern about labour discipline, and a series of decrees were issued imposing stern penalties for absenteeism and other offences and attempting to reduce the very high rate of labour turnover in the factories. This has sometimes been associated with the regime's ideological movement away from an exclusive identification with the working class and the weakened political position of the trade-union leadership. But more likely the main reasons were practical. Industry had to cope with an enormous influx of peasant workers who were not only unskilled but completely unused to factory life and an urban environment. In effect, the First Five-Year Plan had created a new working class – which, unlike the working class of the 1920s, had not put the regime under special obligation by its services in the Revolution and Civil War – and the regime treated it as such.

Education was another area in which discipline was stressed, although here the policy reorientation of the 1930s was in more dramatic contrast to what had gone before. The progressive educational tendencies of the 1920s had run wild during Cultural Revolution, with formal classroom teaching often abandoned in favour of 'socially-useful labour' outside the school and lectures, textbooks, homework and individual testing of academic achievement almost totally discredited. Between 1931 and 1934, these tendencies were abruptly reversed, partly as a result of Stalin's personal outrage when he discovered the disorderly condition of the schools. Examinations, homework, textbooks and rote learning were reinstated, classroom discipline was emphasized, and the authority of teachers and parents over the pupils reinforced. Later in the 1930s, school uniforms reappeared, making boys and girls in Soviet high schools look very like their predecessors in Tsarist gymnasia. The reorganization of higher education was also in many respects a return to traditional, prerevolutionary norms. The old professors recovered their authority; entrance requirements were once again based on academic rather than social and political criteria; and examinations, degrees and academic titles were reinstated.[15]

Even history, a subject banished soon after the Revolution on the grounds that it was irrelevant to contemporary life and had traditionally been used to inculcate patriotism and the ideology of the ruling class, reappeared in the curricula of schools and universities. Mikhail Pokrovsky, an Old Bolshevik and distinguished Marxist historian whose disciples had been very active in the scholarly branch of Cultural Revolution, was posthumously criticized for reducing history to an abstract record of class conflict without names, dates, heroes or stirring emotions. Stalin ordered new history textbooks, many of which were written by Pokrovsky's old enemies, the conventional 'bourgeois' historians who gave only lip service to Marxism. Heroes returned to history: Tarlé's *Napoleon* was an early success, but the rehabilitation extended to great Russian leaders of the past like Ivan the Terrible (purger of the Russian boyars in the sixteenth century) and Peter the Great (the 'Tsar-Transformer', architect of Russia's first modernization at the beginning of the eighteenth century). Russia's historic achievements – even, after the Second World War, its progressive mission as a nineteenth-century imperialist power – became a source of pride rather than a chronicle of exploitation.

The new Soviet patriotism – which contained a large dose of old-fashioned Russian nationalism, manifested itself in many ways. The term *rodina* (motherland), despised by the Old Bolshevik internationalists, came back into common use. In the arts, the campaign against 'formalism' in the mid-1930s had distinct xenophobic overtones, foreshadowing the anti-cosmopolitan campaigns of the late 1940s. Although xenophobia and antisemitism were historically linked, and both were elements in the postwar drive against 'cosmopolitanism', there was no overt antisemitism in the policies of the 1930s. However, the Stalinist leadership clearly had less sensitivity to the Jewish question than the older generation of Bolshevik intellectuals. There were proportionately fewer Jews in the party and its leadership than there had been in the 1920s, just as there were proportionately fewer intellectuals. This was a function of the party's enormous numerical expansion, but it also reflected the First Five-Year Plan drive to recruit and promote workers and peasants – categories that were non-intellectual by definition, and largely non-Jewish in practice.

Motherhood and the virtues of family life were also extolled from the mid 1930s. Despite their reservations about sexual liberation, the Bolsheviks had legalized abortion and divorce shortly after the Revolution and were popularly regarded as enemies of the family and traditional moral values. In the 1920s, the leaders had held to the principle that state intervention in matters of private sexual morality was undesirable, although it had always been assumed that all aspects of a *Communist*'s personal conduct should be open to the scrutiny of his party comrades. In the 1930s, Stalin's 'great retreat' involved not only an assertion of traditional family values, but also an extension of the principle of legitimate scrutiny of personal conduct from Communists alone to the population as a whole.

In the Stalin era, divorce became more difficult to obtain, free marriage lost its legal status, and persons taking their family responsibilities lightly were harshly criticized ('A poor husband and father cannot be a good citizen'). Homosexuality was made a criminal offence; and in 1936, after a long public discussion showing support for both the pro- and anti-abortion viewpoints, abortion was also outlawed. Gold wedding rings reappeared in the shops, and the traditional New Year trees (*elki*, the Russian equivalent of Christmas trees) were revived 'to bring joy to Soviet children'. To Communists who had assimilated the more emancipated attitudes of an earlier period, this all came very close to the dreaded Philistinism of the petty bourgeoisie, especially given the sentimental and sanctimonious tones in which children and the family were now discussed (in the old anti-Philistine days, Lenin's widow had once vigorously protested against the vulgarity of writers who portrayed Lenin as a 'virtuous petty-bourgeois' and 'exemplary family man'; but from the 1930s, this was clearly the right way to portray the Founding Father). However, the policies that were most jarring to Communist intellectuals were often popular with a broader public: the new morality of the 1930s was almost certainly welcomed by the 'Philistine, petty-bourgeois' majority of the Soviet population.[16]

The cause of women's emancipation met a mixed fate in this period. On the one hand, a very large number of women were drawn into the labour force from the early 1930s, and Soviet publicists hailed this a major victory for women's emancipation. With regard to the peasantry, the issue of women's rights was more strongly emphasized than before. Much was made of the fact that women had full individual membership in the kolkhoz, whereas they had not had it in the old village *mir*. Peasant women were encouraged to become tractor-drivers and move into other traditional male spheres of activity. When the women reported conflict with husbands and fathers over their new assertiveness and initiative, even conflicts leading to divorce or outright defiance of parental authority, Soviet officials took the women's side and condemned the men.

On the other hand, the new line was quite discouraging for the educated and usually middle-class women (including Communists) who had been part of the women's movement before and immediately after the Revolution. The old-style liberated woman, assertively independent and ideologically committed on issues like abortion, was no longer in favour. The new message was that the family came first, despite the growing numbers of women who were receiving education and entering professional careers. No achievement could be greater than that of a successful wife and mother. In a campaign inconceivable in the 1920s, wives of members of the new Soviet elite were directed into voluntary community activities that bore a strong resemblance to the upper-class charitable work that Russian socialist and even liberal feminists had always despised. At a national 'meeting of wives' in 1936, the wives of industrial managers and engineers described their successes in cleaning up factory kitchens, hanging curtains in the workers' hostels, advising the working girls on personal hygiene and how to keep out of trouble, and so on. Stalin and the military leader Klim Voroshilov were in attendance, and the wives presented them with traditional Russian shirts embroidered with their own hands. Later, the proceedings were published in a handsome volume with roses decorating the endpapers.[17]

The signs of *embourgeoisement* were not restricted to women, for male elite members were also encouraged to behave in a manner appropriate to their status. In the 1920s, many Communist officials clearly developed a taste for luxury and a sense of belonging to a privileged caste, but they were liable to be criticized for this and, at least in theory, a 'party maximum' kept most Communists' salaries from rising above the average wages of a skilled worker. In the 1930s, however, privileges and a high standard of living became a normal and almost obligatory concomitant of elite status, and the 'party maximum' disappeared. The elite – which included professionals (Communist and non-party) as well as Communist officials[18] – was set apart from the masses of the population not only by high salaries but also by privileged access to services and goods and a variety of material and honorific rewards.

Elite members could use shops that were not open to the general public, buy goods that were not available to other consumers and take their vacations at special resorts and well-appointed dachas. They often lived in special apartment blocks and went to work in chauffeur-driven cars. Some effort was made to conceal these elite prerogatives from the population as a whole; yet at the same time those who held responsible positions were expected to dress and entertain in a certain style, and their subordinates were expected to show deference. It was no more appropriate in the 1930s for a factory worker to use the familiar form of address to the plant manager than for a schoolchild to use it to his teacher, though at an earlier period this form had normally been used among Communists without regard to status and position.

Cultural life was very much affected by the regime's new orientation (just as it was affected, in a different way, by the increasing authoritarianism of the regime). In the first place, cultural interests and cultured behaviour (*kul'turnost'*) were among the visible marks of elite status that Communist officials were expected to display. In the second place, non-Communist professionals – that is, the old 'bourgeois intelligentsia' – belonged to the new elite, mixed socially with Communist officials and shared the same privileges.[19] This constituted a real repudiation of the party's old anti-expert bias that had made the Cultural Revolution possible, and it meant also that the young Communist intellectuals who had been the activists of Cultural Revolution fell out of favour with the party leadership. The Communist intelligentsia trained in the 1920s, with its strange mixture of political militancy and cultural avantgardism, became an anachronism in the Stalinist 1930s. Its basic premiss had been that the revolutionary age demanded a different culture from that of Pushkin and *Swan Lake*. But in the Stalin era, with the old bourgeois intelligentsia staunchly defending the cultural heritage and a newly middle-class audience looking for an accessible culture to master, Pushkin and *Swan Lake* came out the winners.

The emergence of a new Soviet elite raised conceptual problems both for Soviet ideologists and Marxist critics of the Soviet Union. In Marxist terms, the elite could not strictly be classified as a bourgeois class, since it did not own the means of production, although it clearly had the characteristics of a bourgeois status group. The Yugoslav Marxist Milovan Djilas was later to coin the term 'new class' for the Soviet elite.[20] For Soviet apologists, the main problem was to describe Soviet society without suggesting a class hierarchy with a ruling or exploiting class at the top. In the mid 1930s, Stalin solved the terminological problem by stating that the society consisted of two basic classes, the working class and the kolkhoz peasantry, together with a stratum, the intelligentsia or white-collar group.[21]

According to Stalin, there was no longer an exploitative relationship between classes, and presumably therefore no class hierarchy: the three constituent parts of Soviet society were separate but equal. The 1936 Constitution guaranteed equal rights to all citizens of the socialist Soviet state, regardless of class. But even in a society of equals, some may be more equal than others. In official Soviet writings, the 'more equal' group seemed to be the working class, since, in deference to its historic achievements, it was still accorded a 'leading role' in Soviet society. But in practice, of course, it was the group with higher status and greater privileges that was 'more equal' – that is, the intelligentsia stratum or white-collar elite.

Stalin's new regime

In the 1930s, it is generally agreed, a new political system was consolidated in the Soviet Union. Whether this system should be classified as socialist, totalitarian or simply Stalinist[22] remains a matter of debate, and there has been so little agreement on the nature of the regime that even descriptive analysis tends to be controversial. It is possible, nevertheless, to isolate a number of characteristics of the regime in the 1930s that were new or strikingly different from those of the pre-1929 period. Two have already been mentioned: the dropping of class-war ideology, and the emergence of a new, privileged elite of administrators and professionals. Another was Stalin's consolidation of a quasi-dictatorial role, with the consequent changes in the mode of party leadership and organization. Finally, there had been important changes in the role of the secret police and the extent of police repression, producing a large increase in the convict population in prisons and labour camps, and culminating in the monstrous and still baffling episode of the Great Purge of 1937–8.

Some scholars have interpreted these changes as a reversion to the old Russian tradition of autocratic rule and police surveillance – in effect, a political version of the 'great retreat'. Others have been primarily interested in the relationship of Stalinism to Leninism or original Bolshevism. On this question, the orthodox Soviet approach has always stressed continuity, perceiving the political system of the Stalin era as socialist (although post-1956 writings admit the 'distortions' of socialism accompanying Stalin's cult of personality), and thus a legitimate and historically inevitable outcome of the October Revolution. The orthodox Western approach of the postwar period also stressed continuity, though classifying the system as totalitarian dictatorship rather than socialism (see above, p. 4). But there have been recent doubts about continuity, both in the Soviet and the Western camp: some Western scholars have questioned the assumption that Stalinism was a logical or necessary outcome of original Bolshevism,[23] while, on somewhat similar lines, some Soviet Marxists have attempted to rescue Lenin and the Revolution from the odium of responsibility for Stalin's terror.[24]

For historians, however, there is still a great deal to be said for emphasizing continuity. A large part of all historical explanation consists of analysing change in terms of immediate antecedents. To postulate very sharp discontinuities, for example between Lenin's and Stalin's Russia, is sometimes little more than a way of saying that we find Stalin's Russia inexplicable. Yet the Stalinist 1930s are surely not totally inexplicable in terms of the preceding era of revolution: on the one hand, we can discern processes of consolidation, routinization and the imposition of order on a disrupted society; and, on the other hand, we can identify residual 'revolutionary' elements that produce further disruption and undermine the process of stabilization. In historical terms, the Stalin era was the outcome of the Russian Revolution – not the intended, inevitable or desirable outcome, no doubt, but the actual outcome, the only one that exists. Stalinism (regardless of how we define that term) represented a conclusion or settlement of the Russian Revolution. The question is, what kind of settlement? Which of the many different and contradictory revolutionary strains were incorporated?

The first aspect of the revolutionary settlement to consider is Stalin's emergence as Leader (*vozhd'*) of the party and the nation. Stalin is often described as a dictator, since he exercised more or less autocratic powers without having the traditional legitimacy of a monarch. But he never declared himself dictator. In fact, Stalin solved the leadership problem in the manner of Janus, turning one face to the party and the other to the people. For the masses, his image resembled that of the traditional autocrat, the all-powerful Tsar who was father of his people. (Lenin had also been perceived in this way, though it was an image he resisted and the Bolsheviks did not fully appreciate until his death.) For the party, Stalin took over Lenin's leadership role and exploited its considerable ambiguities. He made no formal institutional changes, and observed the convention that he was only the first among equals within the Central Committee and the Politburo. At larger party gatherings, it became customary for Communists to greet Stalin's entrance with wild applause. But Stalin, mindful of Lenin's example, appeared to deprecate such enthusiasm.

Stalin inherited from Lenin an elaborate structure of soviet and internal party democracy that was largely a sham. But the sham became more blatant under Stalin, both because the violations of democratic norms were greater and because Stalin (unlike Lenin) made extravagant and implausible claims about soviet and party democracy. While Lenin had imposed a formal ban on party factions in 1921, Stalin actually succeeded in putting the ban into effect, with the result that potential factions automatically became conspiracies. It was only under Stalin that rank-and-file Communists were kept in virtual ignorance of the discussions of the party leadership, and that the leaders – particularly the supreme Leader – began to cultivate the godlike attributes of mystery and inscrutability.

Stalin's politics of mystery were also the politics of fear. Under Stalin, the secret police greatly expanded its activities, in a manner that had profound consequences for the everyday life of the population as well as the political life of the party. Among the important contributing causes were the mass arrests and deportations that accompanied the liquidation of NEP and collectivization, and the new economic role that the police acquired through the deployment of convict labour. Stalin's police state can also be seen as a reversion to the practices of the late Tsarist period,[25] or as the development of a Soviet precedent in the Cheka terror of the Civil War. In both cases, however, there were qualitative and quantitative differences from the Stalin model. A number of Stalin's major policies, including dekulakization and the Great Purge, could only have been carried out by police action. Despite the precedent of Civil War terror, large-scale and sometimes random terror in time of peace was one of Stalin's political innovations; and, as the theorists of totalitarianism suggest, it was surely an integral part of his formula of rule – an aspect of the remystification of power that the leadership promoted in the 1930s.

It was also Stalin's innovation to use the secret police against the Communist political opponents and, in the Great Purge, against the Communist elite as a whole. As in so many cases, however, Stalin's innovation was not wholly without roots in earlier Bolshevik tradition. Lenin had had no inhibitions about arresting *non*-Communist political opponents, whether or not they had engaged in real conspiracy against the regime. He threatened to shoot Mensheviks and SRs at the beginning of the 1920s, although in practice their punishment was usually less drastic.

Under Lenin, a sharp distinction was drawn between opposition from outside the party and dissidence within it. The Old Bolsheviks held strongly to the principle that internal party disagreements were outside the scope of the secret police, since the Bolsheviks must never follow the Jacobins' example of turning terror on their own comrades. But, admirable though that principle was, the fact that the Bolshevik leaders needed to affirm it says something about the atmosphere of internal party politics. In the early 1920s, when organized opposition outside the Bolshevik Party disappeared and internal party factions were formally banned, dissident groups within the party in effect inherited the position of the old opposition parties outside it, and it was hardly surprising if they began to receive similar treatment. At any rate, there was no great outcry within the Communist Party when, in the late 1920s, Stalin used the secret police against the Trotskyites and then (following the model of Lenin's treatment of Cadet and Menshevik leaders in 1922–3) deported Trotsky from the country. It was a further step to propose the death penalty for leaders of an illegal factional group within the party, as Stalin apparently did in the Ryutin case of 1932, or to arrest *former* Opposition leaders on trumped-up charges of terrorist conspiracy, as Stalin did to Zinoviev and Kamenev after the assassination of Sergei Kirov, the Leningrad party leader, in December 1934. But these actions fall into a logical, if not inevitable, sequence.

The Great Purge may also be put in this sequence, although there is clearly a qualitative leap in ruthlessness and brutality, together with a new element of irrationality which has been explained in terms of Stalin's personal paranoia, the impact of Kirov's murder and the fears and insecurity associated with the growing threat of war. Among the most dramatic aspects of the Purge were the show trials of 1936, 1937 and 1938, in which Old Bolshevik defendants (many of them former oppositionists) confessed to a variety of fantastic crimes and were in most cases sentenced to death, and the court martial of Marshal Tukhachevsky and other military leaders in June 1937, which resulted in their immediate execution as German spies.[26] But this was only the tip of the iceberg.

For two full years in 1937 and 1938, top Communist officials in every branch of the bureaucracy – government, party, industrial, military and finally even police – were being arrested as 'enemies of the people' and disappearing into prisons and labour camps. In the highest administrative and political strata, the casualty rate rose as high as 70 per cent.[27] Waves of fear and terror spread downwards into the population, as citizens were encouraged to denounce each other (but particularly to denounce their bosses) as spies, saboteurs and terrorists. Estimates of deaths by execution or in the camps in 1937–8 alone have run into the millions, though a figure in the low hundreds of thousands seems more plausible;[28] and the labour camp population in 1941 (including common criminals and earlier 'politicals' as well as Purge victims) has been calculated at three and a half million.[29] Many of the Purge victims remained in labour camps until Khrushchev's denunciation of Stalin in the Secret Speech of 1956.

How much the Great Purge had in common with earlier Soviet purges is debatable. 'Great Purge' is a purely Western label for the Stalinist terror of 1937–8. In Soviet usage, the term 'purge' (*chistka*) is not applied to the terror, but to the periodic reviews of party membership and the government bureaucracy that began soon after the Revolution. To be purged from the party simply meant losing party membership; to be purged from a government institution meant losing your job; and the causes ranged from drunkenness to concealment of social origin or oppositionist political activity. However, while purges were a routine matter in the 1920s and 1930s, they were not wholly unconnected with the equally routine process of police arrests of 'enemies'. At least some of those purged from the party and the government bureaucracy in 1929–30 suffered subsequent administrative exile or arrest.

In 1933, after a massive recruitment of new members during the First Five-Year Plan, the party decided to purge its ranks again, mainly, it seems, with the intention of dropping the more illiterate and inactive of the new working-class and peasant recruits. This was done, but in the panic following Kirov's murder at the end of 1934 it was decided that the whole process had to be repeated. Purging of the party continued in 1935–6, in an atmosphere of rising political tension and police activity: it was still in progress in the summer of 1936, when the first show trial of Old Bolsheviks prefigured the onset of the terror and mass arrests of party cadres. Thus the party purge and the Great Purge (which was *not* a purge in the formal sense) were part of a continuum. Taking a broader view, the *possibility* of an aberration like the Great Purge was surely inherent in two well-established Bolshevik practices – that of purging party members and officials on general grounds of political and social unreliability, and that of arresting citizens on similar grounds, with or without evidence of specific criminal acts.

Terror also had revolutionary antecedents. It had been used against 'class enemies' during the Civil War, and again in the Cultural Revolution of the First Five-Year Plan period. For Communists, the use of terror against the party was qualitatively different from the earlier episodes, but not all Soviet citizens would have sympathized with this point of view. Even allowing a qualitative difference, however, it is hard to overlook the fact that the terror of the Great Purge had many similarities with historical events that are usually labelled revolutionary. One example is the Jacobin terror of 1794, in which revolutionary leaders followed aristocrats to the guillotine. Another more recent example is the Chinese Cultural Revolution of the 1960s, which struck down Communist cadres along with professionals and survivors from the old elite. But perhaps the most interesting analogue is the Soviet Union's own Cultural Revolution, which preceded the Great Purge by only a few years. In both cases, suspicion and spy-mania flourished, enemies were unmasked (though they were 'class enemies' in the first case and 'enemies of the people' in the second), and show trials were held in which the defendants admitted abusing their high positions to conspire with foreigners against the embattled revolutionary state. Stalin himself linked the two episodes, and seemed to be seeking revolutionary legitimation for the Great Purge by presenting it as a ruthless democratic rejection of an unworthy elite. 'Bosses come and go,' he said in October 1937, in one of his rare and enigmatic comments on the terror, which was then at its height. 'Only the people is eternal.'[30]

A similar perception was expressed by some analysts of Soviet totalitarianism, who argued that terror and repeated purging of the elite was imperative for a regime bent on the continuous revolutionary transformation of society.[31] This argument had its weaknesses, since in historical fact the Great Purge was not repeated (although some evidence suggests that Stalin may have been planning a repetition in the last year of his life). But it does seem reasonable to see the Purge as Stalin's last effort of social engineering – a final product, however monstrous, of the impulse towards revolutionary transformation that had gained ascendancy in 1917. The question then is, what kind of transformation was intended?

The Great Purge shattered the cohorts of Communist leaders formed in the prerevolutionary underground, the Civil War and the period of collectivization and the First Five-Year Plan. In a sense, it was a classic illustration of the maxim that the revolution devours its children; and (assuming that Stalin's was indeed the guiding hand) this was surely a part of Stalin's intention. But it seems likely that Stalin – and, for that matter, the majority of Soviet citizens – saw the cadres of the mid 1930s less in their old role as revolutionaries than in their current role as bosses. There is even some evidence that Stalin saw them as Soviet boyars (feudal lords) and himself as a latterday Ivan the Terrible, who had to destroy the boyars to build a modern nation state and a new service nobility.[32]

The idea that the Revolution's victories would be secure only after the Soviet regime had produced 'its own intelligentsia' or elite had attracted Stalin since the Civil War days; and during the First Five-Year Plan he had taken active measures to realize it (see above, pp. 133–4). Early in 1937, at the beginning of the Great Purge, he reminded the old cadres that, should they prove treacherous or inadequate, a whole cohort of young Communists and workers sent to higher technical schools during the First Five-Year Plan stood ready to replace them. In the wake of the Great Purge, this group – the Brezhnev generation – was promoted extraordinarily rapidly into the highest echelon of the Soviet administrative and political elite. In 1939, Stalin told the Eighteenth Party Congress that now the Soviet regime had finally acquired the kind of intelligentsia it needed. The newcomers had technical expertise and loyalty, and they had risen from the people. In the words of another spokesman for the party leadership, they were 'yesterday's workers and peasants and the sons of workers and peasants, promoted to command positions'.[33]

While Stalin's comparative evaluation of the old cadres and the new ones can scarcely be taken at face value, he had succeeded in creating a new elite with a core of technical expertise, a degree of revolutionary legitimacy derived from the lower-class origins of many of its members, and little experience of actual revolutionary activity. These qualities were nicely balanced for a revolutionary settlement, which by definition must incorporate contradictions. The new cadres were from the people but no longer of it, for they had been upwardly mobile. They were beneficiaries of the Revolution, but by the same token disposed to be loyal to the regime and most unlikely to be revolutionary. To be sure, only a skilled dialectician could relate Stalin's elite-building to the Revolution's socialist objectives: it recalls the irreverent definition of Soviet socialism as the ending of exploitation of man by man, and its replacement by its opposite. But that 'replacement by its opposite' is, in a sense, what revolutions are all about.

The Russian Revolution, according to Soviet propagandists, has never ended. Even today, banners proclaim that 'Lenin lives! Lenin is with us!' This claim is not made about Stalin, whose body was removed from Lenin's Mausoleum under Khrushchev, though many have shared the fear expressed in a famous poem by Evtushenko that Stalin might rise from the grave. But of course it is true, in figurative terms, that the Revolution survives in the institutions and collective memory of a society that is no longer revolutionary. It is the keystone in Soviet national tradition, a focus of patriotism, a subject to be learnt by children in school and celebrated in Soviet public art.

But the revolutionary myth, like the real Revolution, is not monolithic. It was officially revised in 1956, when Khrushchev denounced Stalin's crimes and a campaign began for a return to 'Leninist norms'. Yet Stalin's grave still stands not far from Lenin's Mausoleum, and ambivalence on his historical contribution has become the standard position for Soviet ideologists. The victorious Revolution had many aspects and phases, whose balance in the myth is constantly shifting. Even the Revolution's losers – aims and leaders that were long ago repudiated or defeated – remain somewhere on the peripheries of consciousness, potentially available for resurrection in a different political climate.

In the late 1950s, for example, Khrushchev, once a beneficiary of Stalin's policies of proletarian 'promotion', remembered and revived some of the policies of the First Five-Year Plan Cultural Revolution. In the 1960s, memoirists from the intelligentsia wrote nostalgically of NEP as a golden age of cultural pluralism and creative ferment. In the 1970s, some Soviet scholars began to recommend something very like the old 'Bukharin alternative' as a model for economic development in the Third World. Lenin's intellectual legacy is constantly re-examined to provide ammunition for all sides in a wide range of policy disputes.

The West, too, has learnt a series of lessons from the Russian Revolution over the past sixty years. For a long time, the most popular lessons were that Communist 'democracy' really means a repressive dictatorship, and that Communist internationalism both serves as a cover for Soviet expansionism and represents a peculiarly insidious threat to the non-Communist world. But others have held that the true lesson of the Russian Revolution is the superiority of a planned economy, or (from a different ideological standpoint) that socialist revolutions do not eliminate privilege and inequality. For Third World intellectuals, the relevant lessons may be about economic development, resistance to colonial exploitation or the building of new, indigenous administrative elites. All of these lessons, of course, are simplified generalizations from Soviet experience which partly reflect the fears, hopes and biases of different groups of observers. But, taken collectively, they reflect the importance of the Russian Revolution to the rest of the world. It remains one of those ambiguous milestones in human history that scholars, politicians and ordinary thinking people keep coming back to decipher.

This book has tried to provide a context for evaluating the various lessons, true or false, that the West has drawn from the Russian Revolution. It has also attempted to show how the Revolution formed later Soviet society, as well as to identify some of the discarded elements of the revolutionary tradition which now lie buried beneath the surface of Soviet society but may yet emerge to influence its present and future development. However, every historian has his or her biases and favourite questions. I have sought to investigate the social dimension of the Revolution, as well as the more familiar political dimension. To the normal questions of why and how the Revolution occurred and what ideals and objectives inspired it, I have added the question of why the revolutionary regime survived. No revolution is ever truly successful, since the revolutionary spirit (no doubt fortunately) always dies. But in cases where the revolutionary regime survives and assumes permanent form, the presumption must be that it has satisfied some social demands and honoured at least some of the revolution's promises. The ways in which the Russian Revolution succeeded, as well as the ways in which it failed, are part of the subject of this book.

Notes

Details of titles included in the Select Bibliography are given only at the first citation

Introduction (pages 1–9)

1. Dates before the calendar change in 1918 are given in the old style, which in 1917 was thirteen days behind the Western calendar which Russia adopted in 1918.
2. Crane Brinton, *The Anatomy of Revolution* (revised ed., New York, 1965).
3. The party's name was changed from Russian Social-Democratic Labour Party (Bolshevik) to Russian [later, All-Union] Communist Party (Bolshevik) in 1918. The terms 'Bolshevik' and 'Communist' were used interchangeably in the 1920s, but 'Communist' became the normal usage in the 1930s.
4. L. Trotsky, *The Revolution Betrayed* (London, 1937).
5. See Stephen F. Cohen, 'Bolshevism and Stalinism', in Tucker, ed., *Stalinism* (New York, 1977).
6. See Walter Laqueur, *The Fate of the Revolution. Interpretations of Soviet History* (New York, 1967), pp. 126–9.
7. Adam B. Ulam, 'The Historical Role of Marxism', in his *The New Face of Soviet Totalitarianism* (Cambridge, Mass., 1963), p. 35.
8. Barrington Moore, *Terror and Progress USSR* (Cambridge, Mass., 1954).
9. N. N. Sukhanov, *The Russian Revolution 1917*, trans. and ed. by Joel Carmichael (New York, 1962), vol. 2, p. 376.

Chapter 1 (pages 10–33)

1. Frank Lorimer, *The Population of the Soviet Union* (Geneva, 1946), pp. 10, 12.
2. A. G. Rashin, *Formirovanie rabochego klassa Rossii* (Moscow, 1958), p. 328.
3. Barbara A. Anderson, *Internal Migration during Modernization in Late Nineteenth-Century Russia* (Princeton, 1980), pp. 32–8.
4. A. Gerschenkron, *Economic Backwardness in Historical Perspective* (Cambridge, Mass., 1962), pp. 5–30.
5. On peasant rebelliousness and working-class revolution, see Leopold Haimson, 'The Problem of Social Stability in Urban Russia, 1905–1917', *Slavic Review*, vol. 23, no. 4 (1964) pp. 633–7.

6. See Marc Raeff, *Origins of the Russian Intelligentsia. The Eighteenth-Century Nobility* (New York, 1966).

7. This is discussed in Richard S. Wortman, *The Development of a Russian Legal Consciousness* (Chicago, 1976), pp. 286–9 and *passim*.

8. See the argument in Richard Pipes, *Russia under the Old Regime* (New York, 1974), ch. 10.

9. On the Populists' prescience on this question, see Gerschenkron, op. cit. 167–73.

10. For a negative view, see Richard Pipes, *Social Democracy and the St. Petersburg Labor Movement, 1885–1897* (Cambridge, Mass., 1963); for a more positive one, see Allan K. Wildman, *The Making of a Workers' Revolution. Russian Social Democracy, 1891–1903* (Chicago, 1967).

11. Quoted from Sidney Harcave, *First Blood. The Russian Revolution of 1905* (New York, 1964), p. 23.

12. For an analysis of Bolshevik and Menshevik membership to 1907, see David Lane, *The Roots of Russian Communism* (Assen, The Netherlands, 1969), pp. 22–3, 26.

13. For an unusually lucid discussion of the split, see Jerry F. Hough and Merle Fainsod, *How the Soviet Union is Governed* (Cambridge, Mass., 1979), pp. 21–6.

14. Haimson, 'The Problem of Social Stability', pp. 624–33.

15. See Roberta Thompson Manning, 'Zemstvo and Revolution: The Onset of the Gentry Reaction, 1905–1907', in Leopold Haimson, ed., *The Politics of Rural Russia, 1905–1914* (Bloomington, Ind., 1979).

16. Mary Schaeffer Conroy, *Petr Arkad'evich Stolypin. Practical Politics in Late Tsarist Russia* (Boulder, Colo., 1976), p. 98.

17. See Dorothy Atkinson, 'The Statistics on the Russian Land Commune, 1905–1917', *Slavic Review*, vol. 32, no. 4 (1973).

18. For a vivid fictional representation of what this meant in psychological terms, see Alexander Solzhenitsyn, *Lenin in Zurich* (New York, 1976).

19. The family tragedy is portrayed with sympathy and understanding in Robert K. Massie, *Nicholas and Alexandra* (New York, 1967).

Chapter 2 (pages 34–60)

1. For a critical historiographical survey of this argument, see Stephen F. Cohen, 'Bolshevism and Stalinism', in Tucker, ed., *Stalinism*.

2. Quoted from W. G. Rosenberg, *Liberals in the Russian Revolution* (Princeton, 1974), p. 209.

3. George Katkov, *Russia, 1917: The February Revolution* (London, 1967), p. 444.

4. A. Tyrkova-Williams, *From Liberty to Brest-Litovsk* (London, 1919), p. 25.

5. Quoted from Allan K. Wildman, *The End of the Russian Imperial Army* (Princeton, 1980), p. 260.

6. Sukhanov, *The Russian Revolution, 1917*, vol. 1, pp. 104–5.

7. Quoted from Leonard Schapiro, *The Origin of the Communist Autocracy* (Cambridge, Mass., 1955), p. 42 (note 20).

8. V. I. Lenin, *Collected Works*, vol. 24 (Moscow, 1964), pp. 21–6.

9. For a careful analysis of membership data for 1917, see T. H. Rigby, *Communist Party Membership in the USSR, 1917–1967* (Princeton, 1968), ch. 1.

10. Wildman, op. cit. In addition to its central theme, the Army in the period February–April 1917, this book offers one of the best analyses available of the February transfer of power.

11. Marc Ferro, *The Russian Revolution of February 1917*, trans. by J. L. Richards (London, 1972), pp. 112–21.

12. Ibid. 121–30.

13. On the July Days, see A. Rabinowitch, *Prelude to Revolution: The Petrograd Bolsheviks and the July 1917 Uprising* (Bloomington, Ind., 1968).

14. Quoted from A. Rabinowitch, *The Bolsheviks Come to Power* (New York, 1976), p. 115.

15. Newspaper interview with General Alekseev (*Rech*, 13 Sept. 1917, p. 3), in Robert Paul Browder and Alexander F. Kerensky, ed., *The Russian Provisional Government 1917. Documents*, vol. 3 (Stanford, 1961), p. 1622.

16. Quoted from Robert V. Daniels, *Red October* (New York, 1967), p. 82.

17. The actions and intentions of major Bolshevik participants in the October Revolution were later subject to a great deal of self-serving revision and political myth-making – not only in official Stalinist histories, but also in Trotsky's classic history-*cum*-memoir, *The Russian Revolution*. See the discussion in Daniels, *Red October*, ch. 11.

18. Leon Trotsky, *The Russian Revolution* (abridged from Trotsky's *The History of the Russian Revolution* by F. W. Dupee), trans. by Max Eastman (New York, 1959), pp. 411–29, 472–4 and *passim*.

19. See, for example, Roy A. Medvedev, *Let History Judge. The Origins and Consequences of Stalinism* (New York, 1973), pp. 381–4.

20. For one interpretation, see John Keep, *The Russian Revolution. A Study in Mass Mobilization* (New York, 1976), pp. 306–81, 464–71.

21. The following analysis is based on O. Radkey, *The Election to the Russian Constituent Assembly of 1917* (Cambridge, Mass., 1950).

Chapter 3 (pages 61–84)

1. For a good, detailed study, see Robert Service, *The Bolshevik Party in Revolution. A Study in Organizational Change, 1917–1923* (London, 1979).

2. T. H. Rigby, *Communist Party Membership in the USSR, 1917–1967* (Princeton, 1968), p. 242; *Vsesoyuznaya partiinaya perepis' 1927 goda. Osnovnye itogi perepisi* (Moscow, 1927), p. 52.

3. Robert C. Tucker, 'Stalinism as Revolution from Above', in Tucker, *Stalinism*, pp. 91–2.

4. Quoted from John W. Wheeler-Bennett, *Brest-Litovsk, The Forgotten Peace, March 1918* (New York, 1971), pp. 243–4.

5. For a narrative history of the Civil War see W. H. Chamberlin, *The Russian Revolution*, vol. 2 (London, 1935).

6. Quoted from Aleksandr I. Solzhenitsyn, *The Gulag Archipelago* I–II (New York, 1973), p. 300.

7. See Alec Nove, *An Economic History of the USSR* (London, 1969), ch. 3. A detailed historiographical discussion is in E. Gimpelson, '*Voennyi kommunizm*' (Moscow, 1973), pp. 239–82.

8. See E. H. Carr, 'The Bolshevik Utopia', in his *The October Revolution. Before and After* (New York, 1969), pp. 56–86.

9. On the situation in the factories, see Keep, *The Russian Revolution*, pp. 263–75.

10. For a detailed account of the economy during the Civil War, see E. H. Carr, *The Bolshevik Revolution, 1917–1923* (London, 1952), vol. 2, especially chs. 16 and 17.

11. For the argument that there was no 'second revolution', see T. Shanin, *The Awkward Class. Political Sociology of Peasantry in a Developing Society: Russia 1910–1925* (Oxford, 1972), pp. 145–61.

12. N. Bukharin and E. Preobrazhensky, *The ABC of Communism*, trans. by Eden and Cedar Paul (London, 1969), p. 355.

13. On continuity between the period of the Stolypin reforms and the 1920s, especially through the presence in the countryside of agricultural specialists working on land consolidation, see George L. Yaney, 'Agricultural Administration in Russia from the Stolypin Land Reform to Forced Collectivization: An Interpretive Study', in James R. Millar, ed., *The Soviet Rural Community* (Urbana, Ill., 1971), pp. 3–35.

14. Bukharin and Preobrazhensky, op. cit. 118.

15. See Sheila Fitzpatrick, *The Commissariat of Enlightenment* (London and New York, 1970), ch. 6. For a well-illustrated introduction to the avant-garde art of the revolution, see Camilla Gray, *The Russian Experiment in Art, 1863–1922* (London, 1962).

16. Quoted from Fitzpatrick, *The Commissariat of Enlightenment*, p. 20.

17. T. H. Rigby, *Lenin's Government. Sovnarkom, 1917–1922* (Cambridge, 1979).

18. Bukharin and Preobrazhensky, op. cit. 272.

19. See Sheila Fitzpatrick, *Education and Social Mobility in the Soviet Union, 1921–1934* (Cambridge, 1979), ch. 1.

Chapter 4 (pages 85–109)

1. E. G. Gimpelson, *Sovetskii rabochii klass, 1918–1920 gg.* (Moscow, 1974), p. 80.

2. Oliver H. Radkey, *The Unknown Civil War in Soviet Russia. A Study of the Green Movement in the Tambov Region 1920–21* (Stanford, 1976), p. 263.

3. On the Kronstadt revolt, see Paul Avrich, *Kronstadt, 1921* (Princeton, 1970).

4. Lenin, Political Report of the Central Committee to the Eleventh Party Congress (March 1922), in V. I. Lenin, *Collected Works*, vol. 33 (Moscow, 1966), p. 282.

5. A. I. Mikoyan, *Mysli i vospominaniya o Lenine* (Moscow, 1970), p. 139.

6. Lenin, *Collected Works*, vol. 33, p. 288.

7. 'Better Fewer, But Better' (2 March 1923), in Lenin, *Collected Works*, vol. 33, p. 488.

8. I. N. Yudin, *Sotsial'naya baza rosta KPSS* (Moscow, 1973), p. 128.

9. *Kommunisty v sostave apparata gosuchrezhdenii i obshchestvennykh organizatsii. Itogi vsesoyuznoi partiinoi perepisi 1927 goda* (Moscow, 1929), p. 25; *Bol'shevik*, 1928 no. 15, p. 20.

10. The 'Testament' (not included in the English *Collected Works*, which is a translation of the Russian 4th edition) is in V. I. Lenin, *Polnoe sobranie sochinenii* (5th ed.), vol. 45 (Moscow, 1964), pp. 435–6.

11. See Robert V. Daniels, *The Conscience of the Revolution* (Cambridge, Mass., 1960), pp. 225–30.

12. The phrase is Robert V. Daniels's. For a clear and concise discussion, see Hough and Fainsod, *How the Soviet Union is Governed*, pp. 124–33, 144.

13. This is the unifying theme of Robert V. Daniels's study of the Communist oppositions of the 1920s, *The Conscience of the Revolution* – although, as his title indicates, Daniels sees the pleas for internal party democracy as an expression of revolutionary idealism rather than as a function of opposition.

14. See Moshe Lewin, *Lenin's Last Struggle* (New York, 1968), for the argument that Lenin's political thinking changed radically in his last years.

15. On the emergence of the Lenin cult, see Robert C. Tucker, *Stalin as Revolutionary 1879–1929* (New York, 1973), pp. 279–88.

16. Lenin, 'Our Revolution (A Propos of the Notes of N. Sukhanov)', in his *Collected Works*, vol. 33 (Moscow, 1966), p. 480.

17. For Bolshevik discussions of the peasantry and the issue of class differentiation, see E. H. Carr, *Socialism in One Country* (London, 1959), vol. 1, ch. 5, and vol. 2, ch. 22, and E. H. Carr and R. W. Davies, *Foundations of a Planned Economy 1926–1929* (London, 1969), vol. 1, part 1, ch. 4.

18. Quoted from Yu. V. Voskresenskii, *Perekhod Kommunisticheskoi Partii k osushchestvleniyu politiki sotsialisticheskoi industrializatsii SSSR (1925–1927)* (Moscow, 1969), p. 162.

19. J. V. Stalin, 'October, Lenin and the Prospects of Our Development', in his *Works*, vol. 7 (Moscow, 1954), p. 258.

20. For these discussions, see E. H. Carr, *Socialism in One Country*, vol. 2, pp. 36–51.

21. For a detailed examination of the debate, see A. Erlich, *The Soviet Industrialization Debate, 1924–1926* (Cambridge, Mass., 1960).

22. See Stephen F. Cohen, 'Bolshevism and Stalinism', in Tucker, ed., *Stalinism*, and *Bukharin and the Bolshevik Revolution* (New York, 1973); and Moshe Lewin, *Political Undercurrents in Soviet Economic Debates: From Bukharin to the Modern Reformers* (Princeton, 1974).

Chapter 5 *(pages 110–34)*

1. See, for example, Adam B. Ulam, *Stalin* (New York, 1973), ch. 8.
2. On the war scare, see Alfred G. Meyer, 'The Great War Scare of 1927', *Soviet Union/Union soviétique*, vol. 5, part 1 (1978).
3. See Sheila Fitzpatrick, 'The Foreign Threat During the First Five-Year Plan', *Soviet Union/Union soviétique*, vol. 5, part 1 (1978).
4. On the Shakhty trial and the later 'Industrial Party' trial, see Kendall E. Bailes, *Technology and Society under Lenin and Stalin* (Princeton, 1978), chs. 3–5.
5. Stalin's statements on the procurements crisis (Jan.–Feb. 1928) are in J. V. Stalin, *Works*, vol. 11 (Moscow, 1954), pp. 3–22. See also Moshe Lewin, *Russian Peasants and Soviet Power* (London, 1968), pp. 214–40.
6. Frumkin's advice is reported in *Za chetkuyu klassovuyu liniyu* (Novosibirsk, 1929), pp. 73–4; Uglanov's recommendations were outlined by him in a speech in Moscow at the end of January, published in *Vtoroi plenum MK VKP(b) 31 yanv. – 2 fev. 1928. Doklady i rezolyutsii* (Moscow, 1928), pp. 9–11, 38–40.
7. Bukharin's biographer concludes that in the latter years of NEP the party was led not by Stalin alone but by a 'duumvirate' of Stalin, the General Secretary, and Bukharin, the party's leading theoretician (Stephen F. Cohen, *Bukharin and the Bolshevik Revolution*, pp. 213–27, 286). This, I think, is to confuse visibility with power, but it has prompted a worthwhile re-examination of Bukharin's political role.
8. See Cohen, op. cit. 322–3.
9. This comment was made by the Urals party secretary Ivan Kabakov, in response to a belated 'rightist' speech that Rykov made in Sverdlovsk in the summer of 1930. *X Ural'skaya konferentsiya Vsesoyuznoi Kommunisticheskoi Partii (bol'shevikov)* (Sverdlovsk, 1930), Bulletin 6, p. 14.
10. J. V. Stalin, *Works*, vol. 13 (Moscow, 1955), pp. 40–1.
11. Stalin's remark is quoted in *Puti industrializatsii*, 1928 no. 4, pp. 64–5.
12. See E. H. Carr and R. W. Davies, *Foundations of a Planned Economy, 1926–1929*, vol. 1, pp. 843–97.
13. David Ryazanov, in *XVI konferentsiya VKP(b), aprel' 1929 g. Stenograficheskii otchet* (Moscow, 1962), p. 214.
14. Alec Nove, *An Economic History of the USSR* (London, 1969), p. 150.
15. Quoted from R. W. Davies, *The Socialist Offensive. The Collectivisation of Soviet Agriculture, 1929–1930* (Cambridge, Mass., 1980), p. 148.
16. Stalin, *Works*, vol. 12 (Moscow, 1955), pp. 197–205.
17. Nove, op. cit. 197 and 238.

18. On 'gigantomania' in the collectivization movement, see R. W. Davies, 'The Soviet Rural Economy in 1929–1930: The Size of the Kolkhoz', in Chimen Abramsky, ed., *Essays in Honour of E. H. Carr* (London, 1974).

19. N. I. Platunov, *Pereselencheskaya politika sovetskogo gosudarstva i ee osushchestvlenie v SSSR (1917–iyun' 1941 g.)* (Tomsk, 1976), p. 220; N. A. Ivnitskii, *Klassovaya bor'ba v derevne i likvidatsiya kulachestva kak klassa (1929–1932 gg.)* (Moscow, 1972), p. 326.

20. Stalin, *Works*, vol. 13, pp. 54–5.

21. Yu. V. Arutyunyan, 'Kollektivizatsiya sel'skogo khozyaistva i vysvobozhdenie rabochei sily dlya promyshlennosti', in *Formirovanie i razvitie sovetskogo rabochego klassa (1917–1961 gg.)* (Moscow, 1964), p. 113.

22. This is the subject of Sheila Fitzpatrick, ed., *Cultural Revolution in Russia, 1928–1931* (Bloomington, Ind., 1978). It should be noted that the term 'cultural revolution' was also used by Lenin ('On Co-operation', 1923), but in a quite different sense.

23. For examples, see E. J. Brown, *The Proletarian Episode in Russian Literature, 1928–1932* (New York, 1953); David Joravsky, *Soviet Marxism and Natural Science, 1917–1932* (London, 1961); Loren R. Graham, *The Soviet Academy of Sciences and the Communist Party, 1927–1932* (Princeton, 1967).

24. See, for example, S. Frederick Starr, 'Visionary Town Planning During the Cultural Revolution', in Fitzpatrick, ed., *Cultural Revolution*.

25. Katerina Clark, in Fitzpatrick, ed., *Cultural Revolution*, p. 198.

26. In January 1929, for example, the Communist editors of *Kooperativnaya zhizn'* were rebuked by Emelyan Yaroslavsky of the party's Central Control Commission for complaining about antisemitic overtones in the campaign against class enemies in the Animal Products Co-operative Union. *Byulleten' TsKK VKP(b) i NK RKI SSSR i RSFSR*, 1929 no. 1, pp. 15–34.

27. See Sheila Fitzpatrick, 'Stalin and the Making of a New Elite, 1928–1939', *Slavic Review*, vol. 38, no. 3 (1979), pp. 381–2.

28. Figures from Fitzpatrick, *Education and Social Mobility*, p. 241.

29. Ibid. 187–8.

Chapter 6 (pages 135–61)

1. Crane Brinton, *The Anatomy of Revolution* (revised ed., New York, 1965), p. 17.

2. Nicholas S. Timasheff, *The Great Retreat. The Growth and Decline of Communism in Russia* (New York, 1946).

3. See James R. Millar, 'What's Wrong with the "Standard Story"?' (from Millar and Alec Nove, 'A Debate on Collectivization'), *Problems of Communism*, July–Aug. 1976, pp. 53–5.

4. Steel output, another basic index of heavy-industrial growth, rose only by a disappointing 50 per cent; machinery production (measured in roubles)

quadrupled, but the 1932 figure was probably inflated by over-pricing. For a summary of Plan fulfilment and useful commentary, see Alec Nove, *An Economic History of the U.S.S.R.* (London, 1969), pp. 191–4.

5. Holland Hunter, 'The Overambitious First Soviet Five-Year Plan', *Slavic Review*, vol. 32, no. 2 (1973), pp. 237–57.

6. See Fitzpatrick, *Education and Social Mobility*, ch. 6 and *passim*.

7. *Sotsialisticheskoe stroitel'stvo SSSR. Statisticheskii ezhegodnik* (Moscow, 1935), pp. 474–5. The figures do not include military personnel.

8. T. H. Rigby, *Communist Party Membership in the USSR* (Princeton, 1965), p. 52.

9. Beyond socialism lay communism, but by the definition established in the 1930s, communism required the withering away of the state, which was clearly impracticable so long as the socialist state was surrounded by hostile capitalist powers.

10. See Fitzpatrick, *Education and Social Mobility*, pp. 210–17; Kendall E. Bailes, *Technology and Society under Lenin and Stalin* (Princeton, 1978), pp. 141–56.

11. 'New Conditions—New Tasks in Economic Construction' (23 June 1931), in J. Stalin, *Works*, vol. 13 (Moscow, 1955), pp. 53–82.

12. I. Ya. Trifonov, *Likvidatsiya ekspluatatorskikh klassov v SSSR* (Moscow, 1975), pp. 341 and 389.

13. Jerzy R. Karcz, 'From Stalin to Brezhnev: Soviet Agricultural Policy in Historical Perspective', in James R. Millar, ed., *The Soviet Rural Community* (Urbana, Ill., 1971), pp. 54–6.

14. Trotsky, *The Revolution Betrayed*.

15. Fitzpatrick, *Education and Social Mobility*, pp. 217–26.

16. On changing attitudes towards the family, see Timasheff, *The Great Retreat*, pp. 192–203. For an intriguing thesis on Soviet 'Philistinism' in the Stalin period, see Vera S. Dunham, *In Stalin's Time. Middleclass Values in Soviet Fiction* (Cambridge, 1976).

17. *Vsesoyuznoe soveshchanie zhen khozyaistvennikov i inzhenerno-tekhnicheskikh rabotnikov tyazheloi promyshlennosti. Stenograficheskii otchet, 10–12 maya 1936 g.* (Moscow, 1936). A similar conference was held the following year for wives of military officers.

18. By 'elite', I mean the group identified by Soviet statisticians of the 1930s as 'leading cadres and specialists' (numbering about 861,000 at the end of 1933), together with those holding comparable positions in spheres excluded from the statisticians' count like party, security and military work, medical practice, the arts etc. The term 'intelligentsia' was often used to describe the specialist and administrative elite in the Stalin era, although as a statistical category it included all white-collar workers.

19. For further discussion of these points, see my article 'Culture and Politics under Stalin: A Reappraisal', *Slavic Review*, vol. 35, no. 2 (1976), pp. 211–31.

20. M. Djilas, *The New Class. An Analysis of the Communist System* (London, 1966).

21. 'On the draft of the Constitution of the USSR' (25 Nov. 1936), Russian text in I. Stalin, *Sochineniya*, vol. 1 (14), edited by Robert H. McNeal (Stanford, 1967), pp. 142–6, 168–9.

22. The label 'Stalinist' is offered by Robert Tucker, in an attempt to avoid the pre-judgement implicit in the totalitarian model and provide a basis for fresh comparative analysis. See his 'Stalinism and Comparative Communism', in Tucker, ed., *Stalinism. Essays in Historical Interpretation* (New York, 1977), pp. xii–xiv.

23. See, for example, Stephen F. Cohen, 'Bolshevism and Stalinism', in Tucker, ed., *Stalinism*. This essay also includes a useful survey of the totalitarian-model literature on the Soviet system and its evolution.

24. The most accessible example is Roy Medvedev's *Let History Judge*.

25. One of the most provocative versions of this argument, placing the emergence of the Russian-Soviet police state in the 1880s, is in Richard Pipes, *Russia under the Old Regime* (New York, 1974), ch. 11.

26. These trials are vividly described in Robert Conquest, *The Great Terror. Stalin's Purge of the Thirties* (London, 1968).

27. In his Secret Speech to the Twentieth Party Congress (1956), Khrushchev reported that 98 out of 139 full and candidate members of the party's Central Committee elected at the last pre-Purge Congress in 1934 were 'arrested and shot (mostly in 1937–8)' (*Khrushchev Remembers*, trans. and ed. by Strobe Talbott, Boston, 1970, p. 572).

28. See discussion in Hough and Fainsod, *How the Soviet Union is Governed*, pp. 176–7.

29. Naum Jasny, 'Labor and Output in Soviet Concentration Camps', *Journal of Political Economy*, vol. 59, no. 5 (1951), pp. 405–19.

30. Stalin, *Sochineniya*, vol. 1 (14), ed. McNeal, p. 254.

31. See Zbigniew K. Brzezinski, *The Permanent Purge* (Cambridge, Mass., 1956).

32. Robert C. Tucker, *The Soviet Political Mind* (New York, 1971), pp. 181–2; Tucker, ed., *Stalinism*, pp. 99–100.

33. For further discussion, see my article 'Stalin and the Making of a New Elite, 1928–1939', pp. 377–402.

Select Bibliography

Anweiler, Oskar, *The Soviets: The Russian Workers', Peasants' and Soldiers' Councils, 1905–1921*, trans. by Ruth Hein (New York, 1974).

Avrich, Paul, *Kronstadt, 1921* (Princeton, 1970). On the uprising of the Kronstadt sailors against the Soviet regime.

Borkenau, F., *World Communism. A History of the Communist International* (Ann Arbor, Mich., 1962). A participant's history, first published in 1938 as *The Communist International*; strongest on the early years up to the mid-1920s.

Bukharin, N. and Preobrazhensky, E., *The ABC of Communism*, trans. by Eden and Cedar Paul (London, 1969). Written in 1919, this is the classic presentation of the ideology of War Communism. The 1969 edition has a very useful introduction by E. H. Carr.

Carr, E. H., *A History of Soviet Russia* (London, 1952–). A rich and detailed multi-volume history, covering foreign policy and the Comintern as well as domestic developments. The individual titles are *The Bolshevik Revolution, 1917–1923*, 3 vols. (London, 1952), *The Interregnum, 1923–1924* (London, 1954), *Socialism in One Country*, 3 vols. (London, 1959) and *Foundations of a Planned Economy, 1926–1929*, 3 vols., vol. 1 co-authored by R. W. Davies (London, 1969–79).

Chamberlin, W. H., *The Russian Revolution*, 2 vols. (London, 1935). Still the best general work on the Revolution and Civil War, 1917–20.

—— *Russia's Iron Age* (London, 1935). A first-hand report on the upheavals accompanying the First Five-Year Plan.

Cohen, Stephen F., *Bukharin and the Bolshevik Revolution. A Political Biography, 1888–1938* (New York, 1973). The standard work; a thoughtful reinterpretation of Bukharin's role.

Daniels, Robert V., *The Conscience of the Revolution. Communist Opposition in Soviet Russia* (Cambridge, Mass., 1960). The best history of factional politics in the 1920s.

—— *Red October. The Bolshevik Revolution of 1917* (New York, 1967). Disposes vigorously of some myths surrounding the October Revolution and the roles of Lenin and Trotsky.

Davies, R. W., *The Socialist Offensive. The Collectivisation of Soviet Agriculture, 1929–1930* (Cambridge, Mass., 1980). The first of a projected five or six volumes on *The Industrialisation of Soviet Russia*: a work in the E. H. Carr tradition by the economic historian who co-authored one volume in Carr's history.

Deutscher, Isaac, *The Prophet Armed. Trotsky: 1879–1921* (London, 1954), and *The Prophet Unarmed. Trotsky: 1921–1929* (London, 1959). The first two volumes of the classic biography: partisan but well-argued and very lively.

Ferro, Marc, *The Russian Revolution of February 1917*, trans. by J. L. Richards (London, 1972).

—— *October 1917: A Social History of the Russian Revolution*, trans. by Norman Stone (Boston, 1980).

Two important works of social history by a French historian.

Fischer, Louis, *The Soviets in World Affairs. A History of Relations Between the Soviet Union and the Rest of the World, 1917–1929* (Princeton, 1951). Classic study by an American journalist who had access to Chicherin, Litvinov and others.

Fitzpatrick, Sheila, *The Commissariat of Enlightenment. Soviet Organization of Education and the Arts under Lunacharsky, October 1917–1921* (London and New York, 1970).

—— (ed.), *Cultural Revolution in Russia, 1928–1931* (Bloomington, Ind., 1978).

—— *Education and Social Mobility in the Soviet Union, 1921–1934* (Cambridge, 1979).

—— 'Stalin and the Making of a New Elite, 1928–1939', *Slavic Review*, vol. 38, no. 3 (1979).

Florinsky, Michael T., *The End of the Russian Empire* (New Haven, 1931). Last in a series by Russian emigré scholars on the social and economic history of Russia during the First World War.

Fülöp-Miller, René, *The Mind and Face of Bolshevism. An Examination of Cultural Life in Soviet Russia* (London, 1927). First-hand report on revolution in art and everyday life, with fine illustrations.

Gill, Graeme J., *Peasants and Government in the Russian Revolution* (London, 1979). On February–October 1917.

Haimson, Leopold, 'The Problem of Social Stability in Urban Russia, 1905–1917', *Slavic Review*, vol. 23, no. 4 (1964) and vol. 24, no. 1 (1965). A very influential interpretative study.

—— *The Russian Marxists and the Origins of Bolshevism* (Cambridge, Mass., 1955).

Hasegawa, Tsuyoshu, *The February Revolution: Petrograd, 1917* (Seattle, 1981).

Haupt, Georges and Marie, Jean-Jacques, *Makers of the Russian Revolution* (London, 1974). A useful collection of autobiographical sketches by Bolshevik leaders.

Hindus, Maurice, *Red Bread* (London, 1931). Report on collectivization in a Ukrainian village, based on first-hand observation.

Hough, Jerry F. and Fainsod, Merle, *How the Soviet Union is Governed* (Cambridge, Mass., 1979). A revision of Fainsod's classic *How Russia is Ruled* (1st ed. 1953, 2nd ed. 1963), with the historical material now separated from the analysis of the political system. Chs. 2–5 give the best available survey of political development from the October Revolution to Stalin's death.

Katkov, George, *Russia, 1917: The February Revolution* (London, 1967). The product of detailed research; idiosyncratic in its fascination with conspiracy theories.

Keep, John, *The Russian Revolution. A Study in Mass Mobilization* (New York, 1976). Revolution in town and countryside, particularly useful on provinces.

Kerensky, A. F., *The Catastrophe: Kerensky's Own Story of the Russian Revolution* (London, 1927). The first and most useful of several accounts of the October Revolution by the head of the government overthrown by it.

Koenker, Diane, *Moscow Workers and the 1917 Revolution* (Princeton, 1981). Social history, thoroughly researched.

Lane, David, *The Roots of Russian Communism* (Assen, The Netherlands, 1969). Treats Russian Social-Democracy, 1898–1907.

Lewin, Moshe, *Lenin's Last Struggle* (New York, 1968). A provocative essay on the late Lenin (1921–4).

—— *Russian Peasants and Soviet Power* (London, 1968). On the first phase of collectivization (to June, 1930).

Medvedev, Roy A., *Let History Judge. The Origins and Consequences of Stalinism* (New York, 1971). An analysis by a Soviet Marxist dissident.

Melgunov, S. P., *The Bolshevik Seizure of Power* (Santa Barbara, 1972).

Meyer, Alfred G., *Leninism* (Cambridge, Mass., 1957). One of the standard Western works on the subject.

Moore, Barrington, *Soviet Politics—The Dilemma of Power. The Role of Ideas in Social Change* (Cambridge, Mass., 1950). An original and stimulating discussion of Leninist ideology and the realities of power.

Narkiewicz, Olga, *The Making of the Soviet State Apparatus* (Manchester, 1970). Rural administration during NEP.

Pethybridge, Roger, *Witnesses to the Russian Revolution* (London, 1964). A good selection of first-hand accounts of 1905 and the February (March) and October (November) revolutions of 1917.

Pipes, Richard, *The Formation of the Soviet Union. Communism and Nationalism, 1917–1923* (Cambridge, Mass., 1954). A standard work, in which the author does not hide his dislike for the regime of which he writes.

—— (ed.) *Revolutionary Russia: A Symposium* (Cambridge, 1968). On 1917: contributors include George Kennan, Richard Pipes, Leonard Schapiro, E. H. Carr, Marc Ferro and Dietrich Geyer.

Rabinowitch, A., *Prelude to Revolution. The Petrograd Bolsheviks and the July 1917 Uprising* (Bloomington, Ind., 1968).

—— *The Bolsheviks Come to Power. The Revolution of 1917 in Petrograd* (New

York, 1976). Detailed narrative histories, with an emphasis on popular support and diversity within the Bolshevik Party not found in many earlier Western works.

Radkey, Oliver H., *The Agrarian Foes of Bolshevism. Promise and Default of the Russian Socialist Revolutionaries, February to October 1917* (New York, 1958).

―― *The Election to the Russian Constituent Assembly of 1917* (Cambridge, Mass., 1950). A short but admirable analysis of the election returns and their significance.

―― *The Unknown Civil War in Soviet Russia. A Study of the Green Movement in the Tambov Region, 1920–21* (Stanford, 1976). On peasant revolt against the Soviet regime.

Reed, John, *Ten Days that Shook the World* (London, 1966). A vivid eyewitness account of the October Revolution in Petrograd by an American leftist, first published in 1926.

Rigby, T. H., *Lenin's Government, Sovnarkom. 1917–1922* (Cambridge, 1979). Unusual in focusing on Lenin as a governmental rather than a party leader.

Rosenberg, William G., *Liberals in the Russian Revolution* (Princeton, 1974). One of the best works on the politics of February–October 1917.

Schapiro, Leonard, *The Origin of the Communist Autocracy. Political Opposition in the Soviet State: First Phase, 1917–1922* (Cambridge, Mass., 1955). A classic work of postwar Sovietology, by a distinguished British scholar.

Scott, John, *Behind the Urals. An American Worker in Russia's City of Steel* (Boston, 1942). Magnitogorsk during the industrialization drive of the 1930s.

Service, Robert, *The Bolshevik Party in Revolution. A Study in Organizational Change, 1917–1923* (London, 1979). Particularly valuable on the impact of the Civil War on the new regime.

Solzhenitsyn, Aleksandr I., *The Gulag Archipelago 1918–1956. An Experiment in Literary Investigation*, vols. 1–2, trans. by Thomas P. Whitney (New York, 1973). Passionate, unconventional both as literature and history, but still a major historical work on the Soviet secret police and the labour camps.

Sukhanov, N. N., *The Russian Revolution 1917*, 2 vols., edited and translated by Joel Carmichael (New York, 1962). By general consensus, the best of the memoirs – wry, shrewd and knowledgeable.

Suny, Ronald G., *The Baku Commune, 1917–1918. Class and Nationality in the Russian Revolution* (Princeton, 1972). An important study, particularly valuable for testing generalizations about the revolution based mainly on Petrograd and Moscow.

Timasheff, Nicholas S., *The Great Retreat. The Growth and Decline of Communism in Russia* (New York, 1946). A stimulating if slapdash work by a Russian emigré sociologist, focusing on the changing social policies of the 1930s.

Trotsky, L., *The Revolution Betrayed* (London, 1937). Trotsky's major critique of Stalin, his old political opponent. Raises themes of bureaucratization and *embourgeoisement* later developed by Djilas, Burnham and others.

—— *The Russian Revolution,* abridged from Trotsky's *The History of the Russian Revolution* by F. W. Dupee, trans. by Max Eastman (New York, 1959). A memoir brilliantly presented as history, source of many *idées reçues* about the Revolution.

Tucker, Robert C., *Stalin as Revolutionary 1879–1929* (New York, 1973). Subtitled 'A Study in History and Personality', this biography has been criticized for its 'psycho-historical' approach, but offers a convincing and in many ways unfamiliar picture of Stalin based on solid scholarship and broad knowledge of Soviet history, politics and ideology. A second volume is in preparation.

—— (ed.), *Stalinism. Essays in Historical Interpretation* (New York, 1977). The major interpretative work on the Stalin period of recent years, with important essays by Robert Tucker and Stephen Cohen. Contributors include Leszek Kolakowski, Moshe Lewin, T. H. Rigby and H. Gordon Skilling.

Ulam, Adam B., *The Bolsheviks. The Intellectual and Political History of the Triumph of Communism in Russia* (New York, 1965). Essentially a political biography of Lenin, ending with his death in 1924. Lively, intelligent and easy to read.

—— *Stalin. The Man and his Era* (New York, 1973). The same genre as *The Bolsheviks.* Gives an excellent sense of Stalin as a political operator.

Valentinov, Nikolay, *Encounters with Lenin,* trans. by Paul Rosta and Brian Pearce (London, 1965). The most vivid personal memoir of Lenin, based on meetings in 1904 when the author was first drawn to the Bolsheviks and then broke with them.

Von Laue, T. H., *Why Lenin? Why Stalin? A Reappraisal of the Russian Revolution, 1900–1930* (Philadelphia, 1964). A stimulating interpretative essay, seeking to explain the revolution in a context of world and European history and within a modernization framework.

Warth, Robert D., *The Allies and the Russian Revolution* (Durham, 1954).

Wildman, Allan K., *The End of the Russian Imperial Army* (Princeton, 1980). A detailed study with many new insights, dealing with the first months of 1917. A second volume taking the story up to October is in preparation.

Wilson, Edmund, *To the Finland Station: A Study in the Writing and Acting of History* (New York, 1959). An elegant essay on Marxism, Lenin and the evolution of Lenin's thought up to his return to Russia in April 1917, by a distinguished American man of letters.

Wolfe, Bertram D., *Three Who Made a Revolution. A Biographical History* (revised ed., New York, 1964). A triple biography of Lenin, Stalin and Trotsky before 1917. A good work of popular history.

Zeman, Z. A. B. (ed.), *Germany and the Revolution in Russia, 1915–1918. Documents from the Archives of the German Foreign Ministry* (London, 1958). A basic source for those interested in the 'German gold' explanation of the Bolsheviks' success.

Index

DATE DUE

AP 18 '84			
MR 18 '85			
DEC 4 '85			
MAR 8 '88			
MAR 28 '89			
GAYLORD			PRINTED IN U.S.A.